ON BEING A REAL PERSON

ON BEING
A REAL PERSON

By

Harry Emerson Fosdick

Harper & Brothers, Publishers

NEW YORK AND LONDON

This book is complete and unabridged
in contents, and is manufactured in strict
conformity with Government regulations
for saving paper.

CONTENTS

Introduction

ABOUT twenty years ago, at the First Presbyterian Church in New York City, my stated responsibility as a member of the staff of ministers was confined to preaching. Desiring more intimate personal relationships with the congregation, and feeling sure that one major test of a sermon is the wish of at least some hearers to talk over their individual problems with the preacher in the light of it, I announced definite hours of conference when I would be available. On one of the first days I found myself dealing with a threatened case of suicide while fourteen other people awaited their turn for interviews.

That I had undertaken more than I had bargained for in thus inviting personal consultation, was soon evident. Having received my education in pre-psychiatric days when the academic study of psychology was a very dry and formal discipline, and such matters as mental therapy, so far as I recall, were never even mentioned in college or seminary, I was utterly untrained for personal counseling. Of this fact I soon became painfully aware. The general run of personal problems on which the minister happens in pastoral calling is very different from the kind presented to him by distracted souls, so troubled that voluntarily they turn to him for help. Some cases, of course, ordinary good sense could deal with, and some were concerned with familiar problems of religious faith, but there were many others, the like of which I had not even known existed, whose genesis and diagnosis I could not guess, and before which I stood helpless, fearing rightly that I might do more harm than good. Doubtless I had heard that there was such a disease as homosexuality, but never knowingly had I met a homosexual, so that when a humiliated youth came to me with that problem, or something that looked like it, involved in his distressing situation, I knew that I must have help.

Dr. Thomas W. Salmon was then in the full swing of his career—the leading American pioneer in the field of mental hygiene. We had become friends in other relationships and in my need I consulted him. Case after case, involving problems beyond my depth, he took on, and then with infinite patience went over them with me, explaining his diagnoses and therapies, illustrating his explanations from kindred or contrasting cases out of his practice, and sometimes turning the patients back to me as a collaborator to help them correct their spiritual attitudes and secure religious resources. My indebtedness to Dr. Salmon is incalculable. He opened a new world to me. Since then, books, a large and varied clientele, and able cooperators have helped to enlarge that world, but to my "clinical" experience with Dr. Salmon I owe the best I have been able to do in personal counseling.

When I undertook the pastorate at the Riverside Church, Dr. Salmon and I hoped to have a clinic there, where the resources of medical science and Christian ministry would be combined in the help of troubled minds, but his untimely death prevented that plan's fruition. Since then I have constantly utilized the increasing resources of psychiatric service in New York City, and I gratefully acknowledge the generous cooperation with which neurologists, psychiatrists, and psychological counselors have habitually met all appeals for help. As I look back on my ministry now, I wish that I could have extended my personal counseling farther, organized it better, and handled it more competently. At times a crowded schedule has reduced it to a minimum. I have never been able to give myself to it as once I dreamed I might, but a steady stream of troubled minds and disturbed emotions seeking help has willy-nilly kept me at it, and nothing in my ministry gives me more satisfaction now than the memory of some of the results.

Such, in brief, is the personal background of this book. More than once in writing it I have asked myself for whom it was being written. Certainly not for professionals in the field of personal counseling! Sometimes I have had in mind my fellow ministers, and others similarly situated, such as teachers, whose vocation is inseparable from the avocation of counseling individuals, and to whom a book like this might be of service. For the most part, however, I have pictured its readers in terms of the many, diverse individuals who have come to me for help. Here I have tried to set down what I have seen going on inside real people, have endeavored to describe their familiar mental and emotional maladies, their alibis and rationalizations, their ingenious, unconscious tricks of evasion and escape, their handling of fear, anxiety, guilt, and humiliation, their compensations and sublimations also, and the positive faiths and resources from which I have seen help come. As I look over my manuscript I see that I have gone on trying to be a personal counselor in this book, habitually thinking, as I wrote, of typical individuals who have consulted me.

Naturally, therefore, this book deals mainly with the problems of those who pass for normal or near normal. Occasionally, in some hapless case, the discerning minister who knows his way around notes the symptoms of some tragic, and it may be hopeless, mental disorder, and suspects that hospitalization is inevitable. Mostly, however, he deals with ordinary people—some mildly disturbed, others distracted, unhappy, fissured personalities, up against circumstances they feel inwardly inadequate to handle, or moods and feelings they do not understand and cannot bear to live with. In writing this book my major hope has been that to some such folk it might bring help.

The reader, therefore, should understand that this is not at all a treatise about personal counseling. I have said little or nothing concerning the techniques of that difficult, delicate art. My thought has been centered not on the counselor but on the people who consult him. They make up a fascinating company, and this book is altogether for them.

Obviously, a book so written suffers the same limitation as does a sermon addressed to a large congregation—it may not find its way into the special crevice of the individual's need. Preaching has been compared with the discharge of a pipette of eye medicine from a third story window into a crowded street in the hope that it will hit someone in the right place. All such books as this, dealing with the intimate problems of individuals, face that kind of disability, and because of that, my opening chapters, especially the first two, are not based on particular case studies but present more general matters involved in all handling of personal life by anyone whomsoever. Any reader, therefore, eager to get at the specific problems of troublesome individual experience, such as fear, guilt, anxiety, and depression, will have to be patient until certain fundamental matters have been presented on which, so it seems to me, all mental and emotional therapy rests.

Nevertheless, it is with individual cases that the book is ultimately concerned. Often I have drawn on my own experience in counseling for illustrative instances, taking care to assure anonymity. When this has been difficult I have sometimes used the published case records of other counselors, covering problems identical with those that I have dealt with. More frequently I have turned to biography and autobiography, and to those novelists, poets, and dramatists who have been, as was said of Shakespeare, circumnavigators of the human soul. Indeed, I have done this so much that I fear some casual reader's misapprehension about the multiplied allusions and quotations with which this book is filled. If one thinks of them as intended to be decorative, or even in a popular sense illustrative, my purpose in using them is completely misunderstood. They are intended to be case studies and so a substantial part of the argument. Nowhere are the common frustrating experiences of personal life more vividly described, our familiar mental and emotional maladjustments more convincingly portrayed, than in biographies and autobiographies, poems, novels, and dramas, and this rich storehouse of psychological self-revelation and insight has been too much neglected.

When Frederick the Great said, "I hope that posterity

will distinguish the philosopher from the monarch in me and the decent man from the politician," he presented an authentic case study in the difficulty of integrating "multiple selves" into unified personality. When Benjamin Franklin in his autobiography wrote, "So convenient a thing it is to be a *reasonable creature,* since it enables one to find or make a reason for every thing one has a mind to do," he was describing "rationalization" long before it was called that. When Flaubert said, "The moment I cease to be indignant, I shall fall flat, like a puppet when you take away the support," he provided a revealing instance of the strangely diverse ends for which basic emotional urges, such as pugnacity, can be used. When Epictetus said, "The condition and characteristic of a vulgar person is that he never expects either benefit or hurt from himself, but from externals. The condition and characteristic of a philosopher is that he expects all hurt and benefit from himself," he gave an authentic description of real psychological experience, displaying an attitude without whose presence in some degree mental therapy breaks down. All similar quotations and allusions used in this book have been thus intended to provide case studies of the problems under consideration.

So far as religion is concerned, all the more because I am a minister I have tried not to be a special pleader. My main purpose in writing this book has not been to present an argument for religious faith. Indeed, from the beginning I determined to deal with that not as much, but as little, as I could. I have tried in writing, as in personal counseling, to begin with people as I have found them, and to confront religion only when, following the trail of their problems and needs, I ran headlong into it. Nevertheless, one does run headlong into it. In dealing with one problem after another, the realistic wants of troubled souls lead to the confrontation of religious questions and to the need of such backing, reorientation, and resource as genuine religious faith provides. Today many psychiatrists are saying that, and never before has cooperation between them and the ministers of religion been more promising. It is from the scientific angle that Dr. W. H. R. Rivers writes: "One of the most striking results of the modern developments of our knowledge concerning the influence of mental factors in disease is that they are bringing back medicine in some measure to that cooperation with religion which existed in the early stages of human progress."

Concerning my indebtedness to many friends who as psychiatrists, neurologists, and psychological counselors have helped with unstinted generosity, I have already spoken. One of the first lessons the minister needs to learn is his own incompetence. Even in the case of bodily ills it is notoriously difficult for a patient to read his own symptoms truly, and in the emotional realm that difficulty is accentuated. Many translate into terms of moral trouble disorders whose real genesis lies in another area altogether. They come to the minister for counsel about their religion or their morals when the root of their maladjustment is in another soil. I once talked with an able and agreeable person about a minor difficulty and was about to close the interview when a chance remark aroused my suspicion. In the next hàlf-hour I uncovered a tragic case of paranoia in its advanced stages, rapidly approaching

violent expression, and calling for immediate hospitalization.

Personal counseling, therefore, like marriage, is "not to
be entered into unadvisedly or lightly." An unwise and
unprepared minister, having it thrust upon him, can
easily do more harm than good, and for any minister who
habitually faces the varied personal problems it presents,
cooperation with specialists is obligatory.

As for the preparation of this book, my indebtedness to
the writings of others is acknowledged in detail in an
appendix of documented references. I am under special
obligation to my friend, Professor Richard M. Elliott,
Ph.D., of the Department of Psychology in the University
of Minnesota, for whose careful reading of the manuscript
and whose wise and stimulating suggestions I am very
thankful. To my personal secretaries I cannot adequately
express my gratitude, and it is particularly due to Miss
Elizabeth Gough, who has superintended the preparation
of the manuscript, checked all references, and made the
Index. The best literary critic I have ever had has been
my wife, and anyone who profits by this book is in her
debt, both for what is in it, and more especially for the
absence of numberless words, phrases, sentences, and
paragraphs that would have been in it had she not ruth-
lessly cut out the excess verbiage.

Coming, as it does, out of personal experience, this
book is necessarily as limited and partial as that experience has been. Nevertheless, for what it may be worth,
here is the story of what one minister has found out about
people's "insides" and what can be done with them.

HARRY EMERSON FOSDICK

January 1, 1943.

ON BEING A REAL PERSON

CHAPTER I

Shouldering Responsibility for Ourselves

I

THE central business of every human being is to be a
real person. We possess by nature the factors out of
which personality can be made, and to organize them into
effective personal life is every man's primary responsibility. To be sure, the word "personality" through a long
history has accumulated many meanings. It is not man's
initial vocation to become a "personage," or to be "per-
sonable," or to achieve what popularly is known as
"personality." When Daniel Webster walked down State
Street in Boston, business was temporarily suspended
while people rushed to the doors and windows to see him
pass, and to the popular imagination he seemed to take
up half the street. Such impressiveness, in common parlance called "personality," is a priceless gift, but to consider its achievement man's main business would be
preposterous.

The basic fact concerning human beings is that every
normal infant possesses the rudiments of personal life. If
all goes well, he will grow up to be a self-conscious organism with capacities for memory, thoughtfulness, purposefulness, and affection, and, being thus a person, man, so

far as we know, is unique in the universe. An organism, conscious of its own being, that can remember, think, purpose, and love, *is* personal. While these attributes in a rudimentary degree are possessed by animals, in man they have attained a development differentiating him from everything else within our ken, and constituting his essential nature. While we are presented at birth, however, with the makings of personal life, their successful organization into unified and efficient personality is one of the most difficult, as it is the most essential task in human experience.

In confronting this task, man's situation is altogether *sui generis.* He is the only creature that can consciously help to create itself. The fulfillment of the possibilities of its species may be the primary function of a seedling tree, but the tree is unaware of that fact and cannot deliberately cooperate. Man alone consciously assists in the fulfillment of his nature. Einstein was born over a grocery store in Ulm, Germany, an infant whose inner consciousness was—to use William James' phrase—a big, buzzing confusion. When one sees Einstein today, an extraordinarily unified personality concerning whom one observer says, "Einstein is all of a piece. . . . There is no division in him," it is difficult to suppose that Einstein himself, with his deliberate purposes and consciously chosen loyalties, had nothing to do with that result. We are not simply creatures; we are self-creators. As Wordsworth put it, "So build we up the Being that we are."

"Of all animals," writes Professor William Ernest Hocking, "it is man in whom heredity counts for least, and conscious building forces for most. Consider that his infancy is longest, his instincts least fixed, his brain most unfinished at birth, his powers of habit-making and habit-changing most marked, his susceptibility to social impressions keenest,—and it becomes clear that in every way nature, as a prescriptive power, has provided in him for her own displacement. . . . Other creatures nature could largely finish: the human creature must finish himself."

That human happiness is at stake in the success or failure of this undertaking seems clear. No external good fortune can bring abiding enjoyment to a half-made, unorganized personality. Without exaggeration it can be said that frustrated, disintegrated, inhibited, unhappy people, who cannot match themselves with life and become efficient personalities, constitute the greatest single tragedy in the world. Wars come and go; economic circumstances alter with time and place; natural handicaps and catastrophes, inherent in human existence, fall with varying incidence on everyone; social inequities are cruel to some, and inherited prosperity ruins others; but through every situation in this variegated scene, in mansion and hovel, war and peace, wealth and penury, domestic felicity and discord, among the uneducated and in university faculties, an omnipresent calamity is found, strangely impartial in its choice of a matrix. Under every kind of circumstance people entrusted with personality, unable to escape it but incapable of managing it, are making a mess of it, and are thereby plunging into an earthly hell.

This statement involves no underrating of the immense importance of external conditions; few people today are tempted to minimize the terrific impact of adverse environment; yet happiness is never caused by circumstance alone and is often created despite it. A well-inte-

[3]

grated person, supported by a sustaining philosophy, organized around worth-while purposes, and aware of adequate resources, can capitalize adversity and can even be "frustrated into sublimity." Such a person, however, must start with life's primary datum—that we have ourselves on our hands, and that the most determining fact in our experience is that hour by hour *we* are getting to be *we*. From other facts we may run away, but after every consciously or unconsciously maneuvered escape, we find ourselves back where we started, with ourselves on our hands. From that inner relationship there is no divorce. From the relentless process by which, for good or ill, *we* become *we*, there is no means of flight. Every circuitous alley of evasion brings us back to life's central demand, with our beatitude or misery dependent on our response to it: Be a real person.

II

The acceptance of this summons as a reasonable responsibility involves the proposition that three factors enter into the building of personality: heredity, environment, and personal response. The importance of the first two we take for granted; they rigorously limit the control of the individual over his own life. As Oscar Ameringer puts it: "Except that I inherited certain characteristics from an unknown number of unknown ancestors, was deeply influenced by persons most of whom were dead before I was born, and shaped by circumstances over which I had no control, I am a self-made man." Nevertheless, the autobiography of Ameringer or of any other indi-

[4]

vidual leaves the strong impression that whether in success
or failure the element of self-making was indubitably
there. Life consists not simply in what heredity and environment do to us but in what we make out of what they do
to us.

> Fate slew him, but he did not drop;
> She felled—he did not fall—
> Impaled him on her fiercest stakes—
> He neutralized them all.

That phenomenon of personal response, however it may
be explained, cannot be explained away.

One of the clearest illustrations of this fact is found in
the very place where its discovery might seem most difficult. At no point do heredity and environment impinge
upon us so intimately as in our own physical organisms.
Some ills of the body, such as certain glandular diseases,
can utterly disrupt the person. We are psychophysical
organisms, and as a building site profoundly influences
the size and kind of house that can be built upon it, so
the body limits or expands the possibilities of the personality associated with it. Yet even in this most interior
impact of inheritance and circumstance on personal life
an astonishing prevalence of disorganized and sprawling personalities with sound bodies, and consummate
personalities with handicapped bodies, confronts the
observer.

Man's inner self is rooted in the body. To be sure, the
personal faculties—mind, memory, hope, affection, purpose—belong in a realm unseeable, intangible, nonmetric.
A man sees not his friend but only the outward integu-
ment, the physical mask that at once conceals and reveals

him. A man never sees himself; no mirror or fluoroscope can make visible that mysterious center of psychic activity which is the real person. Yet this inner self, invisible though it is, is so interlaced with, dependent on, and influenced by, the body, that no discrimination is fine enough to tell where the one ends and the other begins.

Nevertheless, even in this interior impingement of the non-personal on the personal, personality disengages itself and instinctively asserts its separateness and transcendence. So a small boy, scared by a barking dog and asked by his father if he was frightened, answered: "No, I am not afraid, but my stomach is." So Sir Walter Raleigh, faint from illness as he went to the scaffold to be beheaded, said to his friends: "If therefore, you perceive any weakness in me, I beseech you ascribe it to my sickness rather than to myself."

The roster of the world's real persons is astonishingly inconsiderate of sound physical health. Charles Darwin, as he himself said, "almost continually unwell"; Robert Louis Stevenson, with his tuberculosis; Helen Keller, blind and deaf; Stanton Kirkham, bedridden for twenty-five years, yet saying: "As the most barren regions of the Earth yield something to the botanist and the geologist, the most desolate aspects of life are not wholly without interest to the philosopher"—such people illustrate the unlikely settings of efficient personal life. To be sure, some lesions and disorders put an end to all possibility of happiness or efficiency. As our common speech bears witness, flesh and spirit are indiscriminately entangled— "somebody," "nobody," "everybody," "anybody"—our words for ourselves connote the physical. Yet innumerable people, counting ill health no reprieve from the primary demand to be real persons, find abiding satisfaction and achieve admirable personal life despite calamitous physical conditions. Even concerning glandular disorder, that most intimate of maladies, Dr. Starke R. Hathaway in his *Physiological Psychology* says: "After going through the experimental and clinical literature, the thoughtful reader will conclude that the effects of personality upon glands are more impressive and easier to illustrate than are the effects of the glands upon personality."

The secret of this fact lies deep in the nature of personal life. Things act under the influence of stimuli; they may even be said to *react* to stimuli, but persons can *respond*. Reaction is mechanical, while response is personal, and the endeavors of materialists to reduce the latter to the former are unconvincing because in actual experience the two are so radically different. Billiard balls react; persons can do more. A sneeze is a reaction, but the triumphant answers which some personalities make to life's difficult situations cannot be convincingly subsumed under such a category. Socrates' reply to his judges was not a sneeze, but a response.

Whatever may be the evolutionary relationship between bodily reaction and personal response, they are now in practical experience so widely diverse that to identify them is to obscure one of the most significant contrasts in human life. Sir Walter Scott and Lord Byron both were lame, but they took it differently. High-strung, proud, ambitious men, their physical handicap was to each of them a determining factor, but their biographies reveal how dissimilar their responses were. Sir Walter lived a radiant life, while a friend said of Lord Byron:

"He brooded over that blemish as sensitive minds will brood until they magnify a wart into a wen. His lameness certainly helped to make him sceptical, cynical, and savage." If this capacity to confront life with a distinctive personal rejoinder is thus evident even in that most intimate realm where heredity and environment impinge upon us in our physical organisms, we may certainly expect to find it everywhere else.

III

Far from being comfortable, this power of personal response is the basis of all self-blame. We are not responsible for our heredity; much of our environment we cannot control; but if it is true that a third factor enters into the building of personality—the power to face life with an individual rejoinder—then we are responsible for *that*. When such acceptance involves self-condemnation, however, an alibi almost inevitably rushes to the rescue. The fire companies of a city, answering an alarm and converging upon a conflagration to put out the blaze, do not move more swiftly and automatically than do our alibis, hurrying to extinguish our unhappy self-accusations. All of us resemble the lawyer in the New Testament story, concerning whom we read: "But he, desiring to justify himself, said. . . ."

The fact that we are not marionettes, merely reacting to the pull of inheritance and circumstance, but have power to confront life with a personal rejoinder, is often presented as a gospel. It affirms our freedom. It redeems us from automatism. But as our language itself suggests,

[8]

the capacity to make personal *response* involves *respon-sibility,* and man's desire to escape that, especially if it entails self-blame, is deep-seated and inveterate. A college president says that after long dealing with students, he is unsure whether the degree B.A. stands for Bachelor of Arts or for Builder of Alibis.

On the lowest level this desire to escape blame expresses itself in emphasis upon luck. Fortunate people "get the breaks," men say; personal failure is due not so much to mistake as to mischance. That luck represents a real factor in human experience is evident, and he who does not expect ill-fortune as one of the ingredients of life is trying to live in fairyland, but nothing finer has appeared on earth than unlucky people who are real persons. However the fact be explained, the determining element in their experience is not so much what happens to them as the way they take it. In Shakespeare's words they are

> . . . not a pipe for fortune's finger
> To sound what stop she please.

Biography is packed with illustrations of this fact. Glenn Cunningham, who has run the fastest mile on record, in four minutes, four and four-tenths seconds, was crippled in boyhood in a schoolhouse fire. The doctors said he would never walk again. Then they said that only a miracle could enable him to walk. He was out of luck. He began walking by following a plow across the fields, leaning on it for support; and then went on to tireless experimentation to see what he could do with his legs, until he broke all records for his race. Unlucky people who face mischance with a redeeming personal response make a stimulating company.

Obviously the power of this third factor in building personality can be exaggerated. A young child has lately been discussing whether he will be a man or a woman; he balances the relative advantages and disadvantages of being a father or a mother, and chooses now one and now the other. When he grows up he will discover that his possibilities are less extensive than he had supposed. The individual is not an atom, separable from his biological inheritance and his social environment, able to do what he will with his life. Indeed, personality is itself a social product. A human babe, sequestered at birth upon an uninhabited island, suckled, let us say, like Romulus and Remus, by a wolf, granting that he survive, would never develop into a personality. As Professor Josiah Royce said, were a child to grow with no companioning save inanimate nature, "there is nothing to indicate that he would become as self-conscious as is now a fairly educated cat." Indeed, the famous case of Kaspar Hauser, through political machinations cruelly bereft of all human contacts, seems to prove the case. At seventeen years of age when he wandered into Nuremberg he was still so much an infant that he did not distinguish inanimate objects from living beings, and could mutter only a few meaningless phrases. Beginning with the babe's imitation of his mother, it is only in the matrix of social relationships that personal life can grow. "Society," says Professor Rufus M. Jones, "is fundamental, and it is an essential condition for self-consciousness and personality. However contradictory it may sound, it is nevertheless a fact that there could be no self without many selves. Self-consciousness is a possible attainment only in a world where it already exists."

No one, therefore, can intelligently care for personal life without caring about genetics and social reform. In our day, however—one of the most disturbed, difficult, and fateful eras in human history—the massed weight of popular emphasis is naturally given to the environmental conditions that potently affect man's fortunes and that in particular excuse his failures. So insistently are these dwelt upon that many come to think of themselves as their helpless victims. The characteristic novels of every generation, for obvious reasons, reveal important tendencies in its thought. One can tell much about the Victorian Era by reading Dickens, Eliot, and Thackeray. It is significant, therefore, that our modern novels commonly picture men and women as the prey of fate. Human beings trapped by life, fighting a hopeless battle against the conspiracy of tragic mischances, and finally crushed and mangled—how many novels are based on that idea and shaped to that outline! As one literary critic sums it up, the common theme of a whole school of writers is "the individual defeated by the world, and made a sardonic jest of." So one character exclaims, "Tricked by Gad, that's what I was, tricked by life and made a fool of."

Over against this unbalanced emphasis there is serious need that we restore to its proportionate importance our power of personal response. It is severely limited, but it is real. Its universal presence is indicated by the universality of self-blame. A mechanical automaton lacks any basis for self-condemnation. It is not responsible for anything it is or does. All human beings, however, confront the problem of self-accusation. Conscience, inherent in human nature, is as inescapable as mind or emotion. Is it credible that this omnipresent factor of self-blame, rising at times into remorse, one of the most potent forces in man's experience, should be merely an illusion, not based on any fact that makes it valid and legitimate? But if self-blame has validity, it can only be because man possesses the power to face life with a personal rejoinder for which he is responsible and for whose misuses he can rightly be condemned.

At any rate, bad luck is a poor alibi if only because good luck by itself never yet guaranteed real personality. Professor Henry N. Wieman says that a college roommate of his desired to improve his intellectual life. "He procured a large comfortable chair that was thought to be good for study. He got study slippers and a lounging jacket. A book rest was fastened to the arm of the chair to hold the book at the right angle before his eyes. A special lamp was installed and eyeshade, pencils, paper, and revolving bookcase. He would come into the room after the evening meal, take off his coat and put on the jacket, take off his shoes and slip into the slippers, adjust the study lamp, put his book on the book rest, recline in the comfortable chair with his eyeshade over his eyes, and, when everything was perfectly adjusted, he would go to sleep." Life is like that. It is not so simple that good fortune suffices for it. Seeing that sleeping youth in his comfortable study chair, one remembers that *Pilgrim's Progress* came from a prison, as did *Don Quixote,* and Sir Walter Raleigh's *History of the World,* and some of the best of O. Henry's stories. They were written by unlucky people who were, nevertheless, real persons.

IV

On a higher level many today escape a sense of personal responsibility through a general feeling of powerlessness. Like Gulliver in the land of the giants, they find their lives determined by forces so titanic that they lapse into a mood of emotional fatalism. Human experience has two aspects: the objective and the subjective. On the one side is the impact of external events—the universe we live in, the encompassing and sometimes terrific pressure of economic collapse and international collision, and all the fateful changes of fortune in the scenery of which our lives are set. On the other side is our subjective contribution—what we creatively can do about it all so that we become not victims of fate but masters of destiny. In some generations the subjective looms large, as in the early days of modern science when man felt not so much what nature did to him as what he could do with nature. In other generations, like our own, when world-shaking events suggest analogies of flood and hurricane, the objective aspect of human experience waxes tremendously and the subjective wanes.

The consequent mood of emotional fatalism is a convenient alibi. On its popular levels this mood is not thought through but is instinctively felt; like the atmosphere, it presses on us over fourteen pounds to the square inch; it becomes the climate in which we live, as though, dwelling now in the arctic zone, we had ample excuse for not growing wheat. Fatalism is commonly presented as a dour, grim doctrine, robbing us of inner freedom, reducing us to the estate of robots, denying us initiative and creativity. As a matter of fact, fatalism is one of the most comfortable moods in which a man can live. If he is an automaton, he is irresponsible, and so has an unanswerable justification for anything he is or does. His creed is simple and complete: Whatever is, is inevitable. Said a man to his friend, "You are acting like a fool." "Well," was the answer, "if that is what I am, I cannot help it. That is the way fate made me." From that alibi, persistently held, there is no appeal; it is an impregnable defense mechanism. An altogether different outlook on life is suggested by Emerson's comment in his *Journal:* "Henry Thoreau made, last night, the fine remark that, as long as a man stands in his own way, everything seems to be in his way."

Only on the basis of man's profound emotional desire to be dispensed from such responsibility can the historic rise of one system of fatalism after another be explained. Long ago Omar Kháyyám called us

> . . . helpless Pieces of the Game He plays
> Upon this Chequer-board of Nights and Days.

In the Hebrew-Christian tradition an original progenitor of the race was posited as the causal fountainhead of all our woes—

> In *Adam's* Fall
> We Sinned all.

Astrology—its belated devotees still among us—provided a vast system of foreordination whose verbal left-overs linger in our vocabulary. If a man was jovial, it was because he was born under the planet Jove; if mercurial, under Mercury; if saturnine, under Saturn; and as for disaster in general, that was due to a man's "aster," his star. Nor has theology escaped such usage, for Islam and certain forms of Christianity have notoriously provided fatalistic doctrines, according to which man is the helpless victim of divine decrees.

Lyman Beecher was a masterful figure in New England in his day. One week end he was to exchange pulpits with a neighboring minister who held a stiff theory of predestination, while on that point Beecher was for his time a liberal. On Sunday morning both men started from home, each going to the other's church, and met midway. As they paused, the neighboring minister said, "Doctor Beecher, I wish to call to your attention that before the creation of the world God arranged that you were to preach in my pulpit and I in yours on this particular Sabbath." "Is that so?" said Lyman Beecher, glaring at him. "Then I won't do it!" And turning his horse, he returned to his own church.

For intelligent folk, ancient phrasings of predestination have passed away, but many who would agree with Cassius,

> The fault, dear Brutus, is not in our stars,
> But in ourselves, that we are underlings,

are nonetheless impressed by our modern substitutes for old fatalisms. Moreover, there is a kernel of truth in determinism. The universe was here first, and it impinges on us with tremendous incidence, assuming at times the aspect and potency of doom. When one considers the cosmic setting of our lives, our absolute dependence on the maintenance of the earth's heat and moisture, the determining effect on each individual of the race's bi-

[15]

ological evolution, the momentous consequences of heredity, when one confronts the fact that our initial endowments of physique, intelligence, and temperament are genetically predetermined, and when, added to that, one knows by experience and observation how powerfully lives are directed and shaped from babyhood up by conditioning environments, one cannot lightly talk about being the master of one's fate and the captain of one's soul. Unless our conscious experience, however, is fallacious, this is not the whole story. All the more because the truth in fatalism is so momentous, stress is needed on that inner core of personal initiative and response where lies our power to individualize our handling of life. In the conviction that—to use Dostoievsky's phrase—"people are people and not the keys of a piano," is the beginning of human life's distinction and dignity.

Moreover, the facts justify this conviction. The very spectacle of one vast system of determinism after another rising and falling suggests alike their emotional source and their intellectual invalidity. At the center of human life is a realistic, experiential fact—man's capacity for personal response—whose effects in changing environment as well as enduring it, and in altering personal quality as well as putting up with it, are too evident to be denied. As Professor Hocking states it, man "is the only animal that deliberately undertakes, while reshaping his outer world, to reshape himself also." Every road man has ever traveled toward determinism has wound around to face him with this ineluctable fact. Mysterious it is, and difficult to fit into a scheme of general scientific laws, but it is inescapably there.

This accounts for the notable difference in the depiction of personal life between biographies, novels, and dramas on the one side, and a treatise in general psychology on the other. In the former, persons are distinct individuals. There is no possibility of confusing Jesus and Judas, Anna Karenina and Kitty Shcherbatski, Hamlet and the King. One does not think chiefly, if at all, of the uniformities that make them similar, of the regularities of reaction, statable in general laws, that constitute them members of a single class—the human race. The individual diversities rather than the identities command our interest, for biographies, novels, and dramas portray human beings as they actually live. Many a psychological treatise, however, trying—often rather desperately—to be "scientific," starts by abstracting from the infinite diversities of real people those common elements, regular and uniform, which characterize all humans as such. This is what "science" has come to mean—the discovery of law-abiding identities and regularities that belong to a whole class of objects. The values inherent in this process are immense; no intelligent person would belittle them or doubt their worth in the study of personal life; but this specific method of investigation can dangerously obscure the truth unless it is understood to be what it really is— an abstraction, for purposes of special study, of certain general and uniform aspects of human beings, whereas their real lives are essentially dissimilar and various. General psychology as a "science" takes the infinitely heterogeneous mass of humans and abstracts from them all the homogeneity it can find.

This, however, leaves the actual experience of human beings at its pith and marrow inadequately treated. *There* we are more aware of characteristic differences than of identities. *There* the biographies, novels, and dramas tell the truth, dealing as they do with the wide variation of our personal responses. Because of this, Wilhelm Wundt, who may be called the founder of experimental psychology, confessed concerning "laws" in the psychological realm that "there is no validity" in them "which would not allow for exceptions; on the contrary, the number of exceptions is far greater than all cases of agreement." Just as physical science today wrestles with the problem of indeterminacy among the atoms, so any adequate treatment of personality must face the realistic fact of man's capacity not simply to submit to what life does to him but to handle it, reshape it, transform it, even rise above it and win a victory in the face of it. The same fire that burns the wood hardens the steel.

v

On its highest level man's contemporary desire to escape responsibility expresses itself not in emphasis on luck, or in emotional submission to fate, but in a thoroughgoing deterministic theory, ascribing all personal qualities to heredity and environment. What we have called "personal response" is read back into these two primary factors, is regarded as part and parcel of them, inseparable from them, and not to be conceived as a third factor alongside them. In so far as "personal response" seems differentially real, involving the experience of freedom, initiative, and creativity, it is regarded as illusory. The stream of causation runs one way, they say, from inheritance and conditioning circumstance to personal consequence, and it never can return upon itself; personality is an effect, not a creative cause; it has no more initiative than a shadow; when we feel creative we are fooling ourselves; Booth could not have avoided killing Lincoln; St. Francis of Assisi could not have helped being a saint; Tschaikowsky could not have resisted composing the *Sixth Symphony,* and as one enthusiast for this theory put it, "Heliotropism wrote Hamlet." When one is determined to hold this theory, there is no arguing him out of it, for it can neither be finally proved nor disproved.

In our day this theory offers an attractive defense mechanism, all the more persuasive because it seems unemotional, objective, and realistic. From intelligence quotients within, to crippling environments without, it offers defenses for every kind of deficiency, so that no botched life need look far to find an excuse. The youthful science of endocrinology plays up the decisive importance of the glands; educational psychology creates a general impression of unalterable I.Q.'s; psychiatry weighs down our speech with half-understood, ponderous words describing the various *phobias* and *complexes,* so that, as Dr. Henry C. Link says, they become "a vocabulary of defeat"; mechanistic philosophy reduces man to a helpless cog in the cosmic machine; and for very pity's sake, humanitarian sentiment, outraged at social inequities, ascribes human failure and evil to an unjust society. Here is a massing of potent influences focused on one effect: the denial to man of any power over his own life.

One need not question the entire validity of these influences in order to feel chary of their consequence. Even Christians should appreciate the factual elements in materialism, for there is a mechanistic aspect to the

[19]

universe. As for the discoveries of psychology, the techniques of psychiatry, the experimentation of sciences like endocrinology, and the indignant protests of humanitarian good will against social injustice, they are indispensable. Nevertheless, their confluence in our time has created a flood that sweeps many off their feet. The sense of personal responsibility is in danger of being swamped. Individuals, conceiving themselves as victims of heredity and environment, behave as such, and illustrate the remark of a contemporary philosopher that "there is a deep tendency in human nature to *become like* that which we imagine ourselves to be."

The conviction that heredity and circumstance together make us what we are commonly appears in popular thought when an unsatisfactory heritage plus a calamitous environment are used to explain personal failure. When this occurs in the case of a friend, or when humane sentiment broods over social injustice to the underprivileged, the motive of sympathy deepens our desire to exonerate whipped and beaten men and women from responsibility for their fate. Inheritance and environment doomed them, we say; they are the prey of their genes and their surroundings. It would be absurd to deny the truth in such judgments. It is possible to be not so much born as damned into the world, and the effect of evil environment, especially of evil personal environment in the family and in the dominant cultural pattern, robbing children of a decent chance, and disrupting mature character, anyone can see. Nevertheless, the question still remains: Are heredity and environment the *sole* factors in shaping personality?

When, rather than a calamitous heredity and environment, one faces instead superior inheritance and favorable circumstance, there is a better chance to reach an objective judgment. Must an individual with fortunate genes and propitious circumstances necessarily be a well-knit, efficient, and admirable personality? Is *that* fate, willy-nilly, forced upon him? Certainly in the actual process of living it does not seem so. To the favorably born and well-bestead man, the realistic truth, as he experiences it, appears to be that he must make to his fine heritage and advantageous environing a conscious personal response, often costly, onerous, and sacrificial, or else be a disastrous failure. It would be difficult to persuade Mendelssohn that he could not possibly have missed being Mendelssohn, or to convince Pasteur that he could not have fallen short of becoming Pasteur. The experience of painful effort in becoming a real person is too vivid to be escaped. Personal response is too toilsome and difficult to be dropped out of account.

Did Phillips Brooks, well born and fortunately bestead, have to be the man he was? Graduating from college he turned to his chosen vocation, teaching, and made a complete failure of it. By Christmas of the first year the situation was desperate, by January hopeless. He was compelled to resign. "I don't know what will become of me," he wrote, "and I don't care much." "I shall not study a profession." "I wish I were fifteen years old again. I believe I might make a stunning man: but somehow or other I don't seem in the way to come to much now." Was his recovery from his despair, his come-back, his personal response to his life's problem, and the "stunning" consequence, an inevitable effect, foreordained by his genes and his environment? Did *he* have nothing creative and self-determining to do with it?

Any such denial of the factor of personal response, one may be sure, springs from a mechanistic theory of life, inflexibly held, which, despite the testimony of experience, a man is determined to carry through to the bitter end. Because of that he must manage somehow to submerge personal response in heredity and environment so as not to acknowledge anything beyond them—not even that in the Garden of Gethsemane there was more involved than a good inheritance and a favorable conditioning, bringing a consequence in Jesus' prayer as predetermined as a flower's fragrance or a weed's smell. Such theorists picture the world as a clever master of legerdemain, forcing the cards on the individual so that while the world seems to say to us, Choose what you will, and while we *feel* as if we made a volitional selection, in reality the card we pick is always thrust upon us by our heredity and environment, beyond our power to foresee or prevent. Some mechanists try to think that. Nevertheless, the realistic experience of distinctive, purposeful, often arduous personal response remains an inescapable fact to trouble their dreams.

Indeed, when one confronts the experience of good fortune in biological endowment and conditioning circumstance, two propositions emerge. First, good heredity alone does not settle everything, because the better the heredity the more important is a good environment. Superior genes, providing the makings of an alert, vigorous, high-strung, promising personality, make more important, not less, the right kind of environment in which to grow. Second, good heredity and good environment

[22]

together do not decisively settle everything, because the better the heritage and the more fortunate the circumstances, the more important, not the less, becomes the individual's conscious personal response. A priceless violin, made of the best wood, needs the more to be cared for under good conditions; and furthermore, such a violin, so cared for, only makes more important the decisive matter, the irreducible minimum of music's requirement, the personal handling of it. To be sure, no analogy can adequately represent the reciprocal intimacy of body and spirit, but in some such way the better our heredity, the more important is our environment, and the better our heredity and environment together, the more important is our personal response.

When this proposition is translated into terms of biography it rings true. Granted that great personalities may have had a promising hereditary start, and that one can discern the powerful effect of environing conditions on their development, yet Beethoven without Beethoven's personal response would be unimaginable. Always that third factor is crucially present. Helen Keller's victorious spirit certainly does not seem to be the willy-nilly result of heredity and circumstance; she is not the mere "victim" of innate genes and circumstantial conditions. Only an obsessing a priori theory can lead one to brush aside as non-existent or ineffectual her conscious handling of her life's data, her highly distinctive confrontation of life with a personal rejoinder.

Moreover, the disastrous misuse of fine heredity and environment is too familiar a phenomenon to be doubted. Children are not coercively destined to well-integrated personalities because they are well born and well bestead.

Identical twins, of like genes and similar environment, can travel diverse paths to noticeably different personal results. *The better the heredity, the more good environment matters; the better the heredity and the environment together, the more personal response counts.*

If, when heritage and circumstance are thus fortunate, the individual's distinctive handling of life's data is an indispensable factor in building personality, at what stage in the descending scale of such good fortune can one suppose that that factor disappears? If personal response is operative in using a fortunate situation to great ends, is it not also operative when a deplorable situation is mastered, and some man, hard put to it by handicaps and limited in natal endowment, becomes, nonetheless, an admirable person? Here lies man's central responsibility from which he has no right in any situation, by any excuse, to exempt himself. We are willing to accept such responsibility when we succeed; when by dint of decision and effort we achieve a desired end, we are sure we had a share in *that*. No Chopin, writing music in the throes of creative agony, breaking up one quill pen after another and pacing his room in a frenzy, could believe that the finished nocturne was merely the fated result of genes and general environment. His conscious personal share is obvious. We thus accept responsibility when we succeed; we may not slough it off when we fail. We cannot eat our cake and have it too. Indeed, in the face of difficult situations, when life is limited in endowment and threatened by circumstance, we most need to accept our responsibility to be real persons.

VI

The beginning of worth-while living is thus the confrontation of ourselves—unique beings, each of us trusted ✓
with the makings of personality. Every human life involves an unfathomable mystery, for man is the riddle of
the universe, and the riddle of man is his endowment
with personal capacities. The stars are not so strange as
the mind that studies them, analyzes their light, and
measures their distances. Electrons and protons present
no enigma so occult as the ability of human beings to
remember and hope. Human affection, by which we live
in other lives more than in our own, is none the less
recondite because it is familiar. As for personal qualities
such as courage, the new telescope with its two hundred
inch reflector will reveal nothing more amazing than a
character that in the face of successive calamities says, as
one hard-bestead woman did say: "I am like a deeply
built ship; I drive best under a stormy wind."

In particular, personality's ability to project a purpose
into the future and head toward it is unique. Only within
the personal realm are changes caused by conscious plan-
ning. In the realm of inanimate nature, changes come by
pressure and coercion from behind. The moon makes the
tides rise; the sun makes the planets keep their courses;
gravitation makes the rivers run; the chemistry of soil
and sunshine makes the trees grow. In personal life, however, a new process emerges. There the most significant
changes are caused not by coercion from behind but by
consciously chosen purposes projected before. Scientists
seek truth yet to be discovered; prophetic spirits seek

righteousness yet to be achieved; and ordinary folk have a powerful future tense causative in them. They are not so much forced from behind as drawn from before, not so much pushed as pulled. That gap between causation by pressure from behind in all inanimate nature, and causation by chosen purpose in persons is, as another has said, "one of the widest chasms in the world."

Mind, memory, affection, and purposefulness, centered in an ego that is conscious of itself—with this mysterious endowment each of us has been entrusted, and to make the most of it is our primary task. Yet even in the realm of organized knowledge we know more about the stars than about ourselves. In the development of the sciences astronomy came first, and after that geology, biology, sociology, until last of all came psychology. It is man's strange penchant to confront last what lies nearest, and in the practical handling of life multitudes of people become aware of, and wrestle with, every conceivable factor involved in the human situation before they face their primary problem—being a real person.

The insight of Jesus in his parable of the Prodigal is true to the facts—the remaking of that young man's life began "when he came to himself." By the same sign our commonest human tragedy is correctly represented in a recent cartoon: A physician faces his patient with anxious solemnity, saying, "This is a very serious case; I'm afraid you're *allergic to yourself.*"

CHAPTER II

What Being A Real Person Means

I

THE phrase "real person" is not to be taken for granted as though its meaning were plain. Certain qualities, such as courage, fortitude, and dependability are clearly called for in a genuine personality, but beneath such virtues is a deep-running psychological process, and the criteria of success in handling it are not superficially obvious.

One reason for this is that personal life is essentially dynamic and is ceaselessly in motion. The common phrase, "building a personality," is a misnomer. Personality is not so much like a structure as like a river—it continuously flows, and to be a person is to be engaged in a perpetual process of becoming.

> . . . man knows partly but conceives beside,
> Creeps ever on from fancies to the fact,
> And in this striving, this converting air
> Into a solid he may grasp and use,
> Finds progress, man's distinctive mark alone,
> Not God's, and not the beasts': God is, they are,
> Man partly is and wholly hopes to be.

The tests of successful personal living, therefore, must be caught on the run and they always have a tentative and provisional quality. They are not neatly identical when applied to two persons in different situations or to the same person at different ages. Nevertheless, if one is to think intelligently about being a real person, one must know approximately what is meant.

Concerning one criterion there is common agreement. A real person achieves a high degree of unity within himself. He does not remain split and scattered but gets himself together into wholeness and coherence. As the ten trillion cells of the human body must be well organized to produce a smooth-running physique, so the discrete and often conflicting elements of personal experience, such as reflexes, impulses, desires, emotions, thoughts, and purposes, must be co-ordinated to make an effective personality. All other tests of success in personal living hark back to this—a real person is integrated. Some individuals are like a brush heap, a helter-skelter, miscellaneous pile of twigs and branches; others, like a tree, include the same kind of materials, but are organized into a vital, growing entity. As of the body, so of personality as a whole, the major criterion of success is *e pluribus unum*.

The truth of this is revealed, in the first place, in the process of growing up. There is in the body a basic urge toward wholeness, which is another word for health. The nervous system from the start works at its task of co-ordinating the infant's random movements into system and order, and when at last maturity is reached, deliberate attention can be concentrated on some purpose that commands interest, and the whole organism drawn together into that "acme of integration" which appears in creative work.

At the beginning of this process of growth the infant's observable activity seems to be largely made up of *reflexes*—discontinuous, casual, miscellaneous. These reflexes, however, are never as harum-scarum as they seem, and amid their general randomness there is from the beginning a pattern of regularity. Thus the process of personal synthesis starts early, and if the rudimentary reflexes are compared to notes in the musical scale, tunes are soon heard, intermittent, but indicating that composition has begun.

In the next stage of the maturing life a more inclusive combination occurs. The separate groups of habits are taken possession of by *traits* that marshal and arrange them. Specific modes of adjustment to life appear that characterize the individual so that the growing child now has recognizable peculiarities. Between themselves these characteristics are often inconsistent, but they represent areas of increasing synthesis. The various groups of habitual activities are falling under the control of interests, attitudes, dispositions, and sentiments that begin to offer a design for living.

As growth continues, the very conflict between these dissident traits forces a further synthesis. *Selves* appear, each "self" a group of traits fairly consistent within its own range, but differing from, often incongruous with, other "selves" in the same person. There is the "self" one is at home, the "self" one is in the schoolroom, the "self" one is on the athletic field, and later there are the "selves" that diversely appear in business, in the church, on the golf links—each man having, says William James, "as many different social selves as there are distinct *groups* of persons about whose opinion he cares." Often these "multiple selves" are in bitter conflict—Dr. Jekyll against Mr. Hyde—so that, like states that cannot get together under a federal government, they fall apart into disunity and war. Strange and even comical incongruities appear in consequence—

> When the enterprising burglar's not a-burgling—
> When the cut-throat isn't occupied in crime—
> He loves to hear the little brook a-gurgling—
> And listen to the merry village chime.

The process of synthesis in many lives halts at this point. From reflexes to habits, from habits to traits, from traits to "multiple selves," the human organism, as an expanding pattern of activity, moves toward integration, but never reaches it, for it is a flying goal. Fully matured personality is, as General Smuts says, the most significant of all forms of integration, "the highest and completest of all wholes," and to achieve it is as difficult as it is significant. The central criterion of successful personal living is somehow to pass from mere "multiple selves" into the poise, balance, and cohesion of a unified personality.

II

The importance of this criterion is emphasized when one considers not only the process of normal growth, but the tragedy of the abnormal and insane. Says Dr. Charles H. Mayo, "Every second hospital bed in the United States is for the mentally afflicted." Add to this number the mentally and emotionally unstable people who have escaped hospitalization but who find life a curse to themselves and make it a burden to their friends, and the resultant weight of human woe due to personal abnormality is immense. Regarding the diverse kinds of insanity, one generalization holds—the personality falls apart, fails to achieve or loses cohesion, and so breaks up under the tension of internal conflict. The instinct of our language in describing unstable persons is correct: they "go to pieces"; they "fly off the handle"; they become "scatter-brained," "crack-brained," "rattle-pated," and "unhinged"; they cease being well-arranged persons and become "deranged"; they lose centrality and wholeness and are "eccentrics" and "crack-pots"; the word "crazy" itself comes from the French écrasé, meaning "broken" or "shattered." To be sure, the insane may draw themselves together around some idea furnishing a pseudo-pattern for their living—as, for example, that they are Caesar or Napoleon—but this false cohesion is arrived at only by splitting off wide areas of the personality and suppressing them. One way or another, the common mark of the insane is loss of a steady, coherent design that organizes the else harum-scarum miscellany of personal experience into sense and order.

The extreme forms of insanity specialists must handle, but each of us deals continually with the underlying problem of a disorganized life. We too go to pieces. The rattled baseball pitcher, the ruffled man badly flurried because he has mislaid a needed paper or a pair of glasses, the hurried person, trying to do something with too great haste and becoming flustered, the overfatigued person unable any longer to hold himself together, the frightened

[31]

person fallen into a panic, the choleric individual surprised by a burst of temper into loss of self-control—such examples from ordinary life remind us how insecure is our personal integration. We are a highly complex aggregation of many elements, and we easily break up into fragmentariness. A mature and genuine person is a supreme work of art—a symphony, whose constituent factors are noises that by themselves can be raucous and dissonant, and whose glory lies in the way they are put together.

III

The importance of this criterion is further emphasized when we consider that upon our achievement of personal wholeness and unity our happiness depends. "Happiness," says Dr. William H. Sheldon, "is essentially a state of going somewhere, wholeheartedly, one-directionally, without regret or reservation." Certainly, to live a fractional and flustered life, to feel pulled apart and at loose ends, to be all at odds with oneself, is to be unhappy. When, however, even temporarily, life ceases to be thus discordant and becomes "a settled, strong and single wind, that blows one way," the experience is thrilling. To become completely absorbed in an exciting game, to lose oneself under the spell of great drama or music, to have a well-nigh perfectly focused hour of creativity as an artist or of fortunate eloquence as an orator, to find oneself in the thick of a conflict where the whole of oneself goes all out for the sake of a cause deeply believed in, even to forget oneself in the complete enjoyment of

[32]

uncontrollable laughter—such occasions, when life ceases
to be a fraction and becomes an integer, are profoundly
satisfying. The basic urge of the human organism is
toward wholeness. The primary command of our being
is, Get yourself together, and the fundamental sin is to
be chaotic and unfocused.

The importance of this fact for happiness is evident
when one thinks not alone of radiant hours of relatively
complete integration on special occasions, but of the
underlying need of serenity on ordinary days. Every
human being faces at least three kinds of internal conflict that, left unresolved, spoil tranquillity and banish
happiness. For one thing, our desires and ambitions clash
among themselves. We want competing goods that cannot be had together. We wish to travel north and south
at the same time, and desiring thus, it may be, two admirable goals, around each of which strong aspirations
gather, we confront the danger of a split, dismembered
life. A second set of conflicts arises from the collision between powerful urges in ourselves such as sex, pugnacity,
and selfishness on one side, and on the other the prohibitions and conventions of society. No social order can
allow our egocentric impulses to run amok. From birth
we face restraint, reasonable or unreasonable, and this
interference with strong emotional urges becomes in
adolescence and maturity a cause of such frustration as
often tears personal life to shreds. A third set of conflicts
arises from the disproportion of our abilities to our ambitions. Ideals of achievement or of character are an
inevitable part of the human make-up—pictures of ourselves doing or being something that captures our
longing—and when our ability either is or seems to be

inadequate for our ambitions, frustration afflicts the balked and thwarted life so that girls jump from fourteen-story windows because they cannot be movie actresses, and men become disillusioned cynics because they cannot resolve the clash between their first-rate desires and their second-rate competence.

While our very constitution, therefore, urges us to get together, and makes happiness dependent on our doing so, life is continually pulling us apart. Wholeness is not simply a matter of remaining sane or of growing up until our various "selves" are merged into a unified life; it involves as well facing constant inner conflicts between competing desires, accommodating potent emotional urges to the restrictions of society, and handling the lure of personal ideals that collide with a dismaying sense of inadequacy. Difficult, however, though it is to save life from fragmentariness, the penalty for failure is terrific—a harassed, distracted life, drawn and quartered, that knows no serenity.

There is an understandable reason, therefore, why in modern psychological parlance the word "integration" has taken the place of the religious word "salvation." No disorganized personality can be put into any situation so fortunate that by itself it will make him happy, while a well-organized personality can confront with astonishingly satisfying results conditions that seem at first insurmountable. A young woman, stricken in childhood by infantile paralysis, is now a cripple, walking with difficulty even when mechanically aided. Yet in a college with two thousand students she is elected president of the athletic association. Many things she cannot do with her body, but what she can do, in a canoe, at archery, at swimming, she does supremely well. Whatever else lies behind her selection by her fellow students as their athletic leader, and, as well, behind her own satisfying handling of that leadership, she obviously is a real person, inwardly well organized and coherent, able to go somewhere whole-heartedly and one-directionally. Without that, no magic in any environment can confer happiness on anyone, and with that, the power to rise above and master adverse environment is often astonishing. With a true feeling for the nub of the matter, one youth exclaimed: "I want to get organized. I shall never be happy again till I'm organized!"

IV

The importance of integration as a criterion of successful personal life is further emphasized when we consider the meaning of desirable moral character. No virtue is more universally accepted as a test of good character than trustworthiness. Obviously, however, this virtue is more than "moral" in any ordinary sense of that term. Dependability is possible only in so far as the whole personality achieves a stanch unity that can be counted on. The psychological prerequisites of a reliable man are imperative: he cannot halt the integration of his life at some immature stage; he cannot surrender to internal conflict and live a dispersed and random existence; his impulses, emotions, thoughts, and purposes must not remain mere waifs and strays, nor his multiple selves be so diverse that he is one person today and another tomorrow. "Good old Watson!" said Sherlock Holmes to his friend. "You are

[35]

the one fixed point in a changing age." A consistent character, so unified that the quality of its responses is predictable, is commonly interpreted in moral terms, but the psychological processes involved are basic and profound. A man of integrity must first of all be well integrated.

Unreliability is the first fruit of all forms of dissociated personality. When the dissociation is caused by alcohol or opiates, we have the erratic behavior of the drunkard or the drug addict. When it is caused by infantilism, we have the eccentric whims and caprices of childishness. When it reaches the state of stark insanity, it ranges over a wide and terrible field of unpredictable reactions. It may even produce personalities so split into two or more "persons" of contrasting quality that one of them does not remember the actions of the other, and no observer can be sure which of them at any time will be in operation. As for the rest of us, we frequently act "out of character." The general pattern of our lives may involve honesty, truthfulness, and similar qualities—but not always. There are wild, erratic elements in us that behave in incalculable ways. Some of our moods, impulses, and desires are nomads, incorrigibly uncivilized by our main design for living. In so far as we are thus disintegrated, we are not dependable.

This is evident even with regard to a virtue like courtesy. Although politeness is supported by some of the strongest motives that play on human life, how common is the person whose courtesy is unreliable! Polite today, morose and uncivil tomorrow; obliging and well-bred in business, crabbed, churlish, and sulky at home; affable with one's so-called "equals," gruff and snobbish with one's servants; a good sportsman on the golf links, an ill-

[36]

natured jostler in the subway; kindly at church, snarling and peevish in the office; friendly with one's own kind, splenetic and even brutal toward Jews, Negroes, Roman Catholics, Protestants, religious liberals, Fundamentalists, or what not—so unreliable are men even with regard to courtesy. Such inconsistency is never adequately dealt with when treated only as a moral matter. Morality is rooted in psychology; consistency of character is one aspect of a successfully organized personality; integrity is impossible without integration.

In one sense, human nature is happily unpredictable. No one can foresee what may be forthcoming from most unlikely people. When Thomas Edison was seven years old his schoolteacher gave him up as a hopeless case. He heard her tell the inspector that he was "addled," and that it was useless for him longer to attend school. The incalculable possibilities of such a boy are among the chief assets of human nature. Even when character has been corrupted, transformations can occur, opening up futures that cannot be forecast, and this unforeseeable element is one of the glories of personal life. Moreover, even in those whom we count most dependable there is happily a wide range of unpredictability. We cannot tell what new and surprising qualities may yet appear in them. They may be full of unexpected quirks and humors, like a diamond with many facets that surprise and delight us. Indeed, paradoxical though it is, this unpredictability may be one aspect of trustworthiness; to use Shakespeare's lines, we can count upon the fact that

Age cannot wither her, nor custom stale
Her infinite variety.

James M. Barrie describes his official conscious self as hard-headed, practical, and canny, handling day-by-day affairs with prudence and shrewdness; but his other self, whom he calls "M'Connachie," is an impulsive, fantastic, romantic fellow who, when he wishes, takes charge of Barrie and controls his destiny—"M'Connachie is the one who writes the plays." This is not disintegration, but richness and variety of life. In this sense one can share Logan Pearsall Smith's exclamation, "What a bore it is, waking up in the morning always the same person!"

Without contradicting such facts, however, it still is true that predictable character is one of the highest ethical goods. One can tell in advance with what manner of behavior a man with such character will act. He has developed a dependable style. His responses to life are, in their quality, established and well organized; one can count on them; they are not inconstant and vacillating. His various impulses, emotions, desires, and ideas are no mere disparate will-o'-the-wisps, but he has become a whole person, with a unifying pattern of thought and feeling that gives coherence to everything he does. Such men and women are the strength of their friends and the noblest exhibit that human nature gives of itself. In them integration of personality has issued in integrity of character.

v

Were this the whole of the matter the problem would be simpler than it is. Difficult though it be to achieve personal unity, still, if well-organized personality always involved good character, that fact at least would furnish a clear picture of our task. Unfortunately, the situation is more complicated. The alternative to an integrated life that issues in integrity is not necessarily the loose and vagabond living we have been describing. A personality can become powerfully unified on an ethically low level, around unworthy aims. Integrity is impossible without integration, but integration does not necessarily issue in integrity. Napoleon was not a "good" man, but he was a potent personality with immense capacities for sustained concentration. Someone called him "organized victory." To an extraordinary degree he got himself together, focused his life, achieved centrality in his purposes. Psychologically speaking, he was unusually all of a piece. He illustrates the puzzling difference between a *strong* person and a *good* one.

The importance of this contrast appears in man's natural admiration for firm, hard-driving, one-directional, consolidated persons, even when ethically they have little to commend them. Men like Adolf Hitler, burning glasses that intensely concentrate all the elements of personal life into one fiery purpose, become the idol of millions, although they set the world destructively ablaze. In lesser ways this drift of admiration toward compact, well-organized personality, regardless of its ethical quality, is illustrated in every one of us. Let the saints say what they will, they have a sly liking for strong sinners. All exhibitions of power are fascinating, and in personal life integration is power. The chief rival of goodness is not badness in itself, but the attractive spectacle of lives powerfully organized on low levels. Emily Dickinson may scorn "A hateful, hard, successful face," but that kind of face, if only it be forceful, as in Mussolini's case, exercises a powerful fascination. This drift of admiration is man's instinctive tribute to the fact that whether on one level or another, integration is strength.

The possibility of being psychologically well composed and strong, and at the same time ethically dangerous, or even contemptible, presents life with a serious problem. From birth on, our organism tries to pull itself together. Integration is so imperative a need, happiness is so dependent on it, lack of it so obviously leads to failure, misery, or even madness, that man faces an unavoidable urge, one way or another, to collect himself around some center. If, then, it proves too difficult to achieve this gratifying unity on a high level, man tries it on a low one. Some psychiatrists positively encourage this. Conceiving personality's highest good as psychological integration, no matter how it is achieved, they recommend the organization of life on the most convenient and available level that presents itself. One patient, for example, troubled by powerful animal impulses, had also a sensitive spiritual life involving respect for himself, reverence for others, and religious faith. The psychiatrist told him that unless he stopped bothering about his spiritual life, gave up belief in God, became ethically callous, and exploded his animal impulses, he never could be happy. What the psychiatrist was aiming at is plain. He was being "scientific"; regarding ethical considerations as outside his bailiwick, he conceived his business as helping people to the happiness that integration alone can bring; and he was picking what seemed to him the most available level in that particular life. Such counsel, however, far from solving the problem, merely worsens it. Why should it be supposed that eliminating a man's best, and organizing his life around some egocentric impulse, will bring a satisfying unity? The result of that process is a counterfeit integration, often issuing in the most tragic forms of inner conflict.

While, therefore, integration is a major criterion of successful personal living, integration itself needs a criterion. The fanatic is organized—"the man of one idea, whose world has reference only to his obsession, and whose life is impoverished by its pinpoint focus." One way or another, we desperately need to get order and symmetry into our make-up. In a normal person the drive for that never stops while life lasts. If balked on one level, we try another. If we succeed in centering and collecting ourselves around ethically admirable aims, we present human life at its best. If we fail at that, the alternative is not necessarily a loose and vagrant personality. We may be powerfully integrated psychologically, but organized around aims intellectually trivial and ethically sinister.

Indeed, if we are psychologically normal in even a moderate degree, we *are* getting ourselves together. It is not alone the salvation, but the doom of man that he can and does achieve coherence. Each of us is developing a style, as intimately characteristic of the individual as is the style of an artist or a musician. This style is the subtle, elusive, but nonetheless real result of a progressive organization of life, often half unconscious, around some center or centers, good, bad, or indifferent. It is the aroma from our integration, and it can as readily be evil as good.

Multitudes of people of all moral grades achieve a sufficient degree of compactness so that their organizing principles are clear. Charles Dickens exaggerated the distinctive qualities of such persons, but characters like Uriah Heep, Squeers, Micawber, and Mrs. Jellyby illustrate how many and diverse are the unifying patterns in which personal life can arrange itself. As for St. Francis of Assisi and Julius Caesar, Madame Curie and Beau Brummell, Florence Nightingale and Casanova, all such personalities had sovereign traits that gave their lives a recognizable singleness. Integration as a strictly psychological process can have diverse ethical results. It ambiguously makes great saints and powerful sinners.

VI

√A possible misunderstanding of the well-integrated life on high levels is involved in the use of descriptive words such as "singleness," "poise," "unity," "compactness," and "serenity." They may suggest a placid life, with all conflicts resolved, but such a picture of powerful and admirable personality is plainly false. The great souls have been inwardly tortured. With more contradictory and potent elements in them to be organized, with more ideas, stronger feelings, more urgent impulses, and more possibilities of diverse action than ordinary men possess, they have been more racked and torn, not less, and far from being placid, they illustrate Sydney Smith's saying: ∪ "The meaning of an extraordinary man is that he is eight men in one man."

Wagner was, for the most part, no more serene than a stormy sea. Carlyle suffered such inner mutiny while trying to finish his history of the French Revolution that he said to his wife: "They may twaddle as they like about the miseries of a bad conscience: but I should like to know whether Judas Iscariot was *more* miserable than Thomas Carlyle who never did anything *criminal,* so far as he remembered!" Edwin Booth, looking back on a life of pre-eminent success as an actor, said: "Much of my life's struggle has been with myself, and the pain I have endured in overcoming and correcting the evils of my untrained disposition has been very great." Florence Nightingale had a desperate time finding herself, and wrote in her diary, "In my thirty-first year I see nothing desirable but death." Dwight L. Moody said, "I've had more trouble with D. L. Moody than with any other man I know." Beethoven went through perdition with his unruly emotions, and when at last deafness closed in on him his inner struggle is only imperfectly voiced in his exclamation, "If I were only rid of this affliction I could embrace the world! . . . No! I cannot endure it! I will seize fate by the throat; most assuredly it shall not get me wholly down." As for the saints, they all understand Paul, "The good which I would I do not: but the evil which I would not, that I practise. . . . Wretched man that I am!"

To be sure, not all such tormented folk would, in any case, be selected as examples of psychological integration, but they were powerful persons, with a one-directional drive and with sovereign traits that led to sovereign accomplishments. They got themselves together sufficiently to make a concentrated impression on the world. If integration is the high good we have said it is, it cannot mean mere tranquillity, where conflict ceases in an equable and steady calm, but must somehow include the range of fact that such tortured souls reveal. Who of us does not understand the conversation in James M. Barrie's *Sentimental Tommy?* " 'But you must decide!' Grizel almost screamed. 'I needna,' he stammered, 'till we're at Tilliedrum. Let's speak about some other thing.' She rocked her arms, crying, 'It is so easy to make up one's mind.' 'It's easy to you that has just one mind,' he retorted with spirit, 'but if you had as many minds as I have—!' "

✓The key to the solution of this problem lies in the fact that all integration is hierarchical. It involves the domination of some traits and purposes over others, and, like any government, it seldom, if ever, is so consummated as to quiet all dissent. The story runs that Zanchio, King of Navarre, was nicknamed "Tremblant" because his skin would be seen to be all a-quiver as he was being armed for battle. But when his squires tried to make light of the coming danger in order to allay his fears, "You have no perfect knowledge of me," said he, "for if my flesh knew how far my courage will ere-long carrie it, it would presently fall into a flat swoune." Such governance of alien elements by a dominant purpose is involved in all well-organized living. While, therefore, integration does mean singleness and unity—life ending, as another put it, not like a broom, in a multitude of small straws, but like a bayonet, in point and power—it cannot be pictured as placidity. It involves not only the harmonizing of conflicts but also the subjugation of revolts. It involves a scale of values, with some supreme value, or complex of associated values, so organizing life that one gladly foregoes lesser aims, and resists contradictory enticements, rather than sacrifice life's chief aim and highest worth. Moreover, it entails not alone the resolving of conflicts, but, when that is impossible, the toleration of conflicts, the candid, objective, sometimes humorous recognition of them, coupled with steady resolution to put first values first. Men and women, therefore, with a positive "talent for turbulence," have achieved powerfully integrated lives. Seen from the outside, there is nothing vagrant and sprawling about them; they exhibit extraordinary single-ness and unity. Experienced from the inside, their lives involve a constant struggle to preserve the hegemony of their dominant aims over their competing motives, doubts, and fears.

This factor in even well-organized lives is revealed in the temporary disintegrations with which the most steady and poised persons have to deal. Bobby Jones, notable for his coolness on the golf links, said concerning one of his greatest games that he stood in the eighteenth fairway devoutly wishing that his knees would stop knocking together long enough for him to hit the ball. Caruso once delayed for nearly an hour the raising of the cur-tain at the Metropolitan Opera House because he had an attack of stage fright. John B. Gough, a marvelous orator, remarkable for his self-possession, once said that before each address he always felt, "This is the time when I shall fail." To picture integration, therefore, as a welding process that makes of personality a single, consolidated block, is false. Integration is an affair of psychological government, with all the recurrent dissents, tensions, and revolts to which government, however united and strong, is subject. Writers of biography commonly understate this inner fact about their heroes. They naturally select a few dominant patterns and simplify their portrait by an etcher's art. They present a much more orderly and single-minded individual than actually existed. In all strong characters, when one listens behind the scenes one hears echoes of strife and contention. Nevertheless, far from being at loose ends within themselves, such persons may have achieved a powerful concentration of purpose and drive, and far from being organized on low levels, they may have so identified themselves with some supreme value that their names and their cause are henceforth inseparable.

Indeed, to call integration hierarchical is to use too static a figure. Personality is dynamic; it is a going concern; like a river, its unity consists not in the absence of cross-currents and back-eddies but in its total flow and main direction. A river can have rapids and waterfalls, and still move powerfully one way. While, therefore, there are fortunate dispositions gifted with temperamental calm, whose happiness lies in tranquillity, they alone do not exhaust the meanings of integration. Some happiness is not calm but fierce. So David Livingstone, after costly years of toil and suffering in Africa, doing what most of all he wanted to do, said that he had never made a sacrifice in his life. His experience had been full of struggle, inward and outward. He had buried his wife at Shupanga, crying, "Oh my Mary, my Mary! how often we have longed for a quiet home, since you and I were cast adrift at Kolobeng." The unity of his life consisted not in the resolution and ending of all conflict, but in the toleration of certain inevitable conflicts under the dominance of a controlling purpose. Christ himself cried, "Now is my soul troubled; and what shall I say?" and in Gethsemane, "exceeding sorrowful even unto death," he prayed "in an agony" and "his sweat became as it were

[46]

great drops of blood falling down upon the ground," but he was, at the very least, a marvelously integrated person.

Personalities, therefore, fall into three general classes. Some never get themselves together; they either fail to grow up into psychological maturity, or they go to pieces under strain. Others do get themselves together but on low ethical levels; they become egocentric; they acquire absorbing devotions—money, prestige, fame, even alcohol —to the pursuit of which they subjugate all their powers; they fall under the spell of some single and unifying aim, concerning which they feel as Frederick the Great felt about glory—"Glory . . . is folly, but it is folly that you cannot shake off, when once you get it fastened upon you." Still others, however, achieve well-organized lives on high levels. They find values supremely worth serving. Their lives become coherent, steady, one-directional. They identify themselves with something greater than themselves, to which they give themselves. They face inner tension and at times vehement struggle in maintaining the chosen pattern of their lives, but they maintain it. They become predictable characters.

VII

The process by which real personality is thus attained is inward and spiritual. No environmental changes by themselves can so *push* a personality together as to bring this satisfying wholeness within. The achievement of integration carries one deep into the core of selfhood and suggests some such experience as William James described: "The process, gradual or sudden, by which a self hitherto divided, and consciously wrong inferior and unhappy, becomes unified and consciously right superior and happy, in consequence of its firmer hold upon religious realities."

To be sure, fortunate resolutions of inner discord may come through experiences not commonly thought of as religious. William James said of his wife: "She saved me from my *Zerrissenheit* (torn-to-pieces-ness) and gave me back to myself all in one piece." When, however, anyone, starved for lack of such love, asserts that, were a fortunate marriage to befall, he or she would thereby become unified and happy, the personal counselor may well be dubious. In too many homes the possibilities of such love, though richly present, are nullified by some deep-seated individual disintegration. As Novalis said: "Only so far as a man is happily married to himself, is he fit for married life." Fortunate romance and marriage, profoundly desirable as they are, often accentuate the pre-existing *Zerrissenheit*, rather than resolve it. If anyone is to achieve personal wholeness, even so fortunate an environment as a loyal and loving family cannot dispense him from confronting himself in that innermost center whence his basic faiths about life, and his spiritual resources for life, spring.

As for the typical environments of our modern world, even when they are popularly deemed fortunate they disperse and disorganize life rather than collect and unify it. Such is the psychological effect even of our emphasis on individual liberty. In primitive, tribal society, a man was so submerged in the life of his family and clan that individuality hardly existed. Social solidarity was so complete that thinking, feeling, and deciding were for the most part communal functions, and the whole tribe moved together when it moved at all. The break-up of that old cohesive solidarity into our freer societies, with infinitely greater chances for personal self-expression and self-fulfillment, would be regarded by the typical modern as an advance. Obviously, however, it has immeasurably increased the strain upon the individual. In the modern world the individual is thrown back upon himself as never before in history. For his livelihood, for his standing in the community, for his success or failure, for his personal friendships, for his opinions, he is largely on his own.

It is difficult for a Western liberal to imagine a desirable social order that does not preserve and even accentuate such freedom; yet freedom involves, and always will involve, one of the severest tensions that the human organism can sustain. As Thomas Huxley said, "A man's worst difficulties begin when he is able to do as he likes." Our modern society, therefore, even in those freedom-conferring aspects which are acclaimed as a social advance, increases rather than decreases the internal conflicts, confusions, and worries, and makes more difficult, not less, their avoidance or their solution. "Anxiety," said Kierkegaard, "is the dizziness of freedom." The hope of a society that will automatically produce integrated, one-directional, satisfying personality, pushed together by fortunate environment, is utter delusion.

Indeed, nervous prostration is a specialty of the prosperous, and statistics indicate that suicide occurs most frequently among the more well-to-do. Wealth immensely widens the area of individual freedom, and so increasing the multiplicity of possible choices, it often is far more disrupting than satisfying. Granted that "A heavy purse makes a light heart!" Granted that the inequities of our economic disorder deserve the castigation of good men, and that many thwarted lives, distracted, stunted, and crushed, would in a more decent social organization have a chance at worth-while living now denied them! Nevertheless, no financial prosperity by itself can push a personality together, give it centrality and symmetry, lead it up through reflexes, habits, traits, and multiple selves to a united whole, banish from the scene the major areas of inner conflict, and produce a steady and poised man.

> It's no in titles nor in rank;
> It's no in wealth like Lon'on Bank,
>   To purchase peace and rest.

Balk at it, as we moderns may, there is no solution of this inner problem of a unified and whole personality unless we come back to the insights of the great religious seers. So one of our modern Quakers puts it:

Strained by the very mad pace of our daily outer burdens, we are further strained by an inward uneasiness, because we have hints that there is a way of life vastly richer and deeper than all this hurried existence, a life of unhurried serenity and peace and power. If only we could slip over into that Center! If only we could find the Silence which is the source of sound! We have seen and known some people who seem to have found this deep Center of living, where the fretful calls of life are integrated, where No as well as Yes can be said with confidence. We've seen such lives, integrated, unworried by the tangles of close decisions, unhurried, cheery, fresh, positive. These are not people of dallying idleness nor of obviously mooning

[50]

meditation; they are busy carrying their full load as well as we, but without any chafing of the shoulders with the burden, with quiet joy and springing step. Surrounding the trifles of their daily life is an aura of infinite peace and power and joy. We are so strained and tense, with our burdened lives; they are so poised and at peace.

CHAPTER III

The Principle of Self-Acceptance

I

A MODERN novelist describing one of his characters says, "He was not so much a human being as a civil war." This unhappy condition, however it may involve maladjustment to environment, is always complicated by maladjustment to oneself, and such inner discord commonly takes the form of tension between what we are and what we want to be. Every human being sometime faces a situation where on the one side is his actual self, with his abilities and circumstances, and on the other are ideal pictures of himself as he is ambitious to be and of his achievements as he has set his heart on having them; and between the two is such disparity that they have no practicable relationship. When what we are and what we dearly want to be thus face each other in seemingly hopeless disproportion, inward civil war begins.

This is the more serious because man at his best is distinguished by his capacity to have both an actual and a desired self. Even when we run to catch a bus we are not driven, as the bus is, by posterior force, but are drawn from before by an imagined picture of ourselves seated in the bus and going to our destination. Purposive activity, in which the future tense becomes causative, is man's glory, and nowhere more so than in the development of personality. This faculty, however, can function so abnormally that it tears life to pieces. The ideal confronts the actual, and taunts it; our existent selves see our idealized selves tantalizingly out of reach, and are distraught; in view of the unattainable that we wish, we become disgusted and discouraged with the actual that we are.

No well-integrated life is possible, therefore, without an initial act of self-acceptance, as though to say: I, John Smith, hereby accept myself, with my inherited endowments and handicaps and with the elements in my environment that I cannot alter or control, and, so accepting myself as my stint, I will now see what I can do with *this* John Smith. When Margaret Fuller said, "I accept the universe," Carlyle's retort was, "Gad! she'd better!" Accepting the universe, however, is for many people a simple matter compared with the far more intimate act of accepting themselves.

The coxswain of the winning Freshman crew in one of our largest universities was an eighty-seven pound cripple. Stricken with infantile paralysis in boyhood, he had dropped out seven years of schooling. When allowed to study again he made up for lost time, and, determined not to be a cipher among his fellows, he saw in his dwarfed and handicapped body, even while he was in preparatory school, the positive makings of a good coxswain. So, in the university, this midget, with a crippled voice so that he needed a special type of megaphone, and crippled arms so that he needed a special type of steering apparatus, won his race and became the hero of the river. When one considers the varied kinds of personal response conceivable in such a case—rebellion, despair, self-pity, apathy, inertia—and when one imagines the desired selves that must have tantalized the actual self with their unattainable allurements, it is clear that at the center of that boy's positive handling of his problem was a courageous act of self-acceptance. As Rank rightly says: "The neurotic type, which we all represent to a certain extent, suffers from the fact that he cannot accept himself, cannot endure himself and will have it otherwise."

II

Disruptive tension between our actual and desired selves is variously caused. Parents often project into the imaginations of their children ideals and ambitions utterly out of keeping with the aptitudes and abilities of the children themselves. One mother, aspiring to be a singer and frustrated in her own career, transferred her ambition to her daughter. The fierce and baffled desires of her disappointed life were concentrated on her hopes for the girl. Into her daughter's susceptible imagination she poured her own unattainable aspirations, and did it the more persuasively and remorselessly because she conceived her motive as maternal love. The daughter, in consequence, unfitted for the imposed role, found herself at last with an imagination preoccupied by one ambition and a conscience committed to it as a sacred duty, but with an impassable chasm between her actual and her desired self. For the tragic disruption that ensued before the daughter could be brought to accept *herself*, the mother was responsible.

This emphasis is the more needed because popular stress is commonly laid upon the other side. To have large ambitions, to expect the most of ourselves, to attempt even the seemingly impossible and achieve it—is not this the mark of admirable personality? The answer, of course, is affirmative, but that answer needs to be chastened by the fact that the beginning of wise ambition lies in a man's accepting himself as himself and not as someone else, and in trying to make the most and the best of *that* self and not of another. Mistakes at this initial point of departure carry a heavy penalty.

One boy had shone in the limited community where he was born. He was the pride of his large family and alike the handsomest and ablest boy in town. In everything he undertook he was always first, and he grew into young manhood a serious, high-minded youth, headed for one of the major professions but with a dangerous factor in his situation of which he was unaware—a dominant picture of his desired self as always a shining first. Then in a large university he found himself good but not eminent. The expectations of peerless priority, built into him by his family and friends, proved fallacious. He suffered a serious nervous breakdown without knowing why. Only when he found out why, saw clearly the absurd tension between his actual and imagined self, and went through a thorough process of self-acceptance, did he get himself in hand and go on to make a creditable and serviceable use of the self he really had.

Along with the misused influence of families, the pressure of contemporary culture is often responsible for this disruptive strain. From Periclean Greece to modern Nazi-dom, how diverse have been the cultures into which human individuals have been born! Nothing runs deeper in human nature than the desire to be appreciated, and in whatever cultural setting a man grows up, he normally tries to meet its characteristic demands and succeed according to its characteristic standards. Imagine, then, the same individual, with his physical, intellectual, and temperamental peculiarities, born in central Africa, in Florence in the thirteenth century, in the United States today, in Japan! In each case the admired ideals, the standards of success, the preferred types of ambition, call for distinctive pictures of the desired self. These cultural patterns, however, are not necessarily fitted to any particular man. Their acceptance may mean the gross mal-treatment of his aptitudes. Despite the fact that a culture powerfully helps to make a person what he is, he may find, as millions do, that channeling his life down the river-bed where the main appreciations of his current civilization run, involves the denial of everything that he natively was meant to be and do. Such tension, so caused, is one of man's major tragedies.

No individual self-acceptance alone can solve so vast a problem in its public aspects, but multitudes of individuals, recognizing the nature of the difficulty and see-ing clearly what is happening to them, might solve their own problems. Especially in free countries, with many diversities of choice and with various groups whose ap-preciation may be sought, this problem commonly arises in a form that the wise individual can handle. Tschai-kowsky was a lawyer before he became a musician; Gauguin was a banker a decade before he became an artist; Herschel played the organ in a small church and gave lessons to amateur pianists before he became a great scientist. One consulting psychologist even found a ranchman, who had been born a ranchman, who supposed he always must be a ranchman, and who was trying to be a good one although utterly unfitted for it, but who wanted above all else to paint pictures. Daring to accept himself when he was past forty, he actually did paint pictures that were exhibited in leading galleries. If one is going to be a real person, self-discovery and self-acceptance are primary.

Quite apart from the influence of unwise families and the pressure of social cultures, tension between the actual and the desired selves becomes poignant in the presence of serious handicaps. Alec Templeton entertains millions over the radio with his music and amuses them with his whimsicalities. He is stone blind. The first natural response to such crippling disadvantage is an imagination thronged with pictures of the unattainable, and from the contrast between them and the actualities commonly spring resentment, cynicism, self-pity, inertia. The human story, however, has nothing finer to present than handicapped men and women who, accepting themselves, have illustrated what Dr. Alfred Adler called "the human being's power to turn a minus into a plus." Shut out from some desired southern California where orange trees grow, they have found themselves in some Labrador where no orange trees will grow, but like Sir Wilfred Grenfell they have proved that one can not only exist there but can live there illustriously. Always, behind such personal triumph lies an act of self-acceptance. Only so, for example, could Dr. Edward Livingston Trudeau, driven from his profession in New York City by tuberculosis, ever have written: "The struggle with tuberculosis has brought me experiences and left me recollections which I never could have known otherwise, and which I would not exchange for the wealth of the Indies!"

Tension between our existent and our desired selves arises in one of its most dangerous forms from high moral ideals, and nowhere is it more likely to be mishandled. High moral ideals are among man's noblest possessions, but they too are projected pictures of ourselves as we feel we ought to be or strongly want to be, and the disproportion between them and what we actually are can be so great as to disrupt the life. A young man is fascinated by ideals of public service. He reads stories of eminent social servants of the race, pioneers, and missionary heroes, until he pictures himself as one of them. Is not that a high ideal? Yet he may be no more fitted for the role than basswood is fitted to make a battleship. It is a hard task to persuade that kind of idealist to accept himself as he actually is, to change his projected picture of himself accordingly, and to achieve this change so as not to keep him from being a real person but to make him one.

Worth-while and commanding ideals are indispensable, but that does not mean that an apple tree becomes admirable by aspiring to be an elm tree. Innumerable people are thus the victims of misfitted idealism. They are trying to be great or successful or even good in ways that stem out from misapprehension about what they really are. Granted that there are general ideals that apply equally to Peter, James, and John! Yet, if Peter tries to be James, or James John, trouble begins. Each must accept himself to start with, as a tree might first accept its species and then its special habitat, and try to fulfill the possibilities of that. So Jesus is reported to have said to Peter when Peter asked about another man's lot, "What is that to thee? follow thou me."

This does not mean resignation to the actual self. Resignation can be negative, passive, submissive; self-acceptance is positive, active, aggressive. Peter accepts Peter, with his distinctive and restricted endowment, and will see now what can be made of *that*. The great successes in ethical character are so initiated. Gunga Din, in Kipling's poem, was a humbly situated man, of lowly endowment and vocation, but he was a real person: "You're a better man than I am, Gunga Din!"

Moral ideals, stiff, rigid, and promiscuously applied, can do incalculable harm. Unselfishness and loyalty are major virtues, but a daughter under the thralldom of a possessive mother can so picture herself as in duty bound to be unselfish and loyal, that, without doing her mother any real good, her life is blighted and her personality wrecked. Her selfless devotion leads her to undertake as an ideal what neither God, nor her own nature, nor a sound ethic ever intended her for. Ethical ideals in their application are relative to the native endowment and actual situation of the individual. One man may choose ascetic chastity and be a priest; most of us had better accept ourselves and get married. One man may have a calm, equable temperament that need never be ruffled;

another may have to say, as Dr. Stephen Tyng did to one who rebuked him for asperity, "Young man, I control more temper every fifteen minutes than you will in your whole lifetime." One man may be an Erie Canal, another a Mississippi River, and an Erie Canal has no idea how many ways a Mississippi River has of going wrong.

When one considers how variant the differing life-patterns are—the naturally dominant and the naturally submissive, the perfectionists who never get anything right and the rationalizers who never do anything wrong, the exhibitionists who display themselves and the shy who camouflage themselves, the contrite blamers of self and the chronic accusers of others, the passive, whose ideals are privacy, calmness, and security, and the active, whose ideals are power, popularity, and applause—the factual basis for the need of self-acceptance is clear. Wrote John Quincy Adams in his *Diary:* "I am a man of reserved, cold, austere, and forbidding manners: my political adversaries say, a gloomy misanthropist, and my personal enemies, an unsocial savage. With a knowledge of the actual defect in my character, I have not the pliability to reform it." That was written in a low mood of resignation, but the insight behind it is true; whatever Adams did with his life, he had to start doing by accepting the self he actually possessed, and tackling that.

So Ralph Waldo Emerson put it: "There is a time in every man's education when he arrives at the conviction that envy is ignorance; that imitation is suicide; that he must take himself for better, for worse, as his portion; that though the wide universe is full of good, no kernel of nourishing corn can come to him but through his toil

[60]

t plot of ground which is given to him

III

self-acceptance is not achieved and the
the actual and the dreamed-of self be-
e result is an unhappy and sometimes
nse of inferiority. One study of 275 college
d women revealed that over 90% of them suf-
ed from gnawing, frustrated feelings of deficiency.
The areas of their conscious inferiority were manifold—
physical incompetence, ill health, unpleasant appearance,
lack of social charm, failure in love, low-grade intellectual
ability, moral failure, and guilt. To say that this disheartening sense of being inferior springs from inability
to meet the demands of society is only part of the truth.
The social demands strike inward; they conjure up an
imagined self—competent, adequate, superior; the final
tussle is not so much between the individual and the demands of society, as within the individual, between his
dreamed-of self and the self he thinks he actually is.

To be sure, the feeling of deficiency can never be taken
at its face value as a true indication of real lack. The
feeling is relative and subjective. The runner-up in a
championship tennis match may suffer wretchedly from
a sense of inadequacy; and while a witless dolt may be
well content with himself, the winner of a Nobel Prize,
whose dreams completely outdistance his accomplishments, may suffer from an inferiority complex. Not alone
the ill-born, hard-bestead, and handicapped face this

problem, but the well endowed and i
cumstanced.

The seriousness of the problem itself is m
by the unhealthy ways in which it is common

Some deal with it by the smoke-screen method. F
miserably inferior, and not wanting others to know it
shy become aggressive, the embarrassed effusive, and
timid bluster and brag. The boastful, cocky, pushing ma
may seem afflicted with an exaggerated sense of his superiority, whereas in fact he is covering under a masquerade
of aggressiveness a wretched feeling of inadequacy. One
man, hitherto gentle and considerate in his family, suffered a humiliating failure. At once he began to grow a
crust. He became domineering, harsh, dictatorial. Paradoxical though it is, in the days when he felt superior he
behaved humbly and considerately, as though he felt
inferior; when he felt inferior he began to swagger as
though he were superior. Nowhere does the etymological
meaning of personality run more true to form—it originally came from the Latin *persona,* meaning "mask."

Others, like the fox in Aesop's fable, handle the problem of bitterly felt inferiority by calling sour all grapes
they cannot reach. The frail youth discounts athletics;
the debauchee, really suffering from a sense of guilt,
scoffs at the self-controlled as prudes; the failure at school
or college, deeply humiliated, scorns intellectuals as
"high-brows"; the girl without charm exaggerates her
liability, dresses crudely, adopts rough manners, deliber-

ately looks her worst, professing lofty disdain of charm as a triviality. A major amount of cynicism springs from this source. Watch what people are cynical about, and one can often discover what they lack, and subconsciously, beneath their touchy condescension, deeply wish they had.

Others deal with this tension between the actual and the desired self by fantasy. Unable in the real world to secure their longed-for eminence, they retreat into the world of daydream. In school, business, social intercourse, and love they may be obscure and mistreated, but in this other realm, which reverie creates, they walk fortunate and renowned. Daydreaming in itself is a useful faculty; it can furnish both harmless escape from boredom and struggle, and constructive suggestions for positive endeavor; but when it coincides with severe tension between the actual and the idealized self, it is commonly put to abnormal uses. The imagined world, where the self is all it dreams of being, can become more vivid than the real world, and, habitually inhabiting this pictured paradise of fulfilled hopes, the individual can be disqualified for any constructive dealing with his actual self in the existent situation. In the end the pictured world may become so dominant that the real world is no longer clearly seen, and the individual passes over the border into abnormality.

Still others, facing the strain of a wished-for self, tantalizingly out of reach, turn in precisely the opposite

[63]

direction—not to dreams of hopes fulfilled, but to excuses and retreats based on an exaggerated acknowledgment of their inferiority. So one student who was struggling with failure said: "I have thought it over carefully and I have come to the conclusion that I am feeble-minded!" Far from being said with despair, this was announced with relief; it was a perfect excuse; it let him out from all responsibility. Factually it was absurd; emotionally it was abnormal; but as a defense mechanism it promised release from the taunting challenge of his idealized self. Indeed, so ready an escape does this method provide that the human organism often takes to it subconsciously. Baffled by a sense of failure, the individual develops psychic illnesses, pseudo-maladies, neurotic diseases, in the presence of which he is dispensed from any endeavor to be his desired self.

By such unwholesome methods many evade the basic act of healthy self-acceptance. Being Mr. One-Talent, they will be content with nothing except being Mr. Ten-Talent, or, being Mr. Ten-Talent, they tease themselves out of all happy and coherent living because they are not more. They have the admirable quality of aspiration, ambition, emulation, but they misuse it. A Ford car yearning to be a Rolls Royce is absurd, but a Ford car that accepts itself can easily outlast and outserve, if it be well used, a Rolls Royce that is poorly handled, and it can travel some rough and crooked roads where a Rolls Royce cannot go or would be ridiculous if it did.

IV

Among the constructive elements that make self-acceptance basic in becoming a real person is the principle of compensation. Deficiency can be a positive stimulus, as in the classic case of Demosthenes. Desiring above all else to be an orator and help save his people in a desperate emergency, he had to accept himself as a stammerer. He did not, however, conceal his humiliation with bluster, nor decry eloquence as worthless trickery, nor retreat into fantastic dreams of himself delivering orations that would shake the world, nor resign himself to stammering as an excuse for doing nothing. He took a positive attitude toward his limitation, speaking against the noise of the waves, so runs the story, with pebbles in his mouth, until, as the psychologists put it, he "overcompensated." To say that Demosthenes became a great orator *despite* his stammering is an understatement; the psychologists would add that he became a supremely effective orator *because* he stammered. Genius is commonly developed in men by some deficiency that stabs them wide awake and becomes a major incentive. Obstacles can be immensely arousing and kindling.

To be sure, this direct type of compensation, which attacks a hated inferiority and achieves eminence in the very realm where deficiency threatens failure, is not always possible. Not everyone can, like Theodore Roosevelt, start with a frail physique and so over-compensate that he becomes not merely a normally healthy man but a roughrider, a lion hunter, and in general an exaggerated example of rugged living. Even so, however, a substitutionary compensation is almost always possible. The homely girl may develop the more wit and charm because she is homely; the shy, embarrassed youth, with the temperament of a recluse, may be all the more useful in scientific research because of that. Immanuel Kant suffered all his life from a constricted chest that kept him in almost constant pain, to which in his youth he struggled in vain to reconcile himself. One may fairly conjecture that he would never have been the philosopher he was had he not faced this limitation and made the discovery that determined his life's direction: "While I felt oppressed in my chest, my head was clear."

The idea that we are made great by our superiorities and ruined by our inferiorities is a dangerous half-truth. Many are spoiled by their superiorities, are overmastered by them, mishandle them, prove inadequate to deal with the power involved in them, until in the end, like Saul, they fall on their own sword. Many, on the other hand, have their inferiorities to thank for their eminence. Would Steinmetz, with his grossly deformed body, have developed his mind to such extraordinary uses had he been an Apollo? Biography records too many youths who seemed at first the runts of the litter but who became the eminent surprises of their day for chance and accident to be the explanation. Compensation, direct and substitutionary, is an incalculably influential power in the development of personality.

Involved in such successful handling of recognized inferiority is the ability to pass from the defensive to the offensive attitude toward our limitations. Faced with a discouraging contrast between our actual and desired selves, we are naturally thrown on the defensive. Life seems to be against us; we feel under attack by adverse circumstance; emotionally we become apologetic, resentful, fearful, or humiliated. From this defensive attitude spring all kinds of psychological evils. Alibis and evasions, hypersensitiveness, chronic blaming of others, apathy and dejection, nervous and moral collapse—such maladies go back to a defensive emotional attitude toward life. Into such a problem self-acceptance walks as an indispensable element in the solution. John Smith accepts John Smith with his realistically seen limitations, difficulties, and failures, and positively starts out to discover what can be raised on that rocky farm. Multitudes live in pathetic unhappiness and inefficiency, when the shift from the defensive to the offensive attitude, whether in handling a single day's tasks or a whole life's character and career, can work miracles.

John Callender was an officer of the Massachusetts militia and was guilty of cowardice at the Battle of Bunker Hill. One of George Washington's first duties when he assumed command of the American forces at Cambridge was to order the court-martial of Captain Callender. "It is with inexpressible Concern," wrote Washington in his official orders, "that the General upon his first Arrival in the army, should find an Officer sentenced by a General Court Martial to be cashier'd for Cowardice—A Crime of all others, the most infamous in a Soldier, the most injurious to an Army, and the last to be forgiven." The rest of the story, however, runs as follows: No sooner had this tragedy befallen him than Callender re-enlisted in the army as a private, and at the Battle of Long Island exhibited such conspicuous courage that Washington publicly revoked the sentence and restored to him his captaincy. Behind such an experience lies a basic act of self-acceptance—open-eyed, realistic, without equivocation or excuse—along with a shift from a defensive to an offensive attitude, that makes John Callender an inspiriting person to remember.

V

Self-acceptance, however, with the accompanying substitution of a positive for a negative attitude, is often desperately difficult. To achieve it a man needs alike all the practical good sense he can muster and all the spiritual resources he can bring to his help.

For one thing, put to shame by a sense of inferiority because the contrast between the actual and desired selves is humiliating, a man may well begin by reducing to a minimum the things that thus mortify him. Many people are humiliated by situations that need not be humiliations at all. To be lame, to be blind, to have what Ko-Ko called "a caricature of a face," to lack desired ability, to be economically restricted—such things are limitations, but if they become humiliations it is because inwardly we make them so. Even Napoleon had to accept himself—five feet two and one-fourth inches tall, and forty-third in his class at the *Ecole Militaire*. He never liked himself that way. Considering his imperial ambitions, his diminutive stature was a limitation, but had he made of it and of his scholastic mediocrity a humiliation, he probably never would have been Napoleon.

[68]

Life is a landscaping job. We are handed a site, ample or small, rugged or flat, picturesque or commonplace, whose general outlines and contours are largely determined for us. Both limitation and opportunity are involved in every site, and the most unforeseeable results ensue from the handling—some grand opportunities are muffed, and some utterly unpromising situations become notable. The basic elements in any personal site are bound to appear in the end no matter what is done with them, as a landscape still reveals its size and its major shapes and contours, whatever the landscape architect may do. These basic elements, however, are to be accepted, never as humiliations, commonly as limitations, but most of all as opportunities and even as incentives. New York City rejoices in Central Park, but the outcropping rock ledges which were there originally are there still. The landscape architects never tried to eliminate them but they did landscape them; they made a park not so much despite them as by means of them. As Walther Rathenau puts it, "A man must be strong enough to mold the peculiarity of his imperfections into the perfection of his peculiarities."

To be neurotic, for example, is a limitation. The too high-strung, over-sensitive, abnormally tense, and explosive temperament presents baffling problems, and can easily become humiliating. Yet, in a sense, the neurotics make the world go round. Especially is this true in all creative realms. Psychosis itself dogged Van Gogh's heels; his mind teetered on the edge of outright insanity; so far as misery was concerned, his creative genius was, indeed, like a ship on fire at sea for the delectation of the spectators on shore; he illustrates in an extreme form Mill's saying that "Nothing is more certain, than that improvement in human affairs is wholly the work of the uncontented characters." Beethoven had a dreadful time not simply with his deafness, as is familiarly advertised, but with his stormy, neurotic temperament, so that once, seeing a sleeping coachman comfortably snoring, he exclaimed, "I wish I were as stupid as that fellow." The symphonies and concertos, however, came from no sleeping coachman. That park was created out of difficult temperamental elements that could not be eliminated but could be landscaped.

In ordinary life this problem continually confronts us. A single handicap can be turned by morbid attitudes into a humiliation that wrecks both character and career. Physical lacks, temperamental quirks, intellectual inadequacies, social inferiorities, circumstantial restrictions —such elements enter into every life. They are in themselves natural impediments, and the healthy, objective attitude toward them is expressed in Samuel Gridley Howe's motto, carved in the Massachusetts School for the Blind, "Obstacles are things to be overcome." We, however, can so morbidly brood over them that what began as an obstacle—partly limitation, partly opportunity, and partly incentive—can become a sheer humiliation that leaves us cowed and mortified. That result is our own doing. One man developed an inferiority complex that haunted him all his life and ruined his career because he had curly hair of an unusual shade of red, so that when he entered school at the age of five the children gathered round him and laughed at him, and a relative once called him a "funny little fellow." Obsessed by the idea that his hair made him queer, he fell from one humiliating mood into another, and became an abashed, distrustful, inhibited personality who failed in business and was hopeless in social relationships. From such ridiculous extremes to countless more familiar types, this manufacture of abasement out of individual peculiarities and handicaps goes on.

Some situations, especially those involving moral failure and guilt, are humiliating, but the human problem would be incalculably simplified if people would cease creating personal abasement out of clean handicaps and natural limitations, which call not for mortification but for good landscaping. The same kind of situation that one man construes in terms of chagrin and shame another accepts as his portion, and makes rememberable. As Emerson put it, "Do that which is assigned you, and you cannot hope too much or dare too much."

This leads to a further suggestion: The very things that make a man feel inferior can commonly be translated into his distinctive usefulness. "Sublimation" is the technical word for this process, and it means the resolution of conflict by transforming the lower and less desired emotion into driving power for a higher end. So the sexual urge, denied normal expression, is by some transmuted unconsciously into artistic creativity or social service; and pugnacity, which is naturally destructive, is converted into constructive energy, as in Martin Luther, saying, "When I am angry, I can pray well and preach well." In the same fashion, as Dr. Sadler puts it, "Conflict between actual inferiority and the wish for power or superiority may be resolved by accepting one's limitations and making the best of the abilities one possesses."

Indeed, sublimation in this realm is especially rewarding not only to the individual concerned but to the world. *The Survey* says that years ago in a midwestern orphanage was a ten-year-old girl, a hunchback, sickly, ill-tempered, ugly to look at, called Mercy Goodfaith. One day a woman came to the orphanage asking to adopt a girl whom no one else would take, and seeing Mercy Goodfaith, exclaimed, "That's the child I'm looking for." Thirty-five years afterward an official investigator of institutions in another state, after inspecting a county orphans' home prepared a report of which the following is a résumé. The house was exquisitely clean and the children seemed unusually happy. After supper they all went into the living room where one of the girls played the organ while the rest sang. Two small girls sat on one arm of the matron's chair, and two on the other. She held the two smallest children in her lap, and two of the larger boys leaned on the back of her chair. One of the boys who sat on the floor took the hem of her dress in his hand and stroked it. It was evident that the children adored her. She was a hunchback, ugly in feature, but with eyes that almost made her beautiful. Her name was Mercy Goodfaith.

The idea, encouraged by prevalent stress on "intelligence quotients," that the great work of the world is done mainly, if not altogether, by shining geniuses, is mistaken. Some of the most indispensable helpfulness can be rendered only by those who have struggled with inferiority. The extent and depth of their usefulness is achieved not despite their deficiencies, but because of them. They sublimate what might easily be humiliation, into insight, understanding, sympathy, kindliness, efficient ability. Their acceptance of inferiority, far from being dour and stoical, issues in superior usefulness that would have been unattainable by any other route. Who has not been in want of personal help that no fortunate and successful genius could render? How could he serve us? What would he know? How could he understand? It is a matter of profound psychological, as well as theological, significance that not Apollo but one who was born in a stable and died on a cross is called Savior. As Thornton Wilder puts it in one of his dramas, "In Love's service only the wounded soldiers can serve."

With this possibility of converting apparent inferiority into superior usefulness, the problem of self-acceptance achieves a positive aspect. Handicaps and limitations are not simply impediments; they can be made into serviceable instruments.

VI

Such strong and constructive handling of the problem is unlikely, however, without an underlying philosophy that gives life meaning and purpose. In distraught and dejected people the question almost inevitably rises: Why should we bother to accept ourselves and try to create an integrated and useful personality out of limited materials, a disliked assignment, or a botched mess? What is life about and of what importance are we anyway, that a worth-while personality is to be sought in the face of difficulties, with hopeful self-discipline and sacrifice? At that point we run upon one reason for Jung's famous statement: "During the past thirty years, people from all the civilized countries of the earth have consulted me. I have treated many hundreds of patients, the larger number being Protestants, a smaller number Jews, and not more than five or six believing Catholics. Among all my patients in the second half of life—that is to say, over thirty-five—there has not been one whose problem in the last resort was not that of finding a religious outlook on life. It is safe to say that every one of them fell ill because he had lost that which the living religions of every age have given to their followers, and none of them has been really healed who did not regain his religious outlook."

Certainly, irreligion in its ultimate view of personal life is dispiriting—life an accident on one of the minor planets, a haphazard by-product of blind forces. To be gifted with the makings of personality is, in that case, a mysterious fortuity in a world that never intended us and never cared. When, therefore, the problem of self-acceptance becomes acute, when the self is limited in endowment and harassed by circumstance, when troubles make life seem not worth the living, when one has become miserably neurotic, or when in moral failure one has done something "the most infamous in a Soldier, the most injurious to an Army, and the last to be forgiven," irreligion's natural effect is to deepen hopelessness and deplete morale. Why should a man in such a case bother to be a real person in a world where, as one exponent of irreligion says, "Living is merely a physiological process with only a physiological meaning"? This does not mean that the irreligious person cannot discover motives that may pick him up and give him incentive to get himself together. There are many such incentives—human love, personal ambition, a task to be done, a social ideal to be served, desire for appreciation, or even the instinct of self-preservation and a native pugnacity that make one refuse to be downed. Religion as popularly believed in and practiced can be utterly remote from the real problems of struggling persons, while theoretical irreligion can make place for motives that stimulate the individual to "make the most of your best for the sake of others." Granting this, however, it still remains true that nothing more insistently raises questions concerning life's ultimate meaning than hours when self-acceptance is difficult. The more thoughtful a person is, the more inevitably those questions rise. Every personal counselor knows that the decisive factor in many cases is whether or not the afflicted individual effectively wants to be a real person, thinks it worth while to try, cares enough to pay the price. Commonly it would be infinitely easier to give up. Why should he accept this rocky site and try to make a farm of it? What is the use? At this point, Malinowski, the anthropologist, when he surrendered religious faith, truly described the effect as many people experience it: "Modern agnosticism is a tragic and shattering frame of mind."

Probably every person, soon or late, thus finds himself in some "valley of decision" where the "death-wish" and the "life-wish" confront each other. The question then is not whether he will accept himself, but on what terms —as a defeated man who gives up the battle or as a man in the making who will capitalize even his difficulties and deficiencies to achieve real personality. At that point the wisest psychiatrist is often baffled; he cannot out of hand create in the man the one thing indispensable—confidence that it is worth while constructively to tackle himself, and the effective desire and determination so to do. That indispensable element depends on faith of some sort; without it the "death-wish" triumphs. So, one dying man said to a friend who was sympathizing with him, "Don't pity me now! I died twenty years ago."

Whatever else religion at its best has accomplished, it has in numberless cases prevented *that*. It has never promised eminence, genius, freedom from hardship, satisfied ambition, or worldly success, but it has said to every individual: Whatever you may fail at, you need not fail at being a real person; the makings of great personal life include handicaps, deficiencies, troubles, and even moral failures; they too are raw materials out of which strong personalities are made; the universe itself is not a haphazard affair of aimless atoms but is organized around spiritual purposes; and personality, far from being a chance inadvertence, is the fullest and completest way of being alive and the most adequate symbol we have of the nature of God; the world itself is a "vale of Soulmaking," and he who undertakes that task is on the main highroad of creation's meaning and is accepting the central trust of life. Moreover, says religion, as there are personality-creating forces in the universe—else we would not be here—so there are forces that can recreate and empower us, enabling us to endure what we have to stand and become what we ought to be. Professor J. Scott Haldane, of Oxford University, the physiologist, has even said that "personality is the great central fact of the universe."

This message of religion has been phrased in many forms by differing temperaments, and has been variously embodied in the creeds and customs of the churches. Undergirding faith in a God who cares; the consciousness of available power from beyond ourselves; the practice of prayer as a means of communion with the Eternal Spirit; belief in a criterion of judgment higher than man's, which looks not on the outward appearance but on the heart; confidence in the reality of forgiveness, not only human but divine; faith in the eternal significance of life as headed toward a purposeful goal ultimately worth all that it may cost, in achieving which every person may count; belief in personality's survival of death so that to be a real person is of more than temporal concern—such factors in religious faith focus their strong influence on the individual as he decides whether to accept himself as done for or to accept himself as potentially a worth-while person.

One of the ablest women in this country, herself a university graduate and the wife of a university president, was brought up in poverty. She never saw the inside of a schoolroom until she was fourteen years old. She recalls on one occasion when, as a girl, she complained of her hardships, and her mother, who was of pioneer stock, turned on her. "See here," said the mother, "I have given you life; that is about all I will ever be able to give you —life. Now you stop complaining and do something with it." Religious faith is similarly challenging. Life is a sacred trust, it says. Whatever else has been confided to us, our most intimate and inescapable entrustment lies in our capacity to be real persons. To fail at that is to fail altogether; to succeed at that is to succeed supremely,

whatever it cost. Says Noah in the play *Green Pastures,*
"I ain' very much, but I'se all I got." That is the place
to start. Such self-acceptance is realistic, humble, self-
respectful. Irreligion says that a man must accept himself
as basically a physical fortuity, his spiritual life a strange
"sport" of nature in a universe where nothing kindred
corresponds with it and no destiny lies ahead of it. Religion presents another outlook altogether, a positive,
challenging, and stimulating faith, no cushion to lie down
on but a basis for hopeful adventure and a source of
available power in undertaking the most significant responsibility in the known universe—being a real person.

CHAPTER IV

Getting Oneself Off One's Hands

I

IN THE endeavor to achieve integrated personality it is soon evident that merely tinkering with ourselves is not an adequate technique. Indeed, tinkering with ourselves often accentuates one of life's most disruptive forces—egocentricity. A certain "Charm" School, promising to bestow "personality" on its clients, prescribes in the first lesson that one stand before a large mirror and repeat one's own name in a voice "soft, gentle and low" in order to impress oneself with oneself. It is even the nemesis of psychological counseling that turning attention to oneself in the earnest endeavor to improve oneself may only increase obsession with oneself, which is the root of the mischief. Integrated personality is impossible save as the individual finds outside himself valuable interests, in devotion to which he forgets himself. To be whole persons we must get ourselves off our hands.

Egocentricity is the psychological basis for a selfish life. "Selfish," however, is a moral word, invented by the Presbyterians about 1640. It carries with it ethical blame, and its application to a person commonly involves condemnation more than description. Egocentricity, on the other hand, is a factual word; it describes an actual state of mind; right or wrong, there the psychological situation is—an acute awareness of self, so exaggerated that the ego is habitually the focus of attention, until objective interests have a hard time claiming notice or care. George Eliot describes an old-fashioned silver mirror covered with multitudinous minute scratches from generations of polishing, and notes that whenever a lighted candle is brought close to the mirror all the lines arrange themselves in concentric circles around the flame. No matter where the candle is presented to the mirror, the resultant pattern is the same. So an egocentric person faces the world.

From one point of view this may be regarded as failure to grow up. An infant is necessarily egocentric. He is a bundle of his own sensations, clamoring to be taken care of. To be sure, he has vital social relationships; he belongs to his mother, but all he wants her for is food and protection. He does not care for her nor try to understand her *for her sake;* he wants her, and later everyone else within his reach, solely for his own sake. Self-centeredness is the inevitable attitude of early childhood. Says Dr. William Burnham: "The first period up to the age of seven or eight is one in which the ego is dominant. Both the child's behavior and the child's thinking are alike egocentric. It is the child's business to be selfish at this period."

This fact concerning our initial start poses a difficult problem in becoming a real person. For a real person, maturely developed, is not egocentric. He has objective interests; he cares for other people for their sakes; he discovers causes and values for which he lives and might

[80]

even die; he habitually forgets himself in creative work; the richest values of his life lie not so much in what belongs to him as in persons and interests to which he belongs; his enduring satisfactions are found in letting himself go for aims outside himself, and as Jesus said, he finds life by losing it. Thus discovering objective values, interests, and aims, he is pulled together into coherence and unity by his outgoing loyalties. How, then, does one get from infantile self-centeredness to this maturity of a real person?

Many never do. At fifty years of age they still are living on a childish pattern. Moralists censure them as selfish, but beneath the ethical is a psychological problem—they are specimens of arrested development. Says a contemporary novelist about one of her characters: "Edith was a little country bounded on the north, south, east, and west by Edith." Calling Edith unethical does not get us far. Edith suffers from a serious psychological affliction.

II

The disruptive effects of such egocentricity are serious. Like anybody else, the self-centered person wants to be appreciated; indeed, like a spoiled child, he insists on it all the more ravenously, the more self-centered he is; but his egocentricity in any social group makes admiration difficult. He wants reciprocated love, success in his vocation, and all the normal satisfactions of personal friendship, but he is tripped up in every attempt to get them by his extreme awareness of himself.

The egocentrics, therefore, are habitually baffled, frustrated, and unhappy. The more their self-love craves the admiration of others, the more the self on which their care is concentrated is denied the satisfactions that it wants. At the very least, the too self-conscious person— so keenly aware of himself that he supposes everyone else is aware of him—is socially awkward and embarrassed. More people suffer from this than is commonly understood. One investigation in this field had the following result: "If a thousand people of more than average intelligence were asked what, in their opinion, is their greatest personal handicap in life, more than three hundred and seventy would answer 'Self-consciousness and lack of self-confidence.'" Especially among high-strung temperaments with vivid imaginations egocentricity goes to unhappy extremes of self-awareness until the victim, imagining himself the focus of everyone else's attention as well as of his own, is socially embarrassed and confused. The youthful Jean Jacques Rousseau is not untypical: "Fear and shame overpower me to such an extent that I would gladly hide myself from the sight of my fellow-creatures. If I have to act, I do not know what to do; if I have to speak, I do not know what to say; if anyone looks at me, I am put out of countenance."

Furthermore, egocentricity inevitably involves touchiness. Self-love is always hypersensitive—it bridles and snorts on slight provocation. So Olivia says in "Twelfth Night:" "O, you are sick of self-love, Malvolio, and taste with a distempered appetite. To be generous, guiltless and of free disposition, is to take those things for bird-bolts that you deem cannon-bullets."

As the self-focused life goes on into mature age, fears and anxieties attend it. The too self-centered man is a psychological hypochondriac, examining his own pulse, enquiring how he feels, or dreading how he is going to feel. Along with this accumulation of self-engendered troubles, the egocentric person is undermined and disarmed by his malady so that he, of all men, is least prepared to meet trouble. His whole world consists in what happens to him and in the way he feels. To be opposed, therefore, thwarted, misunderstood, ridiculed, or defeated, he cannot endure. Self-centeredness by unavoidable gravitation becomes self-pity. The egocentrics always feel dreadfully sorry for themselves. This easily leads to an obsessing sense of persecution. The final estate of self-centeredness, gone insane, is mad indeed. The ego becomes the center of the world; vast conspiracies of men and nations are massed against the tortured individual; even casual conversations of strangers on the street concern him and him alone; and all the marks on the mirror of life are concentric about his flaming self. The superintendent of the insane asylum in Ibsen's *Peer Gynt* correctly describes the inmates:

> Beside themselves? Oh no, you're wrong.
> It's here that men are most themselves—
> Themselves and nothing but themselves—
> Sailing with outspread sails of self.
> Each shuts himself in a cask of self,
> The cask stopped with a bung of self
> And seasoned in a well of self.
> None has a tear for others' woes
> Or cares what any other thinks.

All the way from social embarrassment to insanity, therefore, egocentricity is ruinous to real personality. At the very best, a person completely wrapped up in himself makes a small package. At the beginning of our discussion we said that no matter what other responsibilities we succeed in escaping, we always come back to find ourselves on our hands. That, however, is not the whole truth. The great day comes when a man begins to get himself off his hands. He has lived, let us say, in a mind like a room surrounded by mirrors. Every way he turned he saw himself. Now, however, some of the mirrors change to windows. He can see through them to objective outlooks that challenge his interests. He begins to get out of himself—no longer the prisoner of self-reflections but a free man in a world where persons, causes, truths, and values exist, worthful for their own sakes. Thus to pass from a mirror-mind to a mind with windows is an essential element in the development of real personality. Without that experience no one ever achieves a meaningful life.

Like all major spiritual ends, being a real person is arrived at not so much by plunging after it as by indirection. A man escapes from himself into some interest greater than himself to which he devotes himself, and so forgets himself into constructive, unified, significant living. Says Henry D. Thoreau's biographer: "He began to escape from his egocentricity, which is sometimes almost offensive in his early Journal. From subjectivity he began to move toward objectivity. His subjectivity began to break up like the ice in Walden in the spring, and strong new interests in the objective world of men and nature flowed up and over."

III

This problem weighs more heavily on some temperaments than on others. Indeed, Jung distinguished two types of people—the "extravert" and the "introvert." The former readily participates in objective practical affairs, is emotionally spontaneous and outgoing, is relatively toughminded when he is disapproved by others, naturally resolves his difficulties not so much by introspection as by external action, is bothered little by self-analysis and self-criticism, and in general is intently interested in the outer world. The latter is keenly conscious of his inner life of ideas and imaginations, is much less hearty, bluff, and unconstrained in his expression of emotions, is sensitive to disapproval, cherishes long the memory of experiences involving personal praise or blame, is given to brooding, introspection, self-analysis, self-criticism, sees all experiences through the coloring medium of his own feelings, and in general is more vividly aware of the subjective than of the objective world. While, however, everybody can recognize these two types, and while each man can judge to which of them he himself is more closely akin, they do not constitute two mutually exclusive temperaments with a clear boundary between. Each of us is more or less both.

Nor is the advantage altogether on either side. The balanced man is a synthesis of the two. The extreme "introvert," unable to escape from his self-centered broodings, has a morbid mind. The extreme "extravert," however, is unhealthy too. He becomes an insensitive blunderer, a bull in a china shop. He is seldom at home with himself. Meditation is to him an alien art, and if religion is, as Professor Whitehead says, "what the individual does with his own solitariness," he has little of it. His typical technique in facing life is to blow on his hands and lustily tackle it. He may be hearty but he is not deep; he may give himself to objective aims but the self he gives has limited dimensions. No exaggerated "extravert" ever wrote a great poem or symphony; he could not possibly be Wilberforce or Lincoln or Pasteur; and in helping his friends, while he may outwardly give indispensable service, he cannot sustain them inwardly in trouble. He commonly comes a cropper when he himself faces situations that his outgoing, explosive energy is unfitted to handle, for then he tries with busy, mercurial activity to deal with profound sorrows or inner conflicts that cannot be so resolved. Fundamentally he lacks a finely-shaded, sensitive emotional life, so that, not inwardly understanding himself, he fails in understanding others. He could profit by St. Augustine's experience: "Because thou wert strayed as a vagabond from thine own heart, so He, who is everywhere, laid hold on thee, and recalled thee to thine inward self."

In presenting the liberating experience by which the egocentric man forgets himself into real personality, we are not asking the "introvert" to become an "extravert." Neither type in its exaggerated form is desirable, and the ideal consummation includes the better elements of both. Abraham Lincoln had a tragic struggle with himself. His inner emotional conflicts were fierce and sustained. In his early manhood he was not a unified and coherent person but a cave of Aeolus, full of storms. He had the makings of neurotic ruin in him, and whether he would be Hamlet, "sicklied o'er with the pale cast of thought," or the Lincoln we know, was an open question with the odds in favor of Hamlet. In 1841 he said, "I am now the most miserable man living. If what I feel were equally distributed to the whole human family, there would not be one cheerful face on earth." He could easily have been an extreme example of the morbid "introvert," but he was not. Obviously he did not solve his obsessing inner problems merely by tinkering with them. He outflanked them. The amazing development of his latter years into great personality came not so much by centering attention on himself as by forgetting himself. The mirrors of his mind turned more and more to windows. His devotion to a cause greater than himself transformed what he had learned in his long struggle with himself into insight, understanding, sympathy, humor, wisdom. He did not so much subjectively get himself together as he was drawn together by objective loyalties. We cannot call him in the end either "introvert" or "extravert." He combined them.

IV

Practical suggestions as to ways and means of getting out of ourselves must start close at home with the body. Many of the worst symptoms of egocentricity, for example, are associated with fatigue. The mentally and nervously exhausted person inevitably becomes acutely conscious of himself. He is tense, hypersensitive, irritable, petulant. The way he feels fills his whole horizon. Let the overstrain go too far and the last barricade is down against invading fears, anxieties, and unhappy memories. Many miserably self-centered folk need not so much a psychiatrist to analyze them or a minister to discuss morals with them as common sense in handling the physical basis of a healthy life.

The modern man needs constantly to be reminded that he cannot slough off his biological inheritance. Our bodies were made to use in hard physical labor. Our forefathers were compelled to use them so or perish. They daily faced strenuous work that called into play their major muscles and sent them to bed at night too healthily tired to fret over imaginary worries. Within a few generations millions of people have been transferred to urban life where hard, energy-consuming, muscular toil is not called for and where the higher brain centers bear the brunt of the burden. Multitudes of men no longer fell forests and plow fields, and multitudes of women no longer spin and weave and put their backs as well as their heads into the heavy tasks of the household. All this may be "progress," but the emotional and moral results for many are disastrous. We cannot outwit our basic biological necessities, ingrained in us by ages of evolution. The egocentricity that we translate into psychological and ethical terms often has a physical cause. To underwork the major muscles and overwork the higher brain centers is a reversal of our physical organism's normal and accustomed functioning, and few if any who try it come off scatheless.

One of the first and healthiest ways, therefore, to escape from morbid subjectivity into wholesome objectivity is through vigorous, energy-consuming physical

output. Any man who has found his appropriate recrea-
tion or exercise where he can let himself go in the lusty
use of his major muscles, knows what a transformation
of emotional tone and mental outlook such bodily expenditure can bring. To be able to forget oneself in a
strenuous game, to revel in a long hike, to work oneself
out with an ax into satisfying weariness, or in milder
ways to find ease of mind by letting the body forcefully
express itself, is an evidence as it is a cause of health. In
dealing with the everyday problems of self-centeredness
and its wretched morbidities, much of our psychiatry and
of our religion is too high and mighty. In many cases
the homely help is close at hand. We may be spirits, but
we are not disembodied; the brain centers that function
in reason and imagination may be our chief glory, but
the brain centers that function in physical exertion have
been here a long time and refuse to be snubbed with im-
punity.

Practically every brain-worker, soon or late, knows
what it means to go to pieces. To say that he has overworked his nerves is often only half the story; he might
have worked his nerves to even larger output if he had
not underworked his muscles. Because of that he finds
himself in a jam and so begins worrying about himself;
fears, anxieties, even panics invade him; he cannot concentrate; he becomes disconnected and is tossed about
by his confusions.

> There was once an old sailor my grandfather knew
> Who had so many things which he wanted to do
> That, whenever he thought it was time to begin,
> He couldn't because of the state he was in.

From this beginning the road slopes down, sometimes sharply, into serious disintegration. The psychiatrist may call the result "psychoneurosis"; the minister may think it downright self-centeredness; but often the cause that started the trouble was physical. Happy the man or woman who, before it is too late, learns that one indispensable escape from morbid subjectivity into healthy objectivity lies through physical exertion!

V

Important as this is, however, it cannot by itself solve any man's problem in outgrowing egocentricity. Lincoln did not by splitting rails alone become a real person. That difficult achievement involves a profounder process—the renovation of one's ideas about one's "self," the radical reinterpretation of the self's meaning, and the wide extension of its boundaries. Asked where he is, a man naturally defines his position in physical terms; like a sailor using latitude and longitude he locates himself geographically where his body is. This, however, is a gross oversimplification of the facts. Where am I? is a much more difficult question to answer than at first appears. Certainly no worth-while person is merely where his body is. His family and friends may be widely scattered; where they are, he is; what happens to them *there* may affect him far more poignantly than anything that befalls him *here*. As Robert Southwell put it long ago, "Not where I breathe, but where I love, I live."

This extension of the self is one of the profoundest mysteries in personal life. Nothing except a person can

[90]

so live outside itself. Objects of loyalty such as democracy can become part of ourselves until what befalls them anywhere befalls us. Causes to which we belong can so absorb us that their success or failure is our own. Patriotism can so affect millions that the life they live within their bodies is willingly surrendered on behalf of the larger national life into which they have extended themselves. Wilberforce can identify himself with the victims of the slave trade, Florence Nightingale with the unnursed wounded in a war, and Jesus can carry this objectification of himself so far that he says, "Inasmuch as ye have done it unto one of the least of these my brethren, ye have done it into me."

All this is basically not ethics but psychology; in its origin it is not so much a moral ideal as an incontrovertible fact about persons. This is the way they are essentially constituted. They can, and do, and if they are to be mature they must, get out of themselves, not by suppressing their egos but by extending them. Jesus' ethic is founded on realistic fact. Granted that in each of us there is an "impregnable core of selfhood"! Granted the truth in Matthew Arnold's lines,

> . . . in the sea of life enisled,
> With echoing straits between us thrown,
> Dotting the shoreless watery wild,
> We mortal millions live *alone*.

Nevertheless, that by itself is only one snapshot out of the panorama of personality. As truly as the body is dwarfed if it does not grow up, so the self is stunted unless it escapes from its self-absorption, objectifies itself, discovers itself in family, friends, interests, and loyalties beyond itself, and so extends itself that its outer boundaries are hard to find.

Falling in love, for example, is certainly natural. It is not first of all a duty but an instinct. Its essential characteristic, however, is that self-sufficiency breaks down, and in a powerful surge of emotion one person identifies himself with another until hyperboles like "one soul in two bodies" are needed to express the consequence. As Mrs. Browning phrased it,

> The widest land
> Doom takes to part us, leaves thy heart in mine
> With pulses that beat double. What I do
> And what I dream include thee, as the wine
> Must taste of its own grapes. And when I sue
> God for myself, He hears that name of thine,
> And sees within my eyes, the tears of two.

For such experiences of the self's extension persons are fundamentally intended. Along with love and friendship, one of the most durable satisfactions in life is to lose oneself in creative work. Every wise man seeks a task to dignify his days. No man can be himself until he gets out of himself into work with which he identifies himself. Even beavers build their dams, bees their honeycombs, and birds their nests. Rooted in a long past, there is in man an impulse to construct, an urge to create, a deep need to invest himself in work that becomes an extension of himself. This is why more people become neurotic from aimless leisure and laziness than from overwork, and this is why unemployment is one of the worst of tragedies, its psychological results quite as lamentable as its economic ills. As Michelangelo said, "It is only well with me when I have a chisel in my hand."

The personal counselor constantly runs upon self-focused, unextended lives, miserably striving to find happiness by attending to themselves. In late years the gospel of self-expression has gained a wide hearing. Popularly it has meant: Explode yourself; let yourself go; knock the bungs from your emotional barrels and let them gurgle! As a protest against petty, prohibitive moralisms, this gospel is easily explicable, and as a means of release to some individuals, tied hand and foot with senseless scrupulosities, it has had its value. The wise counselor pleads not against self-expression but for it; he too wants the uninhibited, outgoing life; but he wants self-expression to be understood and practiced in accord with the realistic, psychological facts. Merely exploding individual emotions for the sake of the momentary self-centered thrill gets one nowhere. Like fire-crackers they go off and nothing comes of it. In the end the constant repetition of such emotional self-relief disperses life, and leaves it more incoherent and aimless than it was before. Even in the sexual realm this is true. Says one of our eminent psychiatrists: "From the point of view of cure, the advice to go and 'express your instincts' is only one degree more foolish than the antiquated advice which used to be given to every neurotic girl: 'All you need is to get married.' In actual experience I have never known a true neurosis cured by marriage, still less by sexual libertinism. But I have personally known many neuroses precipitated by marriage; indeed, I am sometimes tempted to think that half my patients are neurotic because they are not married and the other half because they are!"

Adequate self-expression is a much deeper matter than self-explosion. Its true exponent is not the libertine but the artist, the musician, the scientist, the fortunate mother absorbed in her family, the public-spirited businessman creatively doing something for his community, the philanthropist going all out for the sake of others in need, the teacher saying as Professor George H. Palmer did, "Harvard College pays me for doing what I would gladly pay it for allowing me to do," or characters like Stradivarius, in George Eliot's poem, saying,

> . . . when any master holds
> 'Twixt chin and hand a violin of mine,
> He will be glad that Stradivari lived,
> Made violins, and made them of the best.
> The masters only know whose work is good:
> They will choose mine, and while God gives them skill
> I give them instruments to play upon,
> God choosing me to help Him.

Such personalities, in eminent or humble places, really express themselves, and their common quality is not self-absorption but self-investment. They forget themselves in something objective to themselves, which they appropriate until it becomes part of themselves. As Professor Gordon Allport puts it, "Paradoxically, 'self-expression' requires the capacity to lose oneself in the pursuit of objectives, *not* primarily referred to the self."

Indeed, all durable happiness partakes of this quality. One must lose oneself in music to enjoy it. One must forget oneself in a game to love it. One must go out to one's friends to know friendship's satisfactions. The egocentric person tries to pounce on happiness, but he always

[94]

misses it. As one young woman wrote to explain her suicide: "I am killing myself because I have never sincerely
loved any human being all my life." It is the outgoing self
that breaks open the road which afterward proves to be a
two-way street with worth-while satisfactions returning
on it. Whittier was not only a good moralist but a good
psychologist when he wrote:

> Oh, doom beyond the saddest guess,
> As the long years of God unroll,
> To make thy dreary selfishness
> The prison of a soul!

Obviously, therefore, to call human nature essentially
and altogether selfish is a misstatement. Human nature is
so constituted that it never flowers out until it escapes
from absorbing self-concern. Some of the direst perils
that confront the world today spring not from egocentricity but from man's constitutional urge to overpass it, and
from the attempted satisfaction of that urge in mistaken
ways. The totalitarian state, for example, is made possible
by men's insistent desire to belong to something greater
than themselves—a race or nation in loyalty to which they
lose themselves. All such demands for self-devotion, even
though we call them "pooled selfishness," have this much
sense in them—they recognize, as philosophies of individ-
ualistic license and libertinism do not, that man is essentially made not for egocentricity but for self-investment,
and can never be satisfied without it.

When this deep-seated urge in human nature, highly
used, achieves its consummate expression, it produces
the world's saviors. They live not so much in themselves
as in other people with whom they identify themselves.

As Jesus said, What befalls anyone befalls them. They become the

> . . . nerve o'er which do creep
> The else unfelt oppressions of this earth.

Looked at from without, they seem to sacrifice themselves; from within, their experience is not so much self-sacrifice as self-expansion. They enlarge the little ego into the extended personality. In them Jesus' basic principle is shown to be not alone great ethics but sound psychology—only he who loses life saves it, only he who expends life keeps it, only he who invests life enriches it. Granted that such consummate personalities are comparatively few in number! Nevertheless, they are actually here, and if Aristotle's principle is true that the real nature of anything is revealed in its finest fruitions, they are of major importance to psychology. Any psychological system that explains the actions of decorticated rats but leaves out of account the supreme exhibitions of personality in the expanded self, has lost its bearings.

To be sure, this extended self does not avoid strain, tension, and the risk of disintegration—

> . . . he who lives more lives than one
> More deaths than one must die.

The mother whose life is more in her children than in herself may be broken by what happens to them. The devoted servant of a great cause may be disillusioned and shattered when it fails. The expanded self is no magic formula. Nevertheless, as any wise man with regard to his body would prefer the risks of maturity to the tragedy of arrested development, so he would choose to face the

[96]

problems of an expanded personality rather than the dwarfed life of egocentricity. Any individual who ever achieved a rich, mature, satisfying personal life, did it only in so far as he was drawn together into coherence and significance by objective loyalties with which he identified himself.

VI

The intellectual recognition of this fact, however, cannot by itself solve our problems. No man, simply because he is mentally convinced, can fall to and out of hand expand his little ego into an extended self. The ego can be extremely recalcitrant, in season and out of season clamoring for self-importance. Of the three major figures in modern psychiatry, Freud may roughly be represented as saying that man wants most of all to be loved; Jung that he wants most of all to feel secure; Adler that he wants most of all to feel significant. Leaving the question of priority open, that last desire is insistent in all of us. Every man wants to feel that he counts.

Some forms of morality and religion, identifying this strong desire for self-importance with selfishness and vanity, endeavor to quash it. Certainly, it can issue in strange and sinister consequences. The desire for self-aggrandizement appears in protean forms. We wish to be loved because to be loved makes us feel that we count; we wish to succeed because success makes us feel significant; greed for money is in many a master motive because money brings not only things but *kudos*. Nothing pleases us more than the augmenting of our self-esteem. To gain this end we put on an endless masquerade, concealing our weaknesses, putting our best foot forward, trying to appear better than we are. Analyze the motives of orators, actors, senators, preachers, and often at the source of their vocation's choice is the love of self-display. What philanthropist or public servant has not been disturbed in some moment of introspection by the suspicion that the desire to feel important is a strong motive in his usefulness? Probably no saint or martyr ever altogether escaped its subtle influence. When Charles Lamb said, "The greatest pleasure I know, is to do a good action by stealth, and to have it found out by accident," he revealed how omnipresent is this wish for notice and attention that enhance self-esteem.

If self-aggrandizement is individually thwarted, men pool their efforts to obtain it in clubs, societies, lodges, with paraphernalia and parade. If they cannot achieve it otherwise they resort to bizarre methods of becoming conspicuous. From the child saying "See how fast I run," to the loud dresser, the pompous talker, the pole-sitter, the eager entrants into eating and beauty contests, and countless other searchers for notoriety, the motive of self-display is everywhere at work. Many deserve Thackeray's description of Pendennis, who, "Having a most lively imagination, mistook himself for a person of importance very easily." If other means of satisfying this desire fail, some become criminals and shine as eminent gangsters, rejoicing in their notoriety and angry if the desired kind of publicity is denied them. So Guiteau, President Garfield's assassin, in his prayer on the scaffold indignantly exclaimed, "The American press has a large bill to settle with the righteous Father for their vindictiveness in this matter." Finally, if desperate measures are called for, some become insane, and imagining themselves kings, queens, or multimillionaires, walk in their fantasies, their desire for self-aggrandizement happily satisfied. It is small wonder that ethics and religion habitually look askance at this dangerous motive.

Nevertheless, there is another side to the matter. The finer a family is, the more the home makes every member of it feel that he or she counts. The truer a friend is, the more he makes each recipient of his affection feel significant. The entire democratic way of life is based upon the proposition that everyone's opinion ought to matter. Christ endues with importance an endless stream of otherwise obscure people, filling fishermen, tax gatherers, and prodigals with the elated conviction that the kind of persons they are and the way they live are momentous for themselves, their friends, their communities, and the world. As for philosophy, whenever it escapes the narrow restrictions of materialism and begins to see spiritual values as rooted in ultimate reality, it inevitably, in one form or another, begins to exalt the meaning of persons, even saying with Professor Hocking, "There are no eternal values unless there are eternal valuers." The entire Christian idea of life is thus structurally dependent upon the importance of persons. That is to say, *self-respect*— Tennyson called it "self-reverence"—is alike the basis and the consequence of our most saving institutions at their best and of the most redeeming ideas we have in philosophy and religion. No great living is possible without self-respect, and self-respect is the old, dangerous, misused, and morally reprehensible passion for self-aggrandizement, elevated, sublimated, and put to good uses.

[99]

No elemental instinct in human nature is ever to be contemned. The impulse to self-display can issue in crude vulgarities and vanities or it can enter as an indispensable element into great actors, orators, and musicians. As Dr. Hadfield sums it up, *"Instincts are ennobled by their uses."* A preacher, psychologically analyzed, may be shocked to see how deeply the enjoyment of self-display entered into his choice of a vocation. Why should he be shocked? Phillips Brooks himself said that no man should ever choose the ministry unless he has a "quality that kindles at the sight of men." Without that no man could ever preach well at all, or play like Kreisler, or act like Sir Henry Irving. That instinctive response in itself is not contemptible; it is part of the indispensable psychological make-up of a self temperamentally fitted for certain kinds of work. Only when it gets out of hand, is harnessed to low uses, becomes an obsession indulged in for its own sake, is it deplorable. If it is carried beyond itself in devotion to a serviceable aim, in which it is absorbed, objectified, and forgotten, it is not only indispensable but admirable.

The cynic says that at the fountainhead of every so-called "unselfish" life are self-regarding motives. The cynic is right—but in his cynicism about it he is wrong. We all start, as a race and as individual children, with self-regarding instincts. If that is damning, then we all are damned. The test of us, however, lies not in our original equipment of instinctive urges to self-importance, but in the objective aims and purposes which ultimately capture these forces in us and use them as driving power. All of them can be elevated and transmuted into creatively fruitful self-respect, in which case Professor McDougall's dictum is justified that self-regard "plays the most powerful all-pervasive role in the higher life of man." What differentiates men is not the desire to feel significant, which all share, but their various ways of responding to that desire and satisfying it.

A wise personal counselor, therefore, never tells anyone that he ought not to wish to feel important, but rather endeavors to direct that powerful wish into constructive channels.

The consciousness of being needed makes one feel important. Even a cry for help upon the street is stimulating. An accident has happened; someone is in danger; we can help. For a time, at least, that appeal can lift us out of the lowest mood into self-respect; we cease being ciphers and become integers—we are needed. Said George MacDonald, "Nothing makes one feel so strong as a call for help." A mother feels significant in a family that depends on her; a father feels important when his son turns to him for counsel; as Robert Louis Stevenson said, "So long as we are loved by others, I would almost say that we are indispensable; and no man is useless while he has a friend." The great social workers, missionaries, scientists, feel significant when some area of need opens which they can enter. For a youth to feel that the world has no use for him is one of the most blighting and withering of harms; to feel that he counts because he is wanted is one of the most stimulating of incentives. Dr. Arthur E. Morgan even says: "Lack of something to feel important about is almost the greatest tragedy a man may have." Jesus throughout his ministry kept laying his hand on unlikely

[101]

people, saying, You are needed, and so awakened in them a transforming respect for the importance of their own lives. Self-regard, when it has thus been carried out of egocentricity by an objective call for help, is not ignoble; without it no great thing was ever tried or done.

The consciousness of having personal possibilities makes one feel important. What a man is worth depends not so much on what he is as on what he may become. When, therefore, in a life however marred and commonplace there rises the vision of a personal tomorrow better than today, the sense of significance rises with it. Anything is important that has potentialities. All good homes and schools play upon this motive; no youth ever flowered who lacked it; and as for religion, its power over men, awakening their self-respect with transforming effect, has lain largely in the fact that, as Professor Hocking says, "The great religions have spoken ill of original human nature; but they have never despaired of its possibilities." To feel life grow significant because there is more in us than we have yet elicited is not ignoble. Such saving self-respect is redeemed from mean egocentricity by devotion to a goal and aim beyond our present selves.

The consciousness of standing for something greater than ourselves makes us feel important. The man who carried the message to Garcia felt significant not so much for himself as for what he transmitted. We are not ourselves alone; we can be vehicles and representatives of momentous matters greater than ourselves. A simple wire can transmit a great light; a plain bucket can carry living water. So, a physician is important not for himself alone but as the custodian of a long-accumulated medical tradition; a musician is significant not simply in himself but as the representative of an indispensable cultural heritage; and every plain man or woman can be the trustee and witness of truths, traditions, and causes desperately needed by the world. To stand for something worth standing for and feel life grow significant in its representative capacity—to be a humble flag pole proud of the flag it flies—is not mere egocentricity but a creative function of the expanded personality.

The essential religious experience of communion with God and devotion to his will makes us feel important. The little ego is inflated by what belongs to it; the enlarged self is made significant by what it belongs to. Really to believe in God, therefore, genuinely to worship him, to have the mirror-minded self become all windows in an hour of outgoing adoration, to become conscious of inner union with the Universal Life, of belonging to him, having a part in his purposes, being a trustee of his commissions, having access to his available power, is an experience alike humbling and exalting. It shames the little ego but it expands and dignifies the personality. Such religious experience is the very opposite of egocentricity, but nothing in human history has done more to produce and sustain a saving self-respect.

At least two practical consequences follow from such successful expansion of the self.

For one thing, the person who has thus achieved a healthy objectivity has a natural and saving sense of humor. In anyone afflicted with abnormal self-concern, a deficient sense of humor is an inevitable penalty. The egocentrics cannot stand off from themselves, look objectively and without undue partisanship at themselves and enjoy laughing about themselves. This is notorious in the self-centered period of childhood. Children love laughter, but not when directed at themselves. To be laughed at seems ridicule, and to the child that is agony.

At few points, if any, is the persistence of childishness into adult years more evident than in exhibitions of deficient humor. Only people with expanded selves, who live objectively in other persons and in wide-flung interests, and who, therefore, have horizon and perspective around their egos and can see themselves impartially and without prejudice, can possibly have the prayer answered:

O wad some pow'r the giftie gie us
To see ourselves as others see us!

The egocentric's petition is habitually otherwise:

O wad some pow'r to others gie,
To see myself as I see me.

Nast, the cartoonist, one evening in a social group drew caricatures of each of the company. The result was revealing—each one easily recognized the caricatures of the others but some could not recognize their own. This inability to see ourselves as objectively we look to others, to detect what is funny, comical, even ludicrous in ourselves and to enjoy it, is one of the surest signs of egocentric immaturity.

Aristophanes, in his drama "The Clouds," caricatured Socrates, and when the play was produced all Athens roared with laughter. Socrates, so runs the story, went to see the play, and when the caricature came on he stood up so that the audience might the better enjoy the comic mask that was intended to burlesque him. He was mature. He had got himself off his hands. The determining center from which he viewed life was in so far outside himself that he could see himself with objective impartiality and could enjoy a jest about himself.

All this involves the interesting paradox that man never understands his own ego until he escapes it. As man astronomically never understood the earth until he looked away from it at sun and stars so that he could, as it were, view the earth from a point beyond itself and see it in large relationships, so no person can gain true insight into himself save as he objectifies himself. Self-knowledge, like happiness, cannot be arrived at by direct attack alone. And when it is arrived at through an extended personality that throws horizon and perspective around the ego, it brings with it a healthy impartiality and disinterestedness that make possible the application of the Golden Rule in reverse: Whatsoever you would laugh at in others, laugh at in yourself.

The pervasive results of gaining an extended self are seen in the fact that not only does it thus issue in humor, but in power to bear trouble. As commonly conceived, trouble is an altogether shattering experience. Yet almost everyone has sometime faced a tragedy that pulled him together. He rose to the occasion. The catastrophic situation turned out to be challenging, arousing, even integrating. The whole self came to a point of concentration to handle it. Many people go to pieces over small irritations—they fly off the handle when exasperated; but let a serious trouble come and they steady down, grow cool and collected. One can fairly see them come together and rally themselves to meet the situation.

In those who thus rise to the occasion in serious trouble and marshal their forces to deal with it, one factor commonly is present—*they are thinking about someone else besides themselves.* They are not egocentric. They meet disaster with courage and fortitude for someone else's sake. If they break down, someone else will break down; if they go to pieces, someone else will collapse; if they can "take it," someone else will stand the gaff too. So one young American officer in the first World War wrote home: "You can truly think of me as being cheerful all the time. Why otherwise? I have thirty-eight men, that if I duck when a shell comes, all thirty-eight duck, and if I smile, the smile goes down the line."

A person who has genuinely identified himself with other persons, therefore, has done something of first-rate importance for himself without intending it. The egocentric is notoriously unable to stand up under strain and disaster, and inevitably retreats into self-pity, but the man who has expanded himself into the lives of others will naturally endure for their sakes what he could not brace himself to stand for his own. When General Booth, the founder of the Salvation Army, went blind, his son Bramwell broke the news to him. "You mean that I am blind?" said the general. "I fear that we must contemplate that," his son answered. "I shall never see your face again?" asked the general. "No," said Bramwell, "probably not in this world." The old man's hand moved across the counterpane until it grasped his son's. "Bramwell," he said, "I have done what I could for God and for the people with my eyes. Now I shall do what I can for God and for the people without my eyes." To such personalities disaster is not shattering; for others' sakes they collect themselves to meet it. In this regard the difference between General Booth and Edith, "bounded on the north, south, east, and west by Edith," is immense.

CHAPTER V

Dealing with Fear and Anxiety

I

STEPHEN LEACOCK'S famous rider who "flung himself upon his horse and rode madly off in all directions," is psychologically reduplicated in many people. In them the centrifugal forces are stronger than the centripetal. As one victim of this unhappy estate put it, "I should know myself better if there were not so many of me."

Difficult days in the world at large make more tragic this inner state of conflict. Instability in man's social, economic, and international life is commonly used as an excuse for instability in the individual, whereas it really puts a premium upon his steadiness. A revolutionary epoch when everything else goes to pieces only accentuates the disaster of a personality that cannot hold together.

To be sure, conflict is an inescapable element in human experience and can be good rather than evil. As Robert Louis Stevenson said, "The spice of life is battle." That is to say, when the conflict is between a well-organized, coherent personality on one side, and a difficult external situation on the other, battle can be "spice." A man free from inner disruption may tackle with joy even Herculean tasks. When, however, the man himself is torn apart, his own inner emotional civil war is not at all life's "spice." Only the integrated person, because he does not have to struggle with himself, can struggle effectively and happily with objective difficulties.

Granted that conflict within the individual can never be completely resolved, and indeed ought not to be! So Robert Browning says:

> No, when the fight begins within himself,
> A man's worth something. God stoops o'er his head,
> Satan looks up between his feet—both tug—
> He's left, himself, i' the middle: the soul wakes
> And grows. Prolong that battle through his life!
> Never leave growing till the life to come!

Such indispensable inner struggle the psychologists call "progressive integration." It means the supersedure of a lower center of organization by the formation of a higher one, with an interim of difficulty and even turbulence, but with coherence still as the aim, and a better ordering of life as the outcome. From such a process no one ever should escape. Nevertheless, it remains true that to be all at odds with oneself, one urgent want fighting another, the actual and desired selves hating each other, conscience and conduct clawing at each other amid a general sense of inferiority and guilt, so that from every venture in tackling objective tasks a man comes home at night to bellicose, cacophonous emotions, is not in the least "the spice of life."

Among the most familiar emotions that thus break up man's peace and crumble his personality are fear and anxiety. Yet, far from being man's enemy fear is one of the most indispensable elements in the human make-up. When it becomes terror, panic, chronic anxiety, it is shattering, but it still remains true that the human race never could have come into existence in the first place or have survived at all without fear. Fear is every animal's elemental alarm-system, so sensitively keyed that at the first sign of danger the organism snaps into readiness for flight or fight. This constitutes the evolutionary basis for our human problem—fear is not to be elided but to be controlled and used. Even in its simpler forms we cannot dispense with it; on the streets of a modern city a fearless man, if the phrase be taken literally, would probably be dead or dying before nightfall. Angelo Patri is right in saying, "Education consists in being afraid at the right time."

Only fools are not afraid. Landlubbers, summering on the Maine coast, are singularly free of dreads. They have no idea what a tide can do, or what a heavy sea can mean, or what being lost in the fog without a compass feels like, or how great the difference may be between the true channel and ten feet to one side. The experienced natives of the coast, however, who understand the sea, have a healthy awe of it. So in *Moby Dick,* in the old days of sperm whale fishing, Starbuck, the chief mate, said that he wanted no man in his boat who was not afraid of a whale.

Indeed, fear can be a powerfully creative motive. In a profound sense schools spring from fear of ignorance, industry from fear of penury, medical science from fear of disease. Every saving invention, from a lighthouse to sulfanilimide, and every intellectual advance, whether in engineering or economic theory, has behind it as part of its motivation the desire to avoid or escape some dreaded thing. As the word "love" ranges in connotation from lust and lechery to sacrificial devotion, so fear's meanings cover a wide gamut, from fright and panic through prudence and foresight to awe and reverence, until "the fear of the Lord is the beginning of wisdom."

One of the strange phenomena of the last century is the spectacle of religion dropping the appeal to fear while other human interests have picked it up. From germs to psychoneuroses, the physicians have presented us with a whole series of new dreads, and the entire development of the scientific idea of the reign of law has involved the inescapable and often fearful fact that what we sow we reap. In the sense of foresight, vigilance, circumspection, prudence, precaution, the fear-attitude has been called out, insisted on, and given intelligent implementation as never before in history.

This fact of fear's necessity and usefulness, however, far from solving our problem, underlies its seriousness. If fear were a sheer evil, our situation would be simpler than it is. Just because fear is an indispensable part of our organic structure, and from its primitive forms of physical recoil to its highest spiritual exhibitions in reverent awe no human life is complete without it, its abnormalities are the more perilous. Like fire, it is a great and necessary servant but a ruinous master. When it becomes terror, hysteria, phobia, obsessive anxiety, it tears personality to pieces. Dr. J. A. Hadfield says: "If fear were abolished from modern life, the work of the psychotherapist would be nearly gone."

II

Of primary importance in dealing with fear is the need of getting out into the open the object of our dread and frankly facing it. Human life is full of secret fears, thrust into the attics and dark corners of personality. Sometimes such fears are consciously "suppressed," deliberately put out of sight and hearing, and sometimes they are unconsciously "repressed," until, forgotten altogether, they gnaw at the vitals of life like clandestine diseases of which the victim is unaware. In either case, the first step in dealing constructively with fear is to end its secrecy and confront it openly where we can look at it ourselves and talk about it with others.

Many fears are not of this kind. Multitudes today know clearly what they stand in dread of—unemployment, economic insecurity, illness, war. Their anxious apprehensions concern objective matters, obvious to everyone. Many others, however, are haunted by furtive fears. The tragedy in the early life of Mr. Clifford Beers, narrated in *A Mind That Found Itself,* would probably have been impossible had he brought his secret dread out of hiding and talked candidly about it to some wise friend. His older brother had epilepsy; Clifford attended him in times of need; he picked up the idea that epilepsy was contagious; this dread, secretly hidden in his thinking, obsessed him until outgrowing his control it convinced him that he *had* caught epilepsy, and so he traveled the road of needless, clandestine fear into insanity.

This example, while extreme, illustrates a typical problem with which personal counselors are well acquainted.

One of the chief services of ministers and psychiatrists is to be listening-posts, where crammed bosoms, long burdened with surreptitious fears, can unload themselves. Fear of the dark, of water, of closed places, of open places, of altitude; fear of cats, of Friday the thirteenth, of walking under a ladder; fear of responsibility, of having children, of old age and death; guilty fears, often concerned with sins long passed; fears of inadequacy, coupled with humiliation and shame; religious fears, associated with ideas of a spying and vindictive God and an eternal hell; endless detailed worries, real or imaginary, and sometimes a vague fearfulness, filling life with anxious apprehension without the victim's knowing just what he is fearful of—such wretchedness curses innumerable lives, and the first step toward cure is to end the concealment and carry the whole situation out into the light.

The disruptive effect of such secret, chronic fearfulness is physically based. The adrenal glands were evolved to furnish us in every frightening situation with "a swig of our own internal fight-tonic." A little of it—even in the proportion of one part to one million parts of water—is stimulating; too much of it is poison. A scared man chased by a bull may jump a fence that under normal circumstances he could not possibly scale, but such sudden access of energy cannot be long sustained. All fear is thus an alarm, in response to which the adrenal glands spring into action; and the tragedy of habitual anxiety and dread is that they constitute a continuous false alarm, repeatedly calling out the fire department when there is no fire, turning the invaluable adrenal secretion, epinephrin, from an emergency stimulant into a chronic poison. Because of this people can worry themselves sick or insane.

[113]

Trembling, fainting, nausea, palpitation of the heart, convulsions, and other bodily repercussions from fear are familiar. Fear in all its forms has a direct physical effect.

Many secret, chronic dreads, suppressed or repressed, call for the skilled competence of the psychiatrist, but others the ordinary man can handle if he is wise; and always the first step is to get the problem out into the open. As infants we started with fear of two things only—falling and a loud noise, and all other fears have been accumulated since. To find out where and how we picked them up, to get at their genesis and development until we can stand over against them and objectively survey them as though they were another's and not our own, is often half the battle. Sometimes when abnormal anxieties and dreads are thus objectified they can be laughed off the scene. As in Mr. Beers' case, they are essentially absurd, incapable of standing inspection in the sunlight. Dr. Sadler even says, with perhaps deliberate exaggeration: "Ridicule is the master cure for fear and anxiety."

III

Far from being ridiculous, however, the fear we find ourselves confronting is often justified, the situation so hazardous that no one can doubt its peril. In that case we are commonly defeated by the fallacy that dangerous situations are necessarily undesirable, whereas the fact is that even a fearful danger *if it be frankly and openly faced* can provide one of the most stimulating experiences in life. At first sight our predicament may be terrifying and our initial response consternation. Moreover, there may be ample justification for dismay. Life can be cruel and terrible, and anyone who expects to escape that fact is asking for a life at sea without storms. Emerson even said that "He has not learned the lesson of life who does not every day surmount a fear." One major secret of doing that is to feel the *stimulus* of hazardous occasions rather than the *dread*.

That both factors are there to be abstracted is made evident when we consider that love of danger is one of the strongest motives in man. When life does not by itself present men with enough hazard, they go out looking for it. They seek it even in their sports—mountain climbing, skiing, football, prize fighting. Mankind from its earliest beginnings was nurtured on danger and is unhappy without it. Only so can such enterprises be explained as trying to climb Mount Everest or to reach the Poles. Graham Wallas, thinking of the major explorers of the race, finds in the love of danger one of their strongest motives: "Perhaps, indeed, it is this desire for Fear rather than the impulse of Curiosity which has been the most important single cause of those dangerous journeys."

We have not dealt adequately with the problem of eliminating war until in addition to all the social factors we take into account the strong support war has in man's psychology. War's terrors are hideous, but at the same time its dangers are attractive. General Robert E. Lee said in the midst of one of his bloodiest battles: "It is well that war is so terrible—we should grow too fond of it!" The persistent need of a "moral equivalent of war" springs from the fact that enterprises attractively dangerous, like war but minus war's insane destructiveness, are a *sine qua non* of healthy human life. Many find this in risky researches and explorations, in missionary adventures, in thinking daring thoughts, in pioneering new and unaccepted fields, in championing unpopular causes, or in compelling themselves habitually in daily life to do things they are afraid of. Thus a character in a modern novel says: "If I knew anything, any least little thing, I was afraid of I'd go right off and do it—do it good and hard." At every turn the fact is clear that the love of danger is one of man's deep-seated motives.

When life faces us with danger, therefore, let us make the most of it! If we get out of it only or mainly fearfulness and anxiety, that is our doing. Stimulus also is waiting there to be appropriated if we will. To stand up to a hazardous situation, to refuse suppression and subterfuge in dealing with it, to face it objectively as a seaman does a tempest, to tune in not so much on its terror as on its challenge, to let it call out in us not our fearfulness but our love of battle, is a healthy, inspiriting experience. So Voltaire said: "This world is warfare; I love to carry it on, it puts life into me." And so one humble woman, coming out from a second painful operation on her eyes under local anaesthesia only, knowing that she would never see again, called her two sons to her and said: "Now I'll show you how to take trouble. How you take it is the only thing about it that's important."

IV

A further step in dealing with anxious fear is to remember that it always involves the misuse of the imagination. Even when fear is physically induced, as in delirium tremens, its terrifying power lies in imaginative pictures that occupy the mind. Anxiety as humans experience it is possible only to a highly developed organism endowed with the gift of fantasy. Animals suffer cruelly, but their sufferings for the most part are immediate and real; they do not, so far as we can tell, lie awake at night picturing difficulties that make them panicky about tomorrow. Such apprehensive dread is peculiarly human, a tribute to one of man's supreme endowments—imagination.

Upon this endowment all inventive progress depends, for whatever man creates he first imagines; upon it all ethical life depends, for the beginning of serious goodness lies in a man's imagining himself in another person's place; upon it all spiritual wealth and development depend, for no values ever vitally belong to us until they have captured our imagination. It is equally true, however, that upon this endowment all ruinous anxiety depends, for chronic worry is fear that has taken possession of our habitual imaginings.

This fact is of special importance in an era of worldwide catastrophe. Robert Louis Stevenson during the Franco-Prussian War described himself in Scotland, lying "in the heather on the top of the island, with my face hid, kicking my heels for agony." Only human beings can present to themselves with picturesque and appalling vividness distant ills and world-wide tragedies so as thus to suffer anguish. Out of this capacity come pity, sympathy, a sense of widespread responsibility, but out of it also come mass hysterias and phobias and individual breakdowns. Moreover, imagination can use terrifying facts as a mere starting-point, and moving out into the realm of chimera can fabricate in the present countless unreal objects of dread, and project into the future countless more. Many thus picture to themselves, in fantasy, all conceivable disasters, until life is encompassed by danger and obsessed by fear. The best and the worst in human life spring from our use of this faculty, and alike

> The lunatic, the lover and the poet
> Are of imagination all compact.

Quite apart from world-wide tragedy, ordinary daily experience offers ample opportunity for such vagaries. Our picture-making capacity can fill our minds with visual images of disaster, possible and impossible, until many of us spend our lives bearing troubles, most of which never happen. From hypochondriacs, exhibiting infinite ingenuity in imagining their various ills, to families where habitual anxieties about one another range over the whole field of credible and incredible possibilities, such misuse of imagination curses daily life. As another put it, "An imaginary worry may be unreal, but a worried imagination is very real."

How serious this is, is evident when one considers that in its original function fear was an emergency emotion. An immediate danger was met by an immediate response. First peril, then fear, then epinephrin, then fight or flight, then victory or escape—that was nature's self-preservative arrangement, and in the animal world it works quickly and is soon over. A deer, suddenly aware of danger, springing to attention, his "flag" up and his whole being alert, fleeing with almost incredible leaps, the strength for which his organism has on the instant provided, is a rememberable sight. But afterwards the deer does not worry about it nor indulge in apprehensive anxiety concerning its repetition.

Now, however, comes a being with the same basic physical endowment who has developed a new faculty—imagination. He can picture danger to himself all day and all night long. To the accompaniment of vivid visual images he can rehearse all past perils and can anticipate every conceivable future danger. Such brooding can obsess his mind until he becomes a habitual worrier. Fear with him is no longer a healthy emergency emotion but has become a morbid state of chronic anxiety. The clear recognition of the fact that we ourselves are creating this disaster in ourselves by the misuse of one of our noblest faculties can be, in many cases, a long step out toward freedom.

For one thing, most of us can exercise a considerable measure of control over our imaginations. To be sure, visual images rise unbidden, but all chronic worriers can, if they will, recognize the pet reels of moving pictures which they habitually run through their minds to stimulate anxiety. A cowboy, enraged at the villain in a cinema, began shooting at the screen where the figures moved instead of at the projector where they originated. So we, tormented by the creatures of our imagination, center our attention on the mental screen where their visual procession moves rather than on the inner faculty where we ourselves project these obsessive and abhorred, yet self-created fantasies. Unless our pathological condition is extreme, we can attend to this self-induced origin of our worry and consternation and can exercise over it salutary control. We can change the reels we run upon our minds, substitute for destructive and fearful imaginings, positive and constructive pictures of life, its meaning, and its possibilities, and prove at last that as a man "thinketh in his heart, so is he."

Moreover, we can find in practical action a substitute for morbid imagination. One of the sovereign cures for unhealthy fears is action. Dr. Henry C. Link gives this homely illustration from a mother of six children: "As a young woman I was troubled with many fears, one of which was the fear of insanity. After my marriage and the birth of our first child, these fears still persisted. However, we soon had another child and ended up by having six. We never had much money and I had to do all my own work with practically no help. Whenever I started to worry about myself, the baby would cry and I would have to run and look after him. Or the children would quarrel and I would have to straighten them out. Or I would suddenly remember that it was time to start dinner, or that I must run out and take in the wash before it rained, or that the ironing had to be done. My fears were being continually interrupted by worries about my family, most of which were fears into which I had to put my back. Gradually my fears about myself disappeared, and now I look back on them with amusement."

The range of fact which this woman illustrates furnishes one explanation of the prevalence of nervous and emotional ills among prosperous and leisurely people. They have time to sit around, feeding their imaginations. In wartime they can listen over the radio to every news broadcast and commentator until, unlike a healthy soldier who is in the thick of affairs and who has a job to do that he must practically tackle, they welter in the whole world's worries, become morbidly distraught over dangers concerning which they do nothing practical, and end by adding to mankind's general hysteria without contributing any useful service. In ordinary peacetime such people are the prey of endless imaginary woes, so that it is commonly true that those worry most who have least to worry about. The brooding imagination from which so much of our chronic anxiety comes has a mortal enemy in vigorous effort expended on daily tasks. Says Dr. William Burnham: "The most drastic and usually the most effective remedy for fear is direct action."

V

Nowhere is the danger of secrecy and of morbid imagination more evident than in the realm of guilty fears. All schools of psychiatry agree that behind every "anxiety neurosis" is a sense of guilt. Dr. Stekel italicizes and reiterates the assertion: "*All anxiety is fear of oneself!*" However objective the occasion of dread at first may be, when the resultant fearfulness has dug in, settled

[121]

down, and become chronic, it is fear of oneself—of one's own inadequacy and inferiority, and so of one's failure.

This sense of guilt is commonly morbid; it springs from an unhealthy conscience; there is no just occasion for it; it is part of the disease. As we can have a pervasive feeling of physical discomfort with no specific reason for it known, or a vague, apprehensive anxiety about nothing in particular, so we can suffer a heavy sense of guilty failure without clearly seeing, or seeing only through sick imaginings, what we have been guilty of. This generalized feeling of being "no good" is one of the commonest forms of depression, and in the neuroses and psychoses it ranges over a wide and distressing field of misery.

Often, however, our guilty feelings are specific. We have done something really wrong—violated a trust, betrayed a friend, outraged inner standards of conduct whose validity we can no more deny than a scientist can deny his duty to be honest with his facts. We discover that when we have accepted a code of the utmost moral latitude and have added to this ethical liberality all the alibis and rationalizations we can lay our minds to, there still are standards of right conduct not to be escaped. No latitudinarian interpretations can make Judas Iscariot right, any more than they can make it right for a scientist to fudge his sums or for an artist to do deliberately shoddy work. Some behavior is really wrong, and among the manifold effects of indulging in it fear is one of the most prevalent.

The fears associated with such sins against personality as alcoholism, abnormal sexuality, drug addiction, furious temper, and with more general moral failures involved in the betrayal of friendship, treachery to trust, disloyalty to love, needless mishandling and loss of opportunity, beggar description. The fear of habits we are free to start but are not free to stop, of consequences from our evil falling upon people for whom we really care, of the gravitation by which a wrong once started goes on to disasters we cannot foresee—such dreads gather themselves together into fear of oneself and of having to go on living with oneself. Many suffer such haunted lives, as the Ancient Mariner of Coleridge's poem did when he had slain the albatross—

> Like one, that on a lonesome road
> Doth walk in fear and dread,
> And having once turned round walks on,
> And turns no more his head;
> Because he knows, a frightful fiend
> Doth close behind him tread.

No realistic dealing with the problem of anxious fear, therefore, can omit this central matter: An ethically satisfying life is indispensable if one is to be delivered from harassing dreads. Otherwise, "Conscience does make cowards of us all."

This is particularly evident when the wrong that we have done is secret. We have sinned clandestinely, and no one save ourselves, and maybe our immediate partners, know it. We have in our lives a secret closet, as in Bluebeard's palace where dead things hang, whose discovery we dread. That situation is productive of endless anxiety. As the old legend of Eden puts it, when Adam and Eve had eaten the apple, they concealed themselves "from the presence of the Lord God amongst the trees of the garden," and when discovered, Adam said, "I was afraid . . . and I hid myself." That ancient insight is as modern as the latest psychoanalysis.

The finer a person is, the more such furtiveness torments him. Some wrong, let us say, in the realm of marital infidelity has been secretly committed, and for the best good of the family it should be kept secret. It was an uncharacteristic lapse, unpremeditated, sincerely repented, and not to be repeated. The open knowledge of it would be a heavy and perhaps intolerable burden for the aggrieved wife or husband to endure. The one who did the wrong should carry it, should burn his—or her—own smoke and not becloud the skies of the home with confession. Let him settle the matter with his own soul, with some trusted counselor, with God! Yet while all considerations of good sense, of unselfish thoughtfulness, and of the best interests of the home dictate this policy, the more fine-grained the guilty party is, the more burdensome he finds such secretiveness to be. The strain of clandestine dealing, even when duty imposes it, is one of the most harassing that a sensitive person can endure.

When to this fact of secrecy is added the fear of disclosure, anxiety commonly becomes destructive of all personal coherence and peace. Dealing with lives haunted by the dread of publicity, the personal counselor finds psychological wisdom in Phillips Brooks' words: "To keep clear of concealment, to keep clear of the need of concealment, to do nothing which he might not do out on the middle of Boston Common at noonday,—I cannot say how more and more that seems to me to be the glory of a young man's life. It is an awful hour when the first necessity of hiding anything comes. The whole life is different thenceforth. When there are questions to be feared and eyes to be avoided and subjects which must not be touched, then the bloom of life is gone. Put off that day as long as possible. Put it off forever if you can."

In a detective drama on the stage, where the key to the crime lay in full view of the audience, waiting for someone in the play to notice it, a fairly gasping tension held the theater spellbound whenever anyone of the cast came near it or gave the slightest sign of paying heed to it. Many lives are thus (distraught with anxious dread of being found out) Two lovers, fully intending marriage, both students for doctorates in philosophy, decided not to marry until they had secured their degrees, but meantime to allow themselves full marital privilege. It would be difficult to imagine sexual irregularity more innocent than that. They rationalized the procedure so that no conscious sense of wrongdoing troubled their minds. Yet the young woman came perilously near nervous breakdown, was sent by the physician to the minister, and at last was brought reluctantly to see that nothing was the matter with her except her inability to stand clandestine living. However stoutly she might defend her course, still in the group she lived with she would not want it known. Despite contraceptives, every faintest indication of possible pregnancy was a terror to her. Deeper than her argued consent to her conduct lay the fact that it would not stand the test of publicity. Had she been made of rougher stuff, she could have sloughed off anxiety, but as it was, secretive behavior produced an intolerable strain. She was too fine-grained and sensitive a person to endure furtiveness; what had to be done on the sly was subconsciously repugnant to her; her ethical self-defense was not so strong as her basic need as a high-grade personality to live openly and candidly.

In such a case the cure was simple—a marriage service that did not alter the conduct but did remove its clandestine character. Far more complicated and difficult are most cases of secretive behavior. From major crimes that publicized would put the guilty in jeopardy of the law, to all manner of sly dealings that must be kept in the dark, this fertile cause of apprehensive fear works its disruptive consequence. One way or another, such secretiveness must be ended if a coherent, well-integrated personality is to be achieved. Confession, whether to the aggrieved, to the church, to some wise counselor, or to God alone; restitution, where that is possible; forgiveness, which re-establishes personal relationships upon a basis of candor and mutual understanding—such processes are indispensable to the soul's health. The long tradition of the church in this regard is based on solid facts, and among the most joyful of its "saved souls" have been those whose closets and attics have been cleansed of stealthy sins, until they have lived openly and aboveboard, with nothing secretive to be kept hidden, and so have won some fair chance at an undistracted and satisfying life.

VI

Successful dealing with our morbid fears, however, involves more than the objective confrontation of them, the wise use of our imagination in handling them, and the elimination of guilty furtiveness as one major cause of them; it involves the positive substitution of courage for them, and in ordinary daily life courage springs from two main sources, *unselfishness* and *faith*.

The egocentric self-pitier is naturally a coward. His hypersensitive concern about himself incapacitates him for either brave endurance or daring venturesomeness. When the call for valor or intrepidity comes, his spine turns out to be made, as Mark Twain said, "of boiled macaroni," and this inherent weakness it is not within his power by force of will to overcome. Being still at a childish stage of personal development, self-concerned, self-centered, self-pitying, he inevitably reacts to difficulty and danger not with courage but with alibis and escapes.

Courage is a concomitant of loyalty, devotion, self-commitment. We are naturally brave on behalf of those persons or causes to which we have given ourselves. Beethoven was immersed in his music so that however much he cared about himself, his "self" was indistinguishable from that extended life which included music and his absorbed devotion to it. When, therefore, he faced physical obstacles and public opposition, including bitter attacks that would have cowed a weaker spirit, he was challenged. "A few fly bites," he said, "can not stop a spirited horse." In this sense the New Testament is psychologically right: "Perfect love casteth out fear." To be sure, love also produces fear. Because a mother loves her children, or a patriot his country, or an artist his work, anxiety arises on behalf of the loved object. That, however, is not half the story. A mother's bravery on behalf of her children is notorious, and in every realm when courage rises to great heights, love, loyalty, devotion, self-commitment are at the root of it. It requires an emotion to drive out an emotion, and fear is too power-ful a feeling to be dealt with by the emotional forces of self-centeredness and self-pity. Even the motive of self-preservation, while it can sustain a fierce fight to the death, is never at its strongest and most enduring until the "self" we are trying to preserve is identified with persons, causes, and values to which we are indissolubly joined.

The steamer "Fairfax" and the tanker "Pinthis" col-lided off the Massachusetts coast and the "Fairfax" caught fire. The crew deserted their posts; some of the terrorized passengers leaped into the sea, and it was Lester Kober, a "wiper," who saved the day. He went to the deserted engine room—where he had no obligation to go—because he saw that the source of peril was there. "There was lots of smoke in the engine room, wasn't there?" he was asked at the investigation. "Yes, there was," he an-swered. "And it was dangerous to remain there, wasn't it?" "I don't know, sir. I'm no judge of that." "But you stayed, didn't you?" "Yes, sir." Then, when pressed to state whether he stayed because he thought it was his duty or because he had no more sense, Kober answered simply, "I saw that someone was needed there." From Kober the "wiper" to man's most illustrious exhibitions of moral daring, that answer reveals one psychological prerequisite of courage. Awareness of social need, ab-sorbed interest in meeting it, self-forgetfulness in the face of it—all great courage is of this outgoing quality.

Only so are those characters produced who when they are afraid feel that it makes no difference whether they are afraid or not. Values are at stake so much more im-portant than their fear, that *that* is a secondary matter.

[128]

Of course they are afraid! According to one of Lincoln's stories, two men were charging side by side in a battle of the Civil War. Said one, "Why, you're pale as a sheet; you look like a ghost; I believe you're afraid." Said the other, "Yes, I am, and if you were half as much afraid as I am you'd have run long ago." In this sense Jesus in the Garden of Gethsemane was afraid—his horror at the physical brutality and public shame of crucifixion are part and parcel of the scene's reality—but what difference did that make? By love, loyalty, and self-commitment he was incorporated with a cause that did not indeed eliminate fear but submerged it, made of it a secondary matter, present but not dominant.

Ordinary life is full of occasions when fear needs thus to be recognized, acknowledged, and treated as of no account. Indeed, the dual nature of fear, as both good and evil, is nowhere better illustrated than in a man who dreads so much falling short of his duty that he dreads much less the cost of doing it. In this sense brave spirits often set a fear to catch a fear. From soldiers to whom the time comes, as Coningsby Dawson said, when one's only fear is a supreme fear lest one may fail to do one's duty, to men like the early Calvinists of whom it was said that they feared God so much that they never feared anything else at all, this supersession of fear by fear has been notably illustrated. Obviously, however, this higher fear is not negative but positive; it is an integral part of one's loyalty and devotion; at its best it is love for family, vocation, nation, cause, world, God, that enables one to say, Granted that I am afraid, what difference does that make?

No one lives deeply to whom this experience is not familiar. Fears come and go. They spring out of all sorts of situations, real and imaginary. Everyone dreads a thousand and one difficult, disagreeable, and hazardous duties and endurances. The curse of fear is that it gets itself taken too seriously. The emotions associated with it are so powerful that they naturally seize the stellar role and reduce other feelings to supers and underlings. But fear deserves no such ascendancy. If one has anything positively to live for, from a child, or a worth-while day's work, to a world delivered from the scourge of war, *that* is what matters. Fear is finally put in its proper place only in those persons who, even when they are afraid, feel that whether they are afraid or not is a minor matter.

VII

Alongside unselfishness, faith is a major source of courage. What Jung wrote concerning nervous disorder in general is particularly applicable to anxious fears: "About a third of my cases are suffering from no clinically definable neurosis, but from the senselessness and emptiness of their lives." Personalities thus cursed by futility inevitably face the ultimate fear—*the dread of life itself.* They perceive no sense in it, believe in no abiding meaning running through it, find it, as one of them said, "the most amazing fanfare of purely temporary and always changing and ever vanishing and, in the main, clownish and ever ridiculous interests that it has ever been my lot to witness." Why they should wish to go on with it they cannot see. It is not dying that they dread but living. This futilitarian aversion to life itself is the final fear, and the only cure for it is positive faith.

Even though one goes no farther than Robert Louis Stevenson in saying, "I believe in an ultimate decency of things; ay, and if I woke in hell, should still believe it," such faith has a therapeutic value beyond computation. Because of this the ebbing of religion as an effective force in multitudes of people has been accompanied by an incalculable increase of nervous disorders. If disbelief in religion were merely disbelief in religion, it could be more easily endured, but irreligion, when it is radical and complete, involves disbelief in life itself—its spiritual source, its ultimate meaning, its undergirding purpose, its eternal value.) When one has granted the worth of such proffered substitutes for religion as faith in friends, in personal possibilities, in creative work, in man's power to build a better world, it still remains true that the hour comes to many, and perhaps to most people, when friends die or betray trust, personal possibilities peter out, creative work confronts failure, and building a better world seems dubious, and when, lacking religion's basic belief in God and so in life's spiritual source, intrinsic meaning, available resources, and worth-while destiny, all values seem in the present precarious and in the future doomed. One thoroughgoing modern atheist confesses that the upshot is a "moral nihilism which is fatal to society or that spiritual despair which falls upon the individual victim of an all-embracing materialistic philosophy."

Faith and fear are true opposites—the more of one, the less of the other. Faith is not simply a theoretical belief but is a powerful emotion of confidence and trust. At this point much of our modern psychiatry breaks down. The analyst may take people to pieces, trace hidden sources of emotional disorder, bring detailed easement and some-

[131]

times radical cure, but often, unless he can supply that ultimate faith in life which alone is adequate to cast out the ultimate fear of life, he fails. It was a psychiatrist, Dr. Sadler, who, having said in one place, "Ridicule is the master cure for fear and anxiety," struck a deeper note when he said in another, "The only known cure for fear is *faith*."

Jesus went to the heart of the matter when he set a mustard seed, the smallest thing he knew, over against Mount Hermon, towering 9,000 feet above the sea, and said that faith like a seed could move obstacles like a mountain.

CHAPTER VI

Handling Our Mischievous Consciences

I

INDISCRIMINATE praise of conscientiousness is psy-chologically dangerous. Many people worry themselves into complete disintegration over moral trifles, and others have consciences so obtuse that they can get away with anything. When Richard Croker approached the end of his notorious career as chief of Tammany Hall, he was once asked whether he had any regrets. Meditatively removing his cigar and thinking for a few moments, he said solemnly, "No sir, not one. I do not remember ever having done anything I ought not to have done, for I have done good all my life." Contemplating such a character one is reminded of Shakespeare's phrase, a "conscience wide as hell."

Conscience is a tricky function of personal life; it runs the gamut from callousness to hypersensitiveness; it can league its powerful sanctions with noble conduct or with bagatelles of moral custom; with equal facility it makes saints, lunatics, and bigots. Indeed, by etymology a "bigot" is a man who associates trivialities with religious conscientiousness and says, "By God!" about them. Following one's conscience can be a distracting experience, and numberless people are torn to pieces by it.

In social life the moral ambiguity of conscience is obvious. Galileo, standing for his truth under persecution, was conscientious, but so too were his persecutors. They honestly thought that the new astronomy, making the earth a mere satellite of the sun, would steal from man his special dignity, deny centrality to the human drama, and make it impossible to believe in the infinite value of each human soul. They had no selfish ends to serve in persecuting Galileo—they did it for conscience' sake. Lecky, in his *History of European Morals* says: "Philip II. and Isabella . . . inflicted more suffering in obedience to their consciences than Nero and Domitian in obedience to their lusts."

From such ambiguity spring many sorry tragedies, alike in man's social history and in his personal life. Conscience is a tremendous force. It can say *You ought!* with a voice like thunder, and cry *Shame!* until sleep vanishes and to live with oneself is intolerable. Yet while conscience thus insists that we do right, it does not by itself tell us what is right. Our ideas of what is right come from varied sources —our inherited tradition, our contemporary culture with its prevailing customs and codes, our own passion and self-interest, our excuses and self-justifications, the books we read, the movies we see, the people we admire, the philosophy we hold. A confluence of many streams flows into our ethical judgments, so that conscience, imperiously demanding that we do right, can back up almost any combination of ideas concerning what right is. Thus Columbus on one of his voyages wrote to King Ferdinand:

"In the name of the Holy Trinity, from here we can send as many slaves as can be sold."

This ambiguity of conscience, equally at home in sanctioning the important and the trivial, the socially good and the socially evil, is bewildering. We are supposed to sail by conscience and yet we cannot trust it; instead of relying on the compass to keep our course straight, we must keep our compass straight, and that makes nervous sailing. Every mariner faces this situation, for even stray bits of metal may deflect a compass, and lacking careful checking many a compass faithfully followed has landed its ship on the rocks.

Obvious in the social realm, this problem of handling our mischievous consciences is familiar and disturbing in individual experience as well, and it is an open question whether the more distracting difficulties are met in those who *evade* their consciences or in those who *accept* them.

II

The endeavor to evade conscience springs from strong motives. We profoundly desire to avoid self-blame, and to serve that end we discover many effective devices and techniques. Conscience is easily drugged with self-justifications. Or if we cannot drug it we commonly harness and guide it in accordance with our dominant self-interests. Of one famous statesman it was said that he "followed the dictates of his conscience—as the driver follows the horse." The psychologists call this process "rationalization," and according to Freud's definition, "To rationalize is the unconscious tendency to represent our conduct in the best light, to suppress the real source of our questionable deeds, to depict them as actuated by worthy and disinterested motives, and to represent past occurrences rather as we wish they had been than as they were."

How comforting a process this is anyone can perceive in his own experience. In moral failure self-blame can become intolerable. There are times when, as Huckleberry Finn said, conscience "takes up more room than all the rest of a person's insides," and its condemnations evade our control. This intractable nature of the inner voice, as though it came from beyond ourselves and were unamenable to our wills, gives it often the aspect of deity and makes its condemnations sound like the voice of doom. Nevertheless, we have not been left altogether without resource. When we can no longer endure *being ashamed of ourselves,* we can by rationalization alter our emotional attitude into *being sorry for ourselves.* This is one of the most fateful transformations of attitude in human experience, and it is in constant use.

Yet self-blame, honestly faced and accepted, is one of personality's most necessary functions. After years of work with college students, Dean Robert Wicks, of Princeton, says that whenever a boy has come about-face and settled down to a worth-while life, the boy always has traced the change back to some experience that made him ashamed of himself. In Barrie's play, "Dear Brutus," Purdie says, "It isn't accident that shapes our lives;" and when Joanna answers, "No, it's Fate," Purdie continues, "It's not Fate, Joanna. Fate is something outside us. What really plays the dickens with us is something in ourselves. Something that makes us go on doing the same sort of fool things, however many chances we get." Such acceptance of responsibility within oneself is a necessary ingredient of strong personality, and the alibi-habit by which we evade it is one of the most disruptive we can form. Yet each of us indulges in it, trying to save his feelings by presenting to himself "a carefully draped and judiciously spotlighted portrait of himself."

Two young children, aged five and six, romping boisterously together were carried away by the excitement of their play until one of them kicked the other in the face. Reproved by her father, the child insisted that she had not kicked her sister, but that when she happened to have her foot thrust out, her sister had carelessly run into it with her face. So early the alibi-habit begins, and as life goes on its ramifications are endless. The words "mental" and "mendacity" come from the same stem, and as one sees how widespread and deep-seated is the use of the mind for self-deception, the etymology seems reasonable.

When things began going wrong in the Far Country, one may be sure that the Prodigal Son instead of blaming himself was at first sorry for himself. He blamed his father, who doubtless had made many mistakes. He blamed his mother, and the wisest mothers can do unwise things. He blamed his elder brother, who was evidently a cad. He probably pictured himself as the one superior member of the family, the real adventurer, while all the rest were stick-in-the-muds and stay-at-homes. To be honest with oneself about oneself when that involves self-blame is often desperately difficult. As one psychologist puts it, "Imagine a conceited boy trying to discover he is conceited, when his conceit makes him sure he is not conceited." Doubtless the Prodigal Son, like all the rest of us, for a long time kicked up the dust of self-deceit before "he came to himself," and said, "I will arise and go to my father, and will say unto him, Father, I have sinned."

Euphemism is one of the commonest instruments of rationalization. As Emerson said, "That which we call sin in others is experiment for us." Where others lie, we are clever; where others cheat, we are shrewd and canny; where others are bad-tempered, we are righteously indignant; judging others, we would call their conduct selfish; judging ourselves, we call it practical. Nowhere is this manipulation of names to avoid self-blame more frequent than in the sexual realm. Many a woman who judging others would call what she is doing downright adultery, when judging herself calls it idealistic romance. All of us are tempted to act on emotion or self-interest and then call what we have done by the best name possible.

In personal relationships this alibi-habit commonly takes the form of face-saving. One of the deepest impulses in human life is self-defense. Without it the race could not have survived, and alike its biological rootage and social necessity are obvious. Nevertheless, whether in sociology or psychology, its perversions are notorious. We do not wish to be put in the wrong; we passionately desire to protect ourselves from blame; face-saving becomes the primary concern in all cases of personal conflict, and almost automatically we throw the blame on others in order to protect ourselves.

The story of the Garden of Eden is good psychology. When God charged Adam with disobedience in eating the apple, Adam said, "The woman whom thou gavest to be with me, she gave me of the tree, and I did eat." When God accused the woman, she said, "The serpent beguiled me, and I did eat." What we call "passing the buck" is an ancient process.

Modern psychology has a word for this, "projection." We accuse others of the faults and follies we are most tempted to ourselves. The bully thinks the world is full of bullies; the homosexual perceives homosexuality everywhere; the bad-tempered man is always discovering bad temper in others; the debauchee thinks hardly anybody decent; the liar says all men are liars. One of the simplest ways of avoiding unhappy criticism of our own faults is to discover and denounce similar shortcomings in others. Or if such direct "projection" does not cover the case, we defend ourselves by charging others not with the same delinquencies we are guilty of, but with attitudes that explain, excuse, and justify our own. From an irascible father who always can discover in the children plenty to excuse his petulant temper, to a paranoiac who sees in others threats of violence that justify his own violent desires, the face-savers find scapegoats everywhere.

In few ways, therefore, do men more clearly reveal themselves than in their characteristic condemnations of others. Watch anyone's habitual fault-finding and an important indication of his own personal problem is made available. This explains certain types of fanatical reformers who try to clean up the world in the very areas where they never have been able to clean up themselves; it explains a good deal of prudishness and censoriousness where people cover up their own suppressed difficulties by holy wrath against others' sins in the same realm; and it explains a large number of people who

> Compound for Sins, they are inclin'd to;
> By damning those they have no mind to.

Moral indignation is commonly a smoke screen behind which men hide themselves from themselves. At this point Jesus' ethic is founded on sound psychology: "Judge not, that ye be not judged. For with what judgment ye judge, ye shall be judged. . . . And why beholdest thou the mote that is in thy brother's eye, but considerest not the beam that is in thine own eye?"

One of the most familiar forms of the alibi-habit, resorted to in cases of trouble or of practical failure, is out-and-out self-pity. Handling difficulty, making the best of bad messes, and surmounting even tragic situations is one of life's major businesses, and in a large proportion of cases the real reason why this victory is not won lies inside the individual, in habits of thought and in emotional attitudes for which the individual must take responsibility if there is to be any help. The recognition of this, however, by the individual concerned is difficult. At times we all resemble the Maine farmer laboriously driving his horses on a dusty road. "How much longer does this hill last?" he asked a man by the roadside. "Hill!" was the answer, "Hill nothing! Your own hind wheels are off."

One reason for our insistence on seeking the cause of failure outside ourselves rather than inside is a natural reluctance to examine ourselves. Introspection is difficult. Few people effectively practice it. They are too busy, too obsessed by external affairs, too biased to see themselves fairly, and prying into their own motives, emotions, rationalizations, and escape-mechanisms, bewilders and distresses them. A high school principal received from a mother whose child was just beginning the study of physiology a letter which said, "I don't want my Mary to learn no more about her insides." This not unnatural reluctance at intimate self-examination even in the physical realm is much more understandable in the psychological realm. The outer occasions of our failure we can easily see; the inner causes of it we refuse to examine.

The deeper reason, however, for our self-pity is our dread of self-blame. Having to choose between the two we almost inevitably incline to the first, often with justification. We are not personally to blame for everything that goes wrong with us. Our heredity—we are not responsible for that. Our social environment—often iniquitous in its injustice—we are not solely and individually accountable for that. The world is a coarse-grained place, and other people are often unfair to us, selfish, cruel, sometimes sadistic. Yet, after all, we know the difference between a man who always has an alibi and the man who *in just as distressing a situation* habitually looks inward to his own attitudes and resources—no excuses, no evasions, no passing of the buck. In any matrix of external circumstance he regards himself as his major problem, certain that if he handles himself well, that is bound to make some difference.

One of the basic pre-requisites of great personality is the courage to deny oneself the luxury of alibis. Rossini, the composer, said, "Give me a laundry list, and I will set it to music." We instinctively applaud this quality when we see it in others. If a boy, losing a race, begins at once to excuse himself—I'd have won it if I had not slipped, if I had not got a pebble in my shoe, if . . . if—we may well be concerned about him. But when he says, I was up against a faster man; there is something the matter with my form; I am going to see what I can do about it—we naturally feel proud of the boy. Anyone can recognize the forthright, objective healthy-mindedness of the youth who wrote home to his father after an unsuccessful football game against a rival school, "Our opponents found a big hole in our line, and that hole was me."

It is a difficult problem the counselor faces to persuade a person to give up his favorite alibis and tackle himself. This involves the ability to blame oneself without being morbid about it, to be ashamed of oneself without being discouraged by it, to accept conscience as a judge, a corrective, a guide, a compass to be both checked and sailed by, a friend that alike admonishes and enheartens with constructive leadership. Roads to this end are not always easy to find, but even the start is impossible without a man's frank confrontation of himself as conscience presents him to himself.

Many people critically need the robust and sinewy scorn of their pet excuses that Edmund in "King Lear" expressed concerning a prevalent alibi of his time, astrology: "This is the excellent foppery of the world, that, when we are sick in fortune,—often the surfeit of our own behavior,—we make guilty of our disasters the sun, the moon, and the stars: as if we were villains by necessity; fools by heavenly compulsion; knaves, thieves, and treachers, by spherical predominance; drunkards, liars, and adulterers, by an enforced obedience of planetary influence; and all that we are evil in, by a divine thrusting on: an admirable evasion of whoremaster man, to lay his goatish disposition to the charge of a star! My father compounded with my mother under the dragon's tail; and my nativity was under Ursa major; so that it follows, I am rough and lecherous. Tut, I should have been that I am,

had the maidenliest star in the firmament twinkled on
my bastardizing."

III

Far from solving the problem of conscience, however,
the acceptance of it is often only the beginning of our
difficulty. Many do accept their consciences. They are dis-
astrously conscientious. The sense of duty may be, as
Wordsworth said, the "Stern Daughter of the Voice of
God," but it can get us into endless mischief.

It can attach itself to trivialities. The psychiatrists'
offices fill up with people whose consciences are on the
warpath, harassing them with worry and remorse over
small scrupulosities. One woman heard a sermon on the
text: "Every idle word that men shall speak, they shall
give account thereof in the day of judgment." That text
haunted her. Her conscience became absorbed in remorseful remembrances of all her idle words—the natural chit-
chat of daily conversation, the normal give and take of
friendly intercourse. She was in for it on the day of judgment! Her conversation dried up as though a drought
had struck it; charm and humor left her; she ceased visit-
ing her friends, and they in turn deserted her; she plunged
head foremost into a breakdown from which with difficulty psychiatric treatment at last released her.

Such "conscience complexes" in milder forms are
among the most familiar human ills. Mothers, too meticu-
lous about details, become painfully finicky in dealing
with their children. Youths, facing for the first time the
normal facts of sex, become overscrupulous concerning

entirely natural thoughts and feelings, their secretive and remorseful compunctions overshadowing their entire lives. Bereaved wives or husbands, parents or children, after years of happy home life torment themselves with remorse over small and often imaginary wrongs done to the one who has died. Businessmen, authors, or artists, devoted to their vocations, become overprecise, fastidious, and squeamish, dotting all their i's, but losing their sense of proportion. Religious people attach their sense of right and wrong to utterly petty matters. As for Caspar Milquetoast, habitually making mountains out of molehills, he is popular in the cartoons because he burlesques the familiar in life.

Jesus was dealing with such wayward conscientiousness when he spoke of those who "tithe mint and anise and cummin," and neglect "the weightier matters of the law, justice, and mercy, and faith." With such men he had his major difficulties. They "strain out the gnat," he said, "and swallow the camel!" The Pharisee prayed in the Temple, "God, I thank thee, that I am not as the rest of men, extortioners, unjust, adulterers, or even as this publican. I fast twice in the week; I give tithes of all that I get." He was a conscientious person. The elder brother of the Prodigal, who remained at home and did his duty so satisfactorily to himself that he could boast, "I never transgressed a commandment of thine," was a conscientious person. Simon the Pharisee, who with shocked amazement felt sure that Jesus could not be a prophet because he let a woman of the streets touch him, was very conscientious. The man so interested in righteousness that he tried to get a mote out of his brother's eye, labored under a heavy sense of duty. Conscience so misused becomes inwardly a disease, and outwardly it has produced some of the darkest evils in human history—bigotry, fanaticism, hypocrisy.

In ordinary daily life three types of morbid conscientiousness are familiar. *Compensatory punctiliousness* is one. It would be strange indeed if when a woman worries herself sick over "idle words," there were not in her life somewhere a major disorder about which her conscience ought to be concerned, but from facing which she has saved herself by a trivial substitute. Persons often behave as though they had at their disposal a given amount of moral concern; if they expend this on matters of small moment, none is left over to expend on their real sins. Compensatory conscientiousness, therefore, becomes a common form of self-defense.

A woman seeks the minister's counsel, deeply worried because she cannot pray. A religious person to whom daily devotions have become second nature, she is profoundly disturbed by the sense of futility that makes them wellnigh impossible for her to go through with. She insists on discussing prayer—its theory and theological basis—with evident anxiety to regain her prayer-habit and assuage her distressed conscience. It takes some time for the counselor to bring out the fact that she, a married woman with children, is deeply infatuated with a married man, and while suppressing the infatuation and refusing overt infidelity, faces nonetheless an important moral problem with which her conscience ought to be centrally concerned. Her worry about praying is a substitute motion. It transfers the application of conscientiousness from cause to symptom. As Coleridge put it in "The Ancient Mariner,"

> I looked to heaven, and tried to pray;
> But or ever a prayer had gusht,
> A wicked whisper came, and made
> My heart as dry as dust.

Conscience, which ought to confront us with our real sins, is commonly used to distract our attention from them and to center it on less important matters. Parents, making sorry failures of the major problems of child training, may be punctilious about small details. Men of affairs can be unjust in large matters of social relationship, while being meticulously careful in keeping a selected code of moral rules. Hitler was defended by one German professor on the ground of his almost ascetic individual habits—he is a vegetarian, and does not smoke; and the meanest man in town may pride himself on the fact that he never dances or goes to the theater. Straining out the gnat and swallowing the camel is not only ethically ruinous, but, used as a defense-mechanism, it leads to all manner of evasions and suppressions, and ends sometimes, as in the case of the woman and her "idle words," in anxiety neuroses.

Another exhibition of the morbid sense of duty is the *overstimulated conscience*. Conscientiousness evolved in the human race to serve definite ends; unless socially useful behavior could be inwardly registered in man's ethical judgment and powerfully backed by the sanction of conscience, society could not persist. What thus is socially indispensable becomes psychologically momentous. Some modern psychiatry has emphasized too exclusively the dangers involved in suppressing man's primitive impulses such as sexuality, pugnacity, egocentricity. There is another side to the matter—the danger involved in suppressing his moral sense, without which social life could not go on at all. "Temptation," says Dr. Hadfield, "is the voice of the suppressed evil; conscience is the voice of the repressed good." If life is to be healthy, therefore, conscience must be given its right of way. Thwarted, frustrated, inhibited, repressed consciences are disastrous.

The mischief is that conscience can take advantage of its importance and can overbid its hand. A remorse-ridden man comes to seek help of a counselor. He has done a real wrong, of which he has repented, concerning which he has made confession, and for which to the limit of his power he has made restitution. His conscience, that is, has fulfilled its function and done all that conscience was intended to do. It has compelled the man to self-examination and self-blame, to contrition, confession, and reparation. Nevertheless, his conscience, having finished its task, refuses to recognize that fact. It goes on harassing, nagging, tormenting him, filling his imagination with remorseful memories and beclouding his emotional life with endlessly repeated self-condemnations. No good can come from this plus-activity of conscience, this hang-over of remorse; it spoils the life of the sufferer and darkens the skies of his family and friends. When conscience has fulfilled its function it ought naturally to stop, but commonly it persists, torturing its victim long after the torture has lost all value.

These people who cannot forgive themselves suffer the

more cruelly because they suffer from too much of a good thing—like a jammed automobile horn, which, having fulfilled its rightful function of warning, now keeps up an unintermittent blare. Moreover, this trouble is the more serious because, while a jammed horn is recognized as abnormal, a jammed conscience is often regarded as the voice of God. Upon the contrary, one of the main therapeutic functions of religion is the dissipation of such remorse through the gospel of God's forgiveness. The ancient cry of the Psalmist,

> Blessed is he whose transgression is forgiven,
> Whose sin is covered,

has never ceased in the church, and today the farther we go into the intricate labyrinth of conscience, the more the need of it becomes clear.

Indeed, theology would not be as content as is psychology to regard this strange aberration of surplus remorse as a mere morbidity. Granted that there is no sense in allowing conscience to pester us when no further good can come of it, it is difficult to translate this into actual experience when remorse, no matter how apparently useless, has once begun returning, as Victor Hugo said, like the tide to the shore. That trouble runs deep and calls for radical relief. Quite apart from the formal teachings of religion, a profound intimation is present in multitudes of people that the wrong they have done is more than private to themselves and more than a concern of those whom they have hurt; that it concerns the whole cosmic order of which they are a part and the God of it whose will they have violated; and that, therefore, they never will be able to forgive themselves until they have been forgiven.

However it be dealt with, this surplus self-reproach must be relieved somehow if healthy personal living is to be achieved. When Samuel Johnson was well advanced in years, he returned to his home town, Uttoxeter, and stood for a considerable time on the spot where his father's store once had been, doing public penance for his refusal as a young boy to carry out some task his sire had given him. He never had been able to forgive himself. He illustrates a common form of anxiety, once expressed by a woman who said that her "mind took tight hold of an idea, and just would not let go." When such an obsessive idea is associated with remorse, when the sense of guilt, having long exhausted its usefulness, still persists in haunting memory and imagination, the acceptance of conscience may have worse consequences than its evasion, and by comparison even rationalization may seem therapeutic.

Another malady of man's moral sense is a *negative and gloomy conscience*. A young schoolgirl wrote an essay on Queen Victoria which ran in part as follows: "When Queen Victoria was coronated she took as her motto, I will be good. She followed this motto passionately throughout a long and tedious life." This youngster's idea of "goodness" is easily explicable. In man's moral evolution the sense of duty was first concerned with prohibitions, and this primitive beginning is recapitulated in modern man. Teachers of morals are constantly dealing with this problem from the standpoint of ethics and religion. They endeavor to substitute positive, creative goodness for prohibitory negations—as Paul said, "Love . . . is the fulfilment of the law." All too little recognition, however, is given to the psychological repercussions of an ethic of embargoes and bans when it is accepted by the individual. For many do accept it. They are early indoctrinated with prohibitory laws, in obeying which they are scrupulously conscientious. They do not rebel against this negative ethic or consciously feel inhibited by it. Instead, it becomes their cherished respectability; they may glory in it, estimating their superiority to others in terms of it and counting themselves the better the more they observe their punctilios.

Conscience was intended to produce a good life, radiant, useful, dependable, satisfying, and when instead it produces a life dour, grim, cramped, and gloomy, it is plainly sick. A young man fairly creeps into the minister's presence and painfully asks if he can make confession. When permission is given, a flood breaks loose, a pent-up stream of guilty fears and self-condemnations concerning a minor and familiar matter, in dealing with which the sense of guilt was a needless and harmful intruder. It took two hours to let that flood run out and to substitute for the guilt-response an attitude of intelligent common sense about this small prohibitory detail, but afterwards the youth wrote back, "I am a new man in a new world." He had accepted his conscience, but with ruinous results that registered themselves in needless despondency and gloom. Conscience was intended to make men like Phillips Brooks, of whom a Boston newspaper once said: "It was a dull rainy day, when things looked dark and lowering, but Phillips Brooks came down through Newspaper Row and all was bright."

In such facts as these lies the reason for saying that it is an open question whether the more distracting difficulties are found in those who evade their sense of duty or in those who accept it. A healthy conscience, producing a really good life, is a supreme boon, but it is not to be taken for granted as though conscience in itself were "the voice of God."

IV

The mischievous conscience troubles the personal counselor most when it positively holds up cure. The moralistic approach to a case often makes a therapeutic approach impossible. A young boy steals; stealing is wrong; the boy is to be condemned, admonished, and punished—that is moralism, and it commonly leaves the boy worse off than he was before. A young boy's thievery is always an endeavor on his part to adjust himself to circumstances. To be sure, it is maladjustment, but there is a reason for it, and to discover that reason is the personal counselor's first business. He is not a judge but a physician; his business is not to condemn but to cure. To that end diagnosis, not denunciation, is the first step. In that process moralism's characteristic attitudes are utterly irrelevant to the main business in hand, namely, understanding the boy's problem and helping him to solve it.

The immense difference which modern psychology has made in the treatment of personal derelictions goes back to its introduction of the idea of cause and consequence into the realm of man's inner life. When a good personal counselor sees maladjustment, it is to him not first of all a sin—although it may be sinful enough—but a result,

[151]

with antecedent causes that must be traced until its genesis and development are laid bare, so that through understanding one may find the way to eliminate it. Moralism deals with symptoms and condemns results; psychotherapy diagnoses causes and is concerned with cure.

Divorce presents endless moral problems, but in a large number of broken homes the genesis of the difficulty was not moral at all. A wife with four children desires to divorce her husband, not because she loves another man or because she is discontented with her husband as a friend, but because coition is distasteful to her, always has been, and has now become intolerable, no matter how considerate her husband is. In dealing with that situation moralism is irrelevant and powerless. That state of mind is a psychological consequence, with a long history behind it —going back in this case to a sexual shock in childhood— and the woman herself has been both ignorant of why she feels as she does and impotent to feel otherwise. No lecturing or condemnation can do any good, only understanding, based on a genetic tracing of her maladjustment's growth and issuing in patient re-education of husband and wife together.

This basic fact underlying intelligent psychotherapy is of momentous importance in the patient's attitude toward himself. In dealing with personal maladjustment, moral self-condemnation is often the most misleading factor that can intrude itself. It may appear ethical, well deserved, and indicative of a sensitive conscience, but it can be and frequently is delusive and harmful. Many boys and girls are badly behaved, their misconduct ranging from extreme laziness to extreme excitability and temper, and

[152]

taking forms that bring upon them moral condemnation
from others and moral self-reproach from themselves,
when all the time what they really need is medical treatment. This same shift of attention from moralism to
diagnosis and therapy is called for in cases where misbehavior is neither explicable nor curable save in terms
of its psychological genesis and history.

Conscience makes multitudes of people miserable to
no good effect. For conscience, that has many functions,
can often become absorbed with only one of them—condemnation—so that it becomes harsh, censorious, and
damnatory. This is obvious in the way certain types of
conscientious people treat their fellows. St. Jerome said
of his fellow-Christian, Origen, with whom he differed on
a point of theology: "Had I heard my father, or mother,
or brother say such things against my Master Christ, I
would have broken their blasphemous jaws like those of
a mad dog." St. Jerome was being conscientious, but in
him conscientiousness took the exclusive form of anger
and denunciation, with no curative element of understanding and sympathy. Jesus' conscience was of another
sort. He came not "to condemn the world; but that the
world through him might be saved." He compared himself to a physician, and sinners to the sick. His conscientiousness caused him to be understanding, merciful, curative, saying even to the woman taken in adultery,
"Neither do I condemn thee: go thy way; from henceforth sin no more." Conscience makes some men harsh as
whips and implacable as executioners; it leads others to
be wise, understanding, sympathetic, magnanimous,
merciful. It led one minister in the early days of his
pastorate to excoriate a misbehaving lad brought to him

for counsel so that he raked the boy fore and aft with withering indignation. It led that same minister, years later, with the same kind of boy before him, to go back into the lad's life with a physician's sympathetic insight, trying to see where the trouble came from and to help set it right. In the latter case a letter came afterwards from one of the boy's closest friends: "You would hardly recognize even his physical aspect, he is so changed."

A censorious conscience that can be blighting when one person uses it on another can have a similar effect when a person uses it on himself. In one's treatment of oneself, moralism is often utterly irrelevant to the real problem. An eighteen-year-old girl had an excessive petting party, which she regretted, learned a good lesson from, and then put out of mind. Some thirty years afterwards she came to the minister distracted with remorse about that petting party. She could not forgive herself for it, was obsessed by self-condemnation about it, had gone all to pieces nervously because of it, and, unhelped by physicians, sought the church's reassurance because it was to her so obviously a moral matter. That woman's conscience was clearly pathological, but no counsel, admonition, or comforting assurance could have persuaded her of that. She was a college graduate, a leader in the social and philanthropic life of her community, but she was helpless in the grip of this insane conscientiousness. There was no help for her until her moralism was superseded by insight into her real trouble. She was happily married in a spiritual union so satisfying in its affection and friendship that she could not bear to recognize anything whatever the matter with it. But something was the matter with it— the physical aspects of the marital relation were imperfect and unsatisfying. This, in a sense, she knew, but she could not face it because she insisted that her marriage must be perfect. So she went on with this real dissatisfaction in the sexual life, refusing to recognize it until being thus repressed it went underground, sought out, as it were, the one occasion in her history where sexual shame had been aroused, and, stirring up that old contrition, appeared now as obsessive anxiety about that. This tentative diagnosis by the minister, confirmed by a psychiatrist, issued in a familiar, minor surgical operation, which removed the impediment to satisfactory sexual union— whereupon the obsessive remorse about the thirty-year-old dereliction vanished.

This underground activity of conscience is so familiar that excessive self-reproach is never to be taken at its face-value, but is almost certain to be a symptom of some hidden trouble, in handling which moralism is likely to be irrelevant. To be sure, lying is wrong! Obviously the boy who lies will face condemnation from others, and if he is sensitive, censure from himself. Thus lying brings out from all concerned—parents, teachers, friends, and the boy himself—a massed recognition of the fact that lying is *reprehensible*. All this, however, may do the boy no good. The deeper fact is that his lying is *explicable*. He may blame himself for lying, without understanding why he lies, and his conscience may become so censorious as utterly to crush and wither him. In such a case moralism, acting as a judge who condemns and sentences, increases the disorder; only the attitude of the physician, who diagnoses, understands, and cures, can save the day.

To some this substitution of explicability for reprehensibility in dealing with misbehavior seems only another alibi. Here is a defense-mechanism, they say, blessed with the authority of the psychologists, that dispenses a man from self-blame and furnishes him with an accredited means of self-justification—all his sins are explainable maladjustments. Upon the contrary, this range of fact we have been dealing with puts the most serious and thoroughgoing meaning into the admonition, *Tackle yourself!* All manner of alibis and rationalizations are evasions of that admonition, but so too is morbid self-condemnation. One can blame oneself endlessly without tackling oneself at all. To tackle oneself seriously is to go to the root of the matter, to get all available help that physicians and psychiatrists can supply in understanding it, to assume responsibility for oneself in so thoroughgoing a fashion that one is willing to dig into oneself, bringing to light the hidden and often dark sources of one's own trouble. The paradoxical fact is that remorse itself can be an escape-mechanism. A man can exhaust his whole response to his sin in feeling sorry for it. This, however, is an inadequate attitude, far different from a serious exploration of his inner history, a serious search for his evil's genesis, and a dogged determination not to rest until the sources of his misbehavior are understood and remedied. The recognition of cause and consequence in the inner life issues in no easy evasion, whether on the one side in rationalization or on the other in mere self-blame. It demands, as no other view of the human problem does, that a man in deliberate earnest tackle himself.

For all such mischievous activities of conscientiousness as we have considered, the only ultimate cure is a healthy conscience. Multitudes of people are sick for the lack of that. That we need more conscientious people is a platitude, common but highly questionable. An immense amount of conscientiousness does more harm than good, just as an immense amount of intelligence is harnessed to destructive ends. People possessing a sense of duty allied with important matters of personal and social goodness, producing conduct such that they could will its principle to be law universal, issuing in radiant characters, and predominantly expressing itself not in censoriousness but in saviorhood—such people are real persons. So a young child prayed, "O God, make all the bad people good, and make all the good people nice!"

CHAPTER VII

Using All There Is in Us

I

ONE way or another we must do something with all
the emotional drives native to our constitution.
However we may name, number, and classify them—fearfulness, curiosity, self-assertiveness, self-abasement, sexual
desire, gregariousness, acquisitiveness, pugnacity—such
emotional urges are an essential part of us. If we try to
exorcise any one of them as though it were a devil, then
as in Jesus' parable, seven devils take its place, and the
last estate of that man is worse than the first. If we leave
these emotional drives untended and uncontrolled, they
become vagabonds, never taken possession of by the personality as a whole, and they often cause pandemonium.
Nor can we put these primary motives into the mind's
cellar and forget them, for they will not remain quiet
there; even in the "unconscious" they cause some of the
major riots that disrupt personality.

Curiosity is an emotional urge in all normal people. It
is obvious in early infancy and its manifestations in adult
life are protean. Peeping Toms, prying gossips, inquisi-
tive bores, open-minded truth-seekers, daring explorers,
research scientists are all illustrations of curiosity. To the

Scripture's question, "Doth the fountain send forth from
the same opening sweet water and bitter?" the answer is,
Curiosity does. It expresses itself in meanness and nasti-
ness, in intelligent open-mindedness, in thirst for knowledge, and in daring venturesomeness. Some uses of it produce the most despicable, while others produce the most
admirable, persons, but one way or another there is no
escaping it. Able neither to expel, neglect, nor with im-
punity suppress it, we must do something with it, good,
bad, or indifferent. From this fact, which holds true of all
our native drives, a double lesson comes: first, *no basic
emotional factor in human nature is to be despised;* and
second, *each of them can be ennobled by its use.*

Pugnacity at present seems to be an ineradicable element in our constitution. To call nature

> . . . red in tooth and claw
> With ravine . . .

may be one-sided, since even in the animal world extensive cooperation exists, but still animals must fight
to live, and out of that original matrix man emerged,
equipped emotionally as well as physically for fighting.
Combativeness is thus one of the most deeply rooted emotional drives in human nature. Its ill effects are so obvious,
it so ravages the world—"When we plant war, we raise
hell"—that in any system of ethics pugnacity gets a bad
name, and its elimination sometimes seems the only cure.

This prescription, however, runs into insuperable difficulty. Pugnacity, in the general sense of conduct aggres-
sively maintained in the face of opposition, cannot be
eliminated, and if it could be we should be ruined by its
loss. There are evils in this world that must be fought,

[159]

and when war has been outlawed and its mass murder has become a horrid memory, combativeness will still be necessary to the continuance and advance of human life. The fighting spirit expresses itself not only in unreasoning anger, quarrelsomeness, hatred, and violence, but in competitive sports, in mountain-climbing, in hard work, in the brave facing of personal hazards and handicaps, and in the whole range of attack on entrenched social evils. A small boy, weary of being called his mother's "little lamb," burst out in protest: "Don't call me 'lamb'; call me 'tiger'!" In a world where there are difficulties to overcome, where courage, fortitude, and bulldog tenacity are demanded, and moral battles must be waged against longstanding evils, that kind of protest is in order from childhood up. When Martin Luther, having nailed his theses to the church door at Wittenberg, walked into the imperial council hall of Charles V to face the charge of heresy, an old knight touched him on the shoulder with his gauntlet, saying, "Little monk, you are taking a step the like of which neither I nor many a commander in our fiercest battles, would take."

How deep-seated in us all is this native drive of combativeness is revealed in one of our most private experiences. Let a person become overfatigued until he is nervously ragged, and almost inevitably he becomes the prey of contentious thoughts and feelings. He imagines controversies with other people; he magnifies disputes that may be real, or creates out of whole cloth quarrels that have no basis in fact; he makes up angry conversations with those whom he does not like, and writes imaginary letters full of indictment and indignation. The reason for this familiar experience lies in the fact that a fatigued

body craves stimulant, that a fight, real or imagined, calls
out the stimulant from the adrenal glands, and that when
the tired organism has no actual fight on hand it can always make one up. Endless disasters to personal peace and
social relationships spring from failure to understand
what really is afoot when this inveterate, organically
grounded urge to pugnacity is thus aroused because of
fatigue.

If, however, we give this indispensable emotional drive
gangway, the results are shattering. Bad temper, quarrelsomeness, anger, resentment, hatred, vindictiveness—few
enemies of personal integration are more ruinous than
these. A chronic hatred or even a cherished grudge tears
to pieces the one who harbors it. "A strong feeling of resentment is just as likely to cause disease as is a germ."
Jesus' admonition, "Love your enemies," commonly
taken as almost impossibly ideal, is, upon the contrary,
indispensable practical psychology. If one is so unfortu-
nate as to have an enemy, the worst thing one can do, not
to the enemy but to oneself, is to let resentment dig in,
vindictiveness get control, and hatred become chronic.
The only thing that healthily can be done in dealing with
an enemy is to rise above such ire and anger into positive
good will. This does not involve softness; it does not mean
that a man should ever become a supine door-mat for
others to wipe their feet upon; it does not deny the necessity of coercion ·in dealing with certain types of social
enemies; but it does at least say, as Lincoln said to a man
possessed by vengefulness, "You have more of that feeling of personal resentment than I have. Perhaps I have
too little of it; but I never thought it paid."

A woman sought the minister's help on a comparatively

trivial matter. The symptomatic unhappiness, however, grew so transparent as the conversation proceeded, that the minister looked further and discovered a serious nervous disorder. That too grew transparent, and in the hinterland loomed a towering hatred, cherished by the woman against her sister. The two lived together; the woman had suppressed her animosity, denying it overt outlet and ministering daily to her sister's needs; but for all that a bitter, chronic hatred, accumulating across many years, had increasingly obsessed her. The harm it did her sister, who was largely unaware of it, was negligible compared with the harm it did herself. She explained and justified her animosity so as to make it seem ethical, but what she failed to see was that whether her hatred was ethically justifiable or not was a minor matter compared with the ominous fact that it certainly was a psychological disease. When all practical advice had been given, and everything immediate and sensible that could be recommended had been done, the most important medicine she could have prescribed to her was the Sermon on the Mount.

The tragic effects of misused pugnacity are everywhere. When completely out of control its fury makes men "blind with rage." When left to the unguided caprice of feeling it comes out in bursts of bad temper, irascibility, and contentiousness. When it settles down into cold, calculating vindictiveness, it can make the desire for revenge life's major obsession—as one of Sir Walter Scott's characters says, "Revenge is the highest-flavoured draught which man tastes upon earth." When deeply aroused in childhood pugnacity can become the determining factor in character, inhibiting normal emotions, affecting social

relationships, and coloring the entire philosophy of life.
So one psychological counselor sums up a typical example
of cherished hate: "Samuel Butler's father was a clergy-
man of the old school, whose precept was 'Break your
child's will early, or he will break yours later on.' There
were two results of this method of upbringing. The first
was a wretchedly unhappy boy who said he could remember no feeling during his childhood except fear and
shrinking, who hated his father, and whose whole affectional nature was so warped he was never able to love
and remained a solitary bachelor. The second result was
one of the bitterest novels ever written, *The Way of All
Flesh,* a burning indictment of the father in fictional
disguise, showing him as a sanctimonious, hypocritical
and egotistical bully."

To treat this vast realm of misused pugnacity in ethical
terms alone is inadequate. Of course furious rage, bad
temper, calculating vindictiveness, and chronic hate are
wrong, but more than that, they are morbid. When Edward Everett Hale in his later years said, "I do not think
anybody in the world ever had so many friends as I have
had. However, I once had an enemy, a determined enemy,
and I have been trying all day to remember his name,"
he gave evidence not only of right-mindedness but of
healthy-mindedness. So, too, Lincoln, rebuked for an
expression of magnanimity toward the South during the
Civil War, and told bitterly that he should desire rather
to destroy his enemies, was not only morally but emotionally sound when he answered, "What, madam? Do I
not destroy them when I make them my friends?" Powerful support for the ethic of good will—even for the proposition that "The greatest single therapeutic agent in the

world is love"—is waiting in the psychological approach to the problem of pugnacity.

The tragedy of rage, ill temper, vengefulness, and hatred is that they are the misuse of an emotional drive whose right use is a necessary ingredient of strong character. To employ the technical term, pugnacity can be "sublimated," that is, channeled in personally satisfying and socially useful courses. A boy with no "fight" in him is a weakling. The high-tempered personalities are the most promising. Pugnacity is latent power. Anyone who has seen a gang of youths, the terror of an urban community, taken into a boys' club, translated into an athletic team and set to defeating opponents in some competitive sport, cannot doubt the possibility of sublimating the fighting spirit.

One of the best tenor voices of our generation is that of Richard Crooks. When he was a young child money was lacking in his home for music lessons and he grew up without them. Even so his untrained voice was beautiful, and when twelve years old, he sang at a music festival in Trenton, New Jersey, and Madame Schumann-Heink exclaimed afterwards, "You have the voice of an angel!" The next we see of young Crooks he is working in an ice plant, getting up at three o'clock in the morning to tug ice cakes about, beginning a long, hard battle for money enough to study music. Then a New York church engaged him as soloist, the New York Symphony Orchestra discovered him, and in time the young iceman became Richard Crooks the tenor.

In all such life stories the fighting spirit is involved. No pugnacity means no first-rate achievement in any realm. No combativeness means no pioneering of unexplored continents, no determined conquest of insidious diseases, no discovery of obscure truth, no sturdy dealing with trouble, no patient, sustained endurance of drudgery and routine. In this realm the double truth is plainly illustrated that the basic emotional drives in human nature are not to be despised and that each of them can be ennobled by its use. The New Testament does not eliminate pugnacity but sublimates it. The early Christians were pacifists, refusing service in the Roman armies, but that does not mean that they were through using the indispensable driving power of combativeness. To be "a good soldier of Christ Jesus" in the moral and spiritual struggle which they faced required *that*, not less but rather more than did the murderous trade of war. The same Paul who wrote the Thirteenth Chapter of First Corinthians, came to his life's end, saying, "I have fought the good fight."

II

The multiple possibilities of use and misuse in handling our native drives root back in the essential quality of all emotional life, *sensitiveness*. One of the most important forks in the road of evolution came when some organisms—afterwards clams, oysters, crabs, and lobsters —began putting their skeletons on the outside and their nerves on the inside, while others risked the great experiment of putting their skeletons within and their nerves without. So began a creature, one of whose essential characteristics was exposed sensibility. Concerning this basic quality of all emotional life—sensitiveness—it is obvious

[165]

that we must do something with it one way or another. We cannot dull it without becoming stupid, or elide it without dehumanizing ourselves. All drugging of it by drink or opiates is a transient palliative. To despise it is absurd, for it is man's glory. From good mothers, good friends, and able social servants sensitively putting themselves in others' places, to a poet, saying,

> O what a wild and harmonized tune
> My spirit struck from all the beautiful,

it is plain that without sensitivity there is no creativity. This basic quality of emotional life is inescapably ours, bound to be used or misused one way or another.

Some of its most typical abuses are seen in hypersensitive people—touchy, irascible, peevish, petulant. Wretched themselves, such folk make all with whom they live miserable too. They illustrate the fact that "the corruption of the best is the worst," for they create hell out of the same quality—sensitiveness—that well used makes happiness possible. One of the most important subjects of self-examination concerns the way we handle this primary quality of the emotional life. Let a man discover what he is characteristically touchy about and he will gain valuable insight into his personal problem.

Some are hypersensitive about the superiority or preferment of another. Jealousy torments them. Able to get on well enough with inferiors and equals, they are painfully upset by those who edge ahead of them in the race. A college professor may be kindness itself to a younger colleague so long as he needs counsel and encouragement, but when the colleague begins to stand on his own feet, to make his own way, win wider popularity and larger elections to his courses than the professor himself, an obsessive jealousy may displace all other sentiments. Granted that preferment is often unearned and unjust and that there are ample occasions in the course of a lifetime for feeling hurt! Granted that, within bounds, jealousy itself may perform a protective function, as in guarding the monogamy of a home! Still, as familiarly exhibited, jealousy is a ruinous form of hypersensitiveness—ruinous not so much to its object as to the one who harbors it.

The paradox in the situation is that we ought to be sensitive to excellence. It is a virtue to recognize superiority and rejoice in it, and jealousy is the perversion of this capacity. In the presence of a superior person—one, let us say, who wins a game we wanted to win, or who writes, paints, preaches better than we can—jealousy is sensitiveness twisted into peevishness, petulance, and anger. The only ultimate cure is the right use of the very sensitivity we are wrongly using. As Goethe said, "Against the superiority of another the only remedy is love." The psychologically healthy person rejoices in the excellence of others. Objectively interested in whatever he is giving his life to, he is glad when a musician, teacher, administrator appears who is better than himself. Thereby the world is enriched, and if he can admire and so share in the excellence, he is enriched himself. As another put it, a superior character is a public banquet to which we are all invited.

To be sure, in special instances, particularly in the realm of sexual competition, the emotional battle involved in any such victory over jealousy is very difficult. Nevertheless, however deeply we may be hurt by the success of another who marries the person we wanted to marry, jealousy only bedevils an already tormenting problem. The one who cruelly suffers from it is the one who harbors it. It is self-inflicted torture added to the already accomplished loss of the loved one. It has no healthy function to perform. Envy is always a morbid form of sensitiveness, and the way out is not so much emotional inhibition as emotional redirection. Here too good will is the only ultimate therapy.

William James was writing as a good psychologist when he said: " 'Love your enemies!' Mark you, not simply those who happen not to be your friends, but your *enemies,* your positive and active enemies. Either this is a mere Oriental hyperbole, a bit of verbal extravagance, meaning only that we should, as far as we can, abate our animosities, or else it is sincere and literal. Outside of certain cases of intimate individual relation, it seldom has been taken literally. Yet it makes one ask the question: Can there in general be a level of emotion so unifying, so obliterative of differences between man and man, that even enmity may come to be an irrelevant circumstance and fail to inhibit the friendlier interests aroused? If positive well-wishing could attain so supreme a degree of excitement, those who were swayed by it might well seem superhuman beings. Their life would be morally discrete from the life of other men, and there is no saying . . . what the effects might be: they might conceivably transform the world."

Many people exhibit their hypersensitiveness not so much in jealousy as in extreme touchiness to criticism.

Their *amour-propre* squirms under adverse judgment. Sensitiveness to the opinion of others, without which social life could not go on at all, has in them been perverted into a disease. A good psychiatrist can generally trace such irascible vanity to some definite source. Naturally, anyone suffering from an underlying sense of inferiority cannot bear to have that sore area touched by criticism. Inevitably the extreme egotist is doomed to lap up flattery, and get hopping mad at fault-finding. Obviously the habitual rationalizer, maneuvering his excuses to save his feelings, will resent the opinion of one who sees his mistake but not his alibi. And anyone in whom jealous, vindictive, choleric emotions have gained dominance has so messed up his personal relationships that he will always have a chip on his shoulder and be quick to take offense at censure.

Such abnormal persons take appreciation for granted and regard criticism as an impertinence. The normal person comes much nearer taking criticism for granted and regarding appreciation as velvet. Ralph Waldo Emerson at Middlebury College once made a speech that a minister sitting on the platform deeply disliked. Not having been asked to speak, the minister could not argue against Emerson, but having been asked to offer the closing prayer he could lay for him there, which he did, praying, "We beseech Thee, O Lord, to deliver us from ever hearing any more such transcendental nonsense as we have just listened to from this sacred desk." When Emerson was asked afterwards what he thought about it, he remarked, "The minister seems a very conscientious, plain-spoken gentleman." Such healthy-mindedness as Emerson's in the face of criticism is a necessary factor in a well-integrated personality.

Mere suppression of hypersensitiveness to criticism, however, even were it possible, is not the way out. Sensitiveness to the opinions of our fellows is a basic good, and the ability to welcome criticism and learn from it is fundamental in wise character. To be sure, criticism can be unjust and discouraging and against it one must protect oneself. Nevertheless, sensitiveness to the judgments of others still remains an essential good, not to be eliminated but sublimated.

Nowhere is objectivity with reference to oneself more needed than here. Whatsoever criticism one would listen to with regard to another, let him listen to it with regard to himself! So treated, a man's outspoken enemies are often his best friends, teaching him more unvarnished truth about himself than those who love him would ever tell. Such a man has not ceased being sensitive to the opinions of his fellows, but he is using the quality for well-directed ends—gaining insight into human nature whether in others or himself, achieving mutual understanding and sympathy in his social relationships, neither bulldozed nor embittered by personal criticism but learning from it and magnanimously refusing to take exaggerated offense at it even when it is unjust.

The misuses of sensitiveness are manifold, but in no case is its elimination the remedy. The cure is always positive redirection. "So with all the primal instinctive tendencies," says Dr. Hadfield, "they are all good. . . . There is no such thing as an evil in itself. Evil is not a thing, but a wrong function; it is the use of a good impulse at the wrong time, in the wrong place, towards a wrong end, that constitutes an evil function. . . . *To the psycho-physician there are no vices in their own right, there are only perverted virtues.*"

III

The *will-to-power* is one of our inescapable motives. Adler regards it as central and controlling. Ambition, the desire to overtake our fellows, delight in our own superiority, in having more than our fellows have and in being more than they are—such self-assertive emotions are deep-seated and potent, and their trail across history is sanguinary and pitiless. Nevertheless, without ambition no one would amount to anything. The man in whom the will-to-power has become ruthlessness, sadism, and brutality is both personally sick and socially a menace, but so too is the person who so lacks it that he is a feeble, listless, debilitated good-for-nothing. Ambition is part of our normal native endowment. A child without self-assertiveness is ill; he is not all there; all worth-while achievement involves it. Said William Cowper: "I have (what, perhaps, you little suspect me of) in my nature an infinite share of ambition." Said Admiral Peary about the North Pole: "For more than a score of years that point on the earth's surface had been the object of my every effort. To attain it my whole being, physical, mental, and moral, had been dedicated." And William Booth, founder of the Salvation Army, described his motive for plunging into the slums of "darkest England," as "the impulses and the urgings of an undying . . . ambition in my soul."

The emotional drive that leads us to assert ourselves

[171]

is, in the end, worth what we make of it. If we let it be crushed out of us we become nonentities. If we misuse it we run to self-display, to cutting a figure in the world by hook or crook, to avarice, greed, tyranny. If we use it well, we become dynamic selves amounting to something, with dominant aims served with forceful self-commitment. A man may be ambitious to conquer a neighboring chief and steal his wives, or he may be ambitious to make a neighborhood, through his settlement house, a more decent place in which to live. A boy may be ambitious to be the leading gangster in the city, or like young Henry Wadsworth Longfellow he may say, "I most eagerly aspire after future eminence in literature; my whole soul burns most ardently for it, and every earthly thought centres in it." Self-assertiveness is ethically neutral; everything depends on what is done with it. Like hunting, it began as a primitive necessity. One had to hunt to live. But the hunting impulse now ranges over a wide field, and the thrill of the hunt in astronomical observations, scientific laboratories, in seeking for social solutions and new ways of creating wealth, fascinates more people than its primitive forms ever did. When MacKay, the missionary, arrived in Uganda in Africa, the difference between him and the natives was not that they had ambition and he lacked it. He had more ambition than all of them put together, else he would not have been there.

This drive to amount to something is the very stuff out of which worth-while personality is made. Saul of Tarsus before he became a Christian was a forceful, assertive man, set on being somebody, and he was none the less so afterwards; but the redirection of this strong propulsion

[172]

made his conversion one of the notable events in history.
Without the high use of this primary motive-power,
leadership in any realm is impossible. As for wholeness of
life and satisfaction in living, the wise channeling of this
deep desire to amount to something is of primary importance. Some try to inhibit the desire, praying, "Oh, to
be nothing, nothing!" and unfortunately for themselves
and others their prayer is answered. Some give the desire
gangway and try by varied routes to become lords of creation, often with disastrous ethical and emotional results.
Others re-define what "amounting to something" and
"being somebody" mean—and so illustrate Jesus' saying,
"He that is greatest among you shall be your servant."
They redirect the course of their ambition so that emotional satisfaction, personal wholeness, and social usefulness are achieved.

Self-regard is another native emotion not to be despised
or suppressed but educated, directed, and used. At no
point have conventional moralists done personality more
disservice than in their disparagement of self-love. They
sometimes wield the word "selfishness" like a bludgeon,
cracking down on all forms of self-consideration until
sensitive consciences are persuaded that whatever is to
one's own advantage is likely to be wrong. This unhealthy
dishonoring of one of our most basic emotional drives is
both false to the facts and dangerous to personal and social
welfare. Shakespeare's sound sense cannot be denied—

> Self-love, my liege, is not so vile a sin
> As self-neglecting.

[173]

Indeed, a greater than Shakespeare based his summaries of the moral law squarely on self-regard. "Love . . . thy neighbor as thyself," involves the proposal that we start with the love of self, take its measure, give full scope to its meaning at its best, and then love our neighbor in the same way. "Whatsoever ye would that men should do unto you, even so do ye also unto them," is impossible of fulfillment unless one begins with self-consideration and then extends the same consideration to others. Jesus' ethic plainly involves not the suppression of self-regard but its sublimation.

From self-regard when it goes wrong spring vanity and pride, avarice and greed, meanness and cruelty. Some people live habitually in the spirit with which Mascagni dedicated his opera, *The Masks:* "To myself, with distinguished esteem and unalterable satisfaction." When, however, it is proposed as a remedy that we cease caring for ourselves and care only for others, when self-regard and altruism are thus set over against each other as though they were mutually exclusive, we are faced with a solution both psychologically impossible and ethically false. We cannot stop caring for ourselves. We ought not to stop caring for ourselves. Our initial business in life is to care so much for ourselves that *I* tackles *Me,* determined to make out of him something worth while. That is life's primary demand. If we fail in meeting that, we fail in everything. Nothing that the self can do for others matters save as the self is of such an inherent quality that what it does is worth while. All valuable altruism roots back in a valuable kind of person who is being altruistic. Jesus' principle, therefore, is psychologically unassailable: Unless a man knows how to love himself well, he will have neither criterion nor means for loving his neighbor; unless he has considered profoundly and wisely what he would like done to himself, he will have no test of how he should treat others. Great religion, with far profounder insight than conventional moralism, has always seen this truth and has made its primary appeal candid and unashamed to man's self-regard. To use Emerson's words, "Souls are not saved in bundles. The Spirit saith to the man, 'How is it with thee? thee personally? is it well? is it ill?' "

In baffling practical situations the slaves of selfishness are pathetic, but so too are the slaves of mistaken unselfishness. Here is a typical daughter of a possessive and demanding mother. The daughter has been taught to be unselfishly filial. Her natural love for her mother, her sympathy for her mother's widowed estate, her conscience urging her to give up everything for her mother, have all conspired to her undoing. The other children have gone out into independent homes and left this daughter to support the mother, live with her, be ruled by her, until now in the forties the daughter hardly dares call her soul her own. She is a professional woman with promising artistic abilities, but in all matters where her mother's whims and wishes are concerned she is as timid as a suppressed child. She can have no friends of her own, no plans of her own, no life of her own. Her slightest goings and comings are noted and controlled, and all this is buttressed and enforced by her own conscience, in the name of unselfishness, and by the rest of the children who profit from it, in the name of duty. The pathos in such a situation is that all this devotion has done the mother harm and not good. She ought never to have been allowed, like

[175]

a cuttlefish, thus to wind her constrictive tentacles around her daughter's life. No immediate outward comfortableness can possibly make up for the long-range harm done to the mother herself and to the daughter by this unnatural use of filial affection and this tyrannical appeal to selflessness. When the relationship becomes intolerable— the daughter on the verge of nervous collapse and the mother utterly miserable—one hardly knows which of the two has been more psychologically and ethically wrong, the one because of possessive selfishness, the other because of morbid and misguided unselfishness.

Many people need to have said to them what Ibsen wrote to Brandes, the novelist, when he was a young man: "What I chiefly desire for you is a genuine, full-blooded egoism, which shall force you for a time to regard what concerns you yourself as the only thing of any consequence, and everything else as non-existent. . . . There is no way in which you can benefit society more than by coining the metal you have in yourself."

To be sure, such advice can be misunderstood and misused. This self whom we are to regard highly and make the most of must not be segregated, as though it were a separable unit complete in itself and as though its possessor could be an isolationist in dealing with its problems. The principle of the extended self is critically important here. Nevertheless, the exclamation of one of our college presidents is justified: "A triumphant individual human life is the grandest thing in the universe," and such a personality is impossible save as self-regard is taken for granted, elevated, educated, sublimated. When W. H. P. Faunce was President of Brown University, he knew a rather wild and reckless boy, hitherto impervious to suggestions, who one day in the biological laboratory watched through the microscope the minute creatures that before his very eyes passed from one generation to another. Suddenly, so the boy told Dr. Faunce, he stood up and walked about the room, saying to himself, "I see it now. I am a single link between the generations before me and those who may come after. I will not be a rotten link in that chain!" That was self-regard put to good use. Probably most people pervert this native drive by letting it run wild into rank selfishness. Others, however, running away from self-love and falling into the ditch of self-neglect, need to face Matthew Arnold's challenge:

> Resolve to be thyself; and know that he,
> Who finds himself, loses his misery!

Another primal motive in human nature is *submissiveness*. Protest as we may that human nature is proud, arrogant, assertive, it still remains true that it is also compliant, yielding, docile. Man finds profound satisfaction not alone in exercising mastery over others but in being mastered by others, in following a leader, in becoming an obedient, loyal devotee. If a Hitler exhibits self-assertiveness, millions of his followers, committing mind, conscience, and life itself to his charge, exhibit submissiveness. The hunger of human beings for leadership and for the privilege of subjecting themselves to it, trusting it and giving their all for it, is one of the most potent forces in mankind's experience. So Vandamme said of Napoleon, "That devil of a man exercises on me a fascination that I cannot explain to myself, and in such a degree that, though I fear neither God nor devil, he could make me go through the eye of a needle to throw myself into the fire."

This powerful instinct goes back to man's primitive beginnings, when physical survival depended on the maintenance of a coherent group based upon the mastery of the leader and the subjection of the led, and throughout history some of the strongest influences in man's experience have conspired to intensify it. Social chaos, demanding centralized strength to achieve order and security, makes millions ready to listen to vigorous, self-confident voices and to follow them. The complex nature of the world's problems, beyond the competence of common men even to grasp, makes a leader seem a godsend, and devotion to him a privilege. Within this larger framework of social need, deep-seated emotional needs conspire to evoke and strengthen submissiveness. By attaching ourselves as devotees to powerful persons or groups, we gain backing, security, and a sense of importance; by our docility we absolve ourselves from trying to think through difficult problems and make difficult decisions on our own account; and we escape from ourselves into the satisfying consciousness of sharing a larger life to which by our loyalty we are joined. Far deeper, however, than such statements reach, this submissive instinct runs into the inner secrets of our emotional experience. We love to be mastered, to sit spell-bound by great oratory or great music, to be subdued by magnificent scenery, to feel awe in the presence of commanding personality, to fall in love until we become humble suppliants for the favors of the adored. From the "crushes" of adolescence on, we are natural-born hero-worshipers and "fans," adherents, disciples, lovers, and credulous believers of what we are told.

Submissiveness is, therefore, an inescapable element in our make-up, and something good or evil must be done with it. In its extreme pathological form it becomes "masochism"—that is, positive pleasure in being abused and maltreated, so that one psychiatrist has wryly suggested that if sadistic men could be married to masochistic women, they both could get satisfaction, the one from inflicting cruelty and the other from suffering it. In milder forms submissiveness becomes an escape mechanism. By being shy, timid, yielding, compliant, some try to adjust themselves to life in such fashion as to avoid conflict and tension. Finding it difficult to handle personal relations, it may be in childhood, either by normal good will or by aggressive self-assertion, they retreat to another technique —compliance, obsequiousness, servility. That explains Uriah Heep. In more common forms this tendency is displayed in the aberrations of hero-worship, in the abject devotion of fans to movie stars, in surrender to the leadership of demagogues who possess unlimited self-confidence and booming voices, and in credulity toward any quack nostrum or popular superstition that uses emphatic propaganda.

Here is a powerful emotional drive in human nature, whose misuses are personally and socially tragic, and yet whose elimination is alike impossible and undesirable. The same propensity that gives a Napoleon or a Hitler millions of devotees can give millions of devotees to a true prophet or saint. The ability to follow leadership is basic in all hopes of a better world, and the direction of this capacity into socially redeeming courses is close to the center of mankind's problem. Man has within him *the capacity to belong to someone*. He may insist that he wishes to be free, but if he interprets that desire as meaning an isolated individualism, he denies one of the strongest factors in him, the need of belonging. To yield oneself, to surrender, to be submissive, sounds at first weak, but in its great uses this capacity of self-committal is an elemental human need. Once, after an inspired rehearsal when the whole orchestra rose, again and again cheering Toscanini, the surprised and embarrassed conductor exclaimed, "You see, gentlemen, it isn't me. . . . It's Beethoven!" Do not the "meek," in this sense, "inherit the earth"? Toscanini's significance lies not alone in what he has mastered but in what has mastered him.

Here lies the explanation of the tragic failure facing many popular endeavors after personal freedom. People refuse the normal obligations of family and friends, explode their animal impulses regardless of social welfare, become self-seekers, uncommitted egoists without loyalties and devotions, all in the name of freedom. No souls are more miserable than these, not because they have violated an imposed ethical code but because they have violated an inherent psychological demand. Life is not whole without love, fealty, devotion, worship. The "man without a country" is typical of one of life's most wretched estates—he belongs to nothing. The feudal system is socially outmoded but psychologically it had much to recommend it—everybody belonged to someone in an ascending series of loyalties and obligations. Now that individualism has replaced such stratification of society, and

fealty, once imposed perforce, must be freely chosen,
many persons are miserable who under feudalism might
well have found happiness. Then they would have *belonged,* whether they would or no, but now they have
found no satisfaction for their deep need of self-committal.

Here, again, psychology confirms the deepest intuitions
of the ethical seers. Man is made for self-surrender—Toscanini to Beethoven, the mother to her babe, the lover
to the loved, friend to friend, the scientist to his research,
the social servant to his cause, the saint to his Master.
Throughout life at its best this basic impulse to self-submission runs, as ennobling when well used as it is debas-
ing when it is perverted. All superior achievement has
this motive in it—whether it be John Masefield, a mill
hand in Yonkers, reading Keats for the first time and overcome by the conviction that his life belonged to poetry, or
Jesus in the Garden, praying, "not my will, but thine, be
done"—and neither a good citizen in daily life nor a
martyr dying for his cause is conceivable without it.

The sight of people harnessing their self-submission
to unworthy objects is familiar. They give themselves
away right and left; their self-surrenders are constant and
pathetic—to alcohol and lust, to vanity and pride, to
avarice and covetousness, to their stray whims and caprices, to quacks and charlatans, to the world's demagogues and dictators. All this, of deep concern to sociology
and ethics, is of concern also to psychology. Here is one
of man's primal emotional drives going wrong, and the
cure lies not in its elimination but in its redirection. The
impulse to self-submission, far from being weak, is dyna-
mite.

Great religion, therefore, has gone to the heart of the matter when it has called for self-surrender to the Highest.

> Make me a captive, Lord,
> And then I shall be free;
> Force me to render up my sword,
> And I shall conq'ror be.

That is excellent psychology.

Probably it is in the realm of *sexual desire* that sublimation is talked about most and understood least. Not all demands of the human organism can be sublimated. In satisfying physical hunger there is no substitute for food; in satisfying the impulse to breathe there is no substitute for oxygen. One cannot refine such desires until they appear in alternative and sublimated forms through which the organism finds satisfaction and content. When sex is thought of in its narrowest sense, as the specific tension of a distended gland, it belongs in this class. Such physical sex-hunger, so organically caused, cannot by itself be stepped up into a transcendent form that will be satisfied with something other than the relief of its specific tension. So long as nature, therefore, prepares boys and girls physically for marriage in their middle teens, and society postpones marriage until the middle twenties, there is bound to be a sexual problem, and were this disparity between nature and society removed, the problem would still remain in multitudes of lives, not to be altogether solved by any talk about sublimation.

To the youth troubled by this elemental biological need, many sensible things can be said: that chastity is

not debilitating and that sexual indulgence is not necessary to health; that distracted attention and absorbed
interest in competing concerns are good therapy; that
the general unrest accompanying unsatisfied sexual tension can often be relieved by vigorous action, fatiguing
the whole body; that sexual desire is natural and right,
to be accepted with gratitude and good humor as part
of our constitutional equipment, and not sullied with
morbid feelings of guilt at its presence; that nature, when
left to itself, has its own ways of relieving the specific
sex-tensions; and that in difficult special cases good psychiatrists and physicians can often be of help.

Sex, however, is far more deep-seated and pervasive
in personality than any distended gland suggests. All the
relationships of the family—maternal, paternal, and filial
—are grounded in this larger meaning of sex, all fine
affection and friendship between brothers and sisters, and
men and women, and all extensions of family-attitudes
to society at large, as in the love and care of children.
Out of primitive man's reproductive function came children; with the birth of children came the first experience of creativity; out of their prolonged infancy came
the first demand for sustained gentleness and self-sacrifice; out of the trinity thus formed, father, mother, child,
came the primary social group with its emotional and
ethical conditions of survival. To use the word "sex"
intelligently, therefore, means to connote by it more than
a specific sensory excitement. Before one is through tracing out its ramifications, it involves the whole affectional
life of man, and a major part of his motive power in every
realm of creativity.)

When a man's life is thus thought of as a whole, with

the pervasive influence of sex suffusing his entire affectional and creative experience, sublimation becomes meaningful. It is possible for him to choose a way of living that will channel his affections, devotions, and creative energies into satisfying courses so that his personality *as a whole* finds contentment, even though specific sexual desires are left unfulfilled. So an unmarried woman, denied motherhood, can discover in nursing, teaching, or social service an outlet for her maternal instincts that brings to her personality an integrating satisfaction. Interwoven with the sexual life are many of our major motives such as the desire to be appreciated and loved, or the need of belonging to someone and of having someone belong to us, and these drives can be elevated and educated until, taken as a whole, we are gratified by their satisfaction even though for one reason or another sexual desire in its narrower sense is not satisfied. Even such a dangerous tendency as homosexuality can be denied overt expression, and redirected so as to eventuate in some of the best work done on earth by men for boys, or by women for girls, not only with admirable social effect but with a high degree of satisfaction to the personalities thus saved by sublimation.

The misuses of sex are too notorious to need description. Promiscuity is no solution of the problem, either for the individual or for society. Even Lenin, not to be suspected of puritanical inhibitions, rebuked his followers for indulging in it, saying: "Of course thirst cries out to be quenched. But will a normal person under normal conditions lie down in the dirt on the road and drink from a puddle? Or even from a glass with a rim greasy from many lips? But most important of all is the social aspect. Drinking water really is an individual concern. Love involves two, and a third, a new life, may come into being. That implies an interest on the part of society, a duty to the community." Not only ethically but emotionally the most satisfying expression of man's sex life comes to its consummation in a monogamous family, where two people love each other so much that they do not wish to love anyone else in the same way, and where they throw around the children the security and happiness of a dependable home. This is the ideal from the standpoint both of social welfare and of personal satisfaction. When through self-control in the pre-marital stage and fortunate relationships in marriage this is attained, the sex life is crowned with its highest conceivable success and happiness.

That this involves restraint on the native drive of sexual desire is obvious. All "primary instincts" have to be, in this sense, inhibited. No one can give pugnacity unrestricted expression on the ground that to restrain it is to inhibit a native impulse and is psychologically unhealthy. All our primary impulses must be restrained if only because their own mutual conflicts compel it. Picture a life in which all the native urges explode themselves together—self-regard and gregariousness, pugnacity and submissiveness, fear and self-assertiveness—and obviously pandemonium would reign. The popular idea, therefore, that the restraint of basic emotional drives is in itself unhealthy is nonsense. Such restraint is compelled by the emotional drives themselves. Left to their own devices they propel the life every which way, until whirl is king, or until one of them, gaining ascendancy, masters the others and puts constraint upon them. The choice before us is not whether our native impulses shall be restrained and controlled but how that shall be done in the service of an integrated life.

So far as the sex life is concerned the central consideration to be kept steadily in mind is that the personality *as a whole* ought to be satisfied by its expression. The specific sex-tensions come as comparatively late arrivals; at puberty they ask to be fitted into a total personal pattern already existent. The uncontrolled neurotic type of individual at once demands the crude satisfaction of the newly arrived appetite. Regardless of consequence upon his personal integrity as a whole, he gives gangway to this fresh, obtrusive desire that seems to him to present an imperative and non-postponable demand. The psychologically healthy person holds up the importunate urgency of this aggressive stranger and insists on a criterion of action—namely, that not the new appetite alone but the whole personality must be satisfied. This is the crown of a fortunate marriage; not alone a single impulse but the total personal life, body, mind, and spirit, is fulfilled. Upon the other hand, to explode sex, in its narrower sense, only to discover that some of the most profound and valuable elements of personal life have been violated, far from satisfying man's emotional needs, utterly disintegrates the man himself.

This emphasis upon the satisfaction of the whole person is indispensable if sublimation is to be successful in handling any of our primary motives. No one can hopefully start out to sublimate his various urges one by one, deciding to turn his curiosity, gregariousness, fearfulness, pugnacity, self-regard, self-assertion, or submissiveness into satisfying and useful courses, if he thinks of these emotional drives merely as separate units and deals with them as isolated problems. Always there must be a central core of personality, a more or less single self, whose satisfaction as a whole is to be sought, if sublimation is to be successful. One of our novelists says of a character: "Jenny at the theatre and Jenny here and now were different persons. Different? Why, there were fifty Jennys." Now fifty Jennys in one person cannot successfully sublimate any native emotional drive. Before the elevation and redirection of these ambiguous urges can be achieved, there must be, one way or another, *Jenny-as-a-whole,* who from within has assumed charge of the muddled situation and is seeking a life that taken altogether will be satisfying and useful. Sublimation is no neat trick that can be swiftly used to change an unruly instinct into an asset and a satisfaction. It takes a *person* to sublimate.

Nevertheless, even for one who can be described as "fifty Jennys," there is hope in what we have been saying —no native emotional drive in human life is in itself evil; none of our primary motives is to be eliminated or crushed; all of them are indispensable material, to be used in creating a complete person; each of them can be dignified and ennobled by our handling of it; none of them is incapable of being sublimated into personally satisfying and socially worth-while motive power. Many a deeply fissured life, grasping this truth, has succeeded at last in achieving a high degree of centrality, coherence, and happiness.

CHAPTER VIII

Mastering Depression

I

ONE of the commonest causes of personal disorganization is despondency. Shocks are dramatic, and some people, shattered by an emotional explosion, can name the time and occasion when their "trauma" occurred. Many more people, however, are inwardly softened up and gradually prepared for dissolution by depressed moods. Their condition is illustrated by General Jordan's remark to General Beauregard at the Battle of Shiloh: "General, do you not think our troops are very much in the condition of a lump of sugar thoroughly soaked with water, but yet preserving its original shape, though ready to dissolve?"

· There are types of melancholia where it is positively dangerous to urge the victim by trying hard to overcome his despondency. In neurasthenia, where shock, overstrain, or chronic fatigue has brought on genuine nervous prostration, trying hard is the worst possible therapy. It is precisely what one tries hard with that is sick. The critical need, even if it takes wisely administered sedatives, is to get the patient to stop trying hard, to let go, relax, and rest back. In this situation, religion can be of incalculable service, for it is often of small use to tell a soul to rest back when he has nothing to rest back on, and a practical, working religious faith at the very least meets that need.

The Slough of Despond, however, has varying depths, and most people, escaping its more dismal morasses, become mired in its shallows. Their moody dejections are not altogether beyond their control, and a resolute tackling of their problem can often bring transforming results.

A first suggestion for dealing with this problem is: *Take depression for granted.* One who expects completely to escape low moods is asking the impossible. Not only is there plenty in life to be depressed about, but by its very nature emotional tone has an up-and-down gamut. Like the weather, it is essentially variable. As the negro folk-song has it:

> Sometimes I'm up, sometimes I'm down,
> Oh, yes, Lord!

Some temperaments are more given to low moods than others are, just as some climates have an unusually large proportion of cloudy days. As long ago as 400 B.C. Hippocrates classified man's temperaments under four heads: *phlegmatic*—slow, impassive, lethargic, heavy; *choleric*—quick, ardent, fiery, passionate; *sanguine*—warm, cheerful, buoyant, enthusiastic, optimistic; *melancholic*—sober, somber, grave, sad. This classic list is not now commonly used, but each of us can more or less clearly locate himself under one of its categories.

Given our choice, we might naturally select the sanguine temperament, but the wisdom of that is questionable. Out of that class, when its typical qualities are exaggerated, come the Pollyannas, the whatever-is-is-right people, and the whole race of wishful thinkers. The familiar saying that a pessimist is one who has to live with an optimist is soundly based. The sanguine temperament presents problems of possible misuse and degeneration quite as real as those presented by the melancholic. That Florida and Southern California have a maximum proportion of sunshiny days, and that Boston and London cannot compete with them in that regard, is no reason why all should wish to migrate to the fairer climate or should contemn the good and interesting uses of their own.

Never despise your temperament! Its basic quality was genetically determined and one way or another you must live with it and make something of it. If, in general, it belongs to the melancholic class, you are in good company. Thomas Gray, who wrote the "Elegy Written in a Country Churchyard," had a typical sober, dark-hued temperament. "Low spirits are my true and faithful companions," he said, "they get up with me, go to bed with me, make journeys and returns as I do." What he did with this basic endowment, however, was worth doing.

> The Curfew tolls the knell of parting day,
> The lowing herd wind slowly o'er the lea,
> The plowman homeward plods his weary way,
> And leaves the world to darkness and to me.

That is not gay but it is beautiful, and it never could have come from a merely blithe and sprightly man.

Nowhere does the principle of self-acceptance apply more obviously than here. Alike our general temperamental cast and type, and the inevitable ups and downs of emotional tone, are part of the material of living. To rebel against it is absurd; to surrender to its wayward and disintegrating abnormalities is fatal; to take low moods too seriously, instead of saying, This also will pass, is to confer on them an obsessive power they need not have; to take both our basic temperament and our variable moods for granted and make something worth while out of them is wisdom.

II

A second suggestion is of daily importance: *We can identify ourselves not with our worse, but with our better, moods.* When for any reason there are "fifty Jennys" in one person, the problem's solution involves at least one basic process: The *ego,* the central "I," must choose with which among all these "Jennys" it will decisively identify itself. One "Jenny" may be hopeful, another crestfallen, one friendly, another vindictive, one confident, another fearful; and all these foci of feeling may co-exist in the same person in unresolved contradiction. Deep within us all, however, is the capacity to begin the solution of the problem. The "I" can choose *this* and not *that* mood as representing the real self; it can identify itself with confidence rather than fear, with hopefulness rather than disheartenment, with good will rather than rancor. Among all the moods that ask for recognition the *ego* can say, in effect: *This* and not *that* is my true self; *this* I accept as my own and *that* I disclaim; with *this* I will identify myself.

Many a youth finds himself in the throes of a difficult crisis, discouraged by unjust treatment, beset by sullenness and gloom. Not long ago he had started out among his young companions

> . . . with the rays
> Of morn on their white Shields of Expectation,

and confidence and courage are not altogether dead in him. The gist of his struggle is within himself as his "I" faces the fateful alternative, With which of these two sets of emotions shall I identify myself? One or the other of them he will, in the end, deliberately or by the drift of inner gravitation choose as his own. With one of them his "ego" will ally itself until it is claimed as part of the person and becomes incorporate into the self.

We confront here what Tennyson called

> . . . this main-miracle, that thou art thou,
> With power on thine own act and on the world.

Miracle or not, it is a fact of experience, nowhere more evident than in the far-reaching effects of this inner power of self-identification. The Prodigal Son was not one self, but two—debauchee and son. With which of these two selves would he identify himself? Of which would he say, This is really I? Everything depended on that inner process of self-allocation until, having stood, like the donkey, hesitant between two haystacks, he chose sonship as his real self. At this point in many persons the whole process of integration begins. Starting with a motley mixture, the "ego" assumes sufficient control to claim certain elements in that mixture as his own. He possesses himself of at least some part of himself, identifying it with himself. This process underlies the fact that, as Senor Ortega says, "Man, willy-nilly, is self-made, autofabricated."

In dealing with despondency this power can be turned to therapeutic use. We all have low moods but we do not need to identify ourselves with them. Even a little introspection reveals in all of us that along with our morose, cynical, and disheartened foci of feeling are other foci where gratitude, confidence, and hope are natural. John Bunyan says that even Giant Despair fell into fits on sunshiny days. All slaves of depression have this in common: They have acquired the habit of identifying their real selves with their low moods. Not only do they have cellars in their emotional houses, as everybody does, but they live there.

Anyone can observe within himself the process by which this result is reached. Whether for solid or imaginary reasons or for no ascertainable reason at all, a blue mood comes. We might, if we would, recognize it and pass on as though it were extraneous to us, like clouds that come and go. If we have been wronged by some, we have been faithfully loved by others; if some circumstances are depressing, doubtless others are encouraging; and in any case surrender to gloom is no solution of our problem. Nevertheless, instead of *facing* depression, we *identify ourselves with it*. We say, in effect, This is my real self. Thus we obliterate from our consciousness the hopeful elements, and incorporate despondency as the pith and marrow of ourselves.

A healthy person believes in the validity of his high hours even when he is having a low one. As a sailor on a foggy day still believes in what he saw when the skies were clear, so a wholesome mind trusts the validity of better hours even when depression has closed in. He identifies himself with his *ups,* not his *downs.* As all the water in the seven seas cannot swamp a ship unless it gets inside the ship, so all the despondency we face cannot swamp our spirits unless we let it in. While each of us, therefore, has depressed hours, none of us needs to be a depressed person.

III

This leads to a third suggestion: *When depression comes, tackle yourself and do not merely blame circumstance.* Circumstances are often so tragic and crushing as to make dejection inevitable. To be sad in bereavement, disheartened by disappointment, dismayed by the world's greed and cruelty, disconsolate when personal trust is betrayed, and even sullen under abuse, is natural. One who does not spontaneously react to evil circumstance in some such fashion is hardly normal. Nevertheless, to deduce from the presence of misfortune the right to be a despondent person, is a fatal error. Said a sympathetic friend, "Affliction does so color the life." "Yes," responded the young woman, hopelessly crippled by infantile paralysis, "and I propose to choose the color."

In any depressing situation the decisive element is not so much the situation itself or the natural emotional reaction to it as the kind of person who stands up to meet the experience and do something with it. Whatever circumstances surround a misanthrope, he will see and emphasize their seamy side. As Horace put it long ago,

[194]

"Unless the vessel is clean, whatever you pour into it turns sour." It is the *ego* itself, with its acquired slants and attitudes, that determines the issue. Life is an assimilative process in which we transmute into our own quality whatever comes into us.

> It's a very odd thing—
> As odd as can be,
> That whatever Miss T. eats
> Turns into Miss T.

To say that depressing circumstances make depressed persons has an important measure of truth in it, but to say that depressed persons can make depression out of any circumstances whatsoever goes deeper into the problem as it immediately confronts the individual.

This truth is especially pertinent in a tragic era when the world is upset by catastrophic events, and the psychiatrists' offices are filled with those who cannot stand the strain. Not to be depressed by such public calamities as afflict mankind would reveal an insensitive spirit. In this sense depression is in order, and one who does not face it betrays an inadequate and even a maimed mind. Nevertheless, the more depressing the time, the more people are needed who maintain their morale in spite of it and attack life with constructive courage. Such people face all the facts that the discouraged face and feel them just as poignantly, but in confronting the world they do not forget to confront themselves. They are not merely mirrors to reflect a tragic situation but persons who have their say concerning the meaning of that situation to themselves and others. The catastrophic eras in history have produced two types of personality—the cowed, disillusioned, and emotionally disintegrated, and the courageous, coherent, and creative. Some people are merely thermometers, registering the temperature; others are thermostats, not only registering the temperature but setting in motion processes by which it is controlled and changed. Many today, emotionally shaken, blame their disorganization on the sad estate of the world whereas their real problem is within themselves. As D. H. Lawrence wrote concerning one of his characters, "Poor Richard Lovatt wearied himself to death struggling with the problem of himself, and calling it Australia."

The refusal to adopt adverse situations as excuses for surrender to despondency is called for not alone by tragic external events but by intimate personal experiences such as growing old. Depression is a common accompaniment of old age. The depletion of vital energies, the termination of accustomed tasks, the death of family and friends, the increasing ills of the body, the disillusionments that long experience accumulates, the unhappy practical circumstances that old age often confronts—such factors make despondency a characteristic problem of the elderly.

There is, however, another way of growing old. "I have no regrets for youth," writes Logan Pearsall Smith. "Gladly would I go on living at my present age, and with my present interests, for uncounted years. To become young again would seem to me an appalling prospect. Youth is a kind of delirium, which can only be cured, if it is ever cured at all, by years of painful treatment. . . . When I think of that brother and sister fifty years ago at Harvard,—endowed, it may be, with the grace of youth, but full otherwise of ignorance and folly,—I cannot but prize more highly our present state. Our bones are ripening, it is true, for their ultimate repose, but how small a price, after all, is that to pay for the knowledge we have acquired of the world and men, for the splendid panorama of literature and the arts which years of travel and study have unrolled before us, and above all for those adequate conceptions in whose possession, according to Spinoza's wisdom, true felicity consists." Radiant old age is one of the finest gifts anyone can bestow on his friends, and obviously it is a spiritual achievement.

Whatever the situation, therefore, and however naturally disheartening it may be, it is a great hour when a man ceases adopting it as an excuse for despondency and tackles himself as the real problem. No mood need be his master. He is bound to have occasions when he understands the meaning of the old proverb, "Every mile is two in winter," but at this point the analogy between moods and weather breaks down. Weather is beyond our control; moods, however recalcitrant and rebellious, need not escape the jurisdiction of the central self.

IV

The fourth suggestion goes beyond self-tackling and says: *Remember others.* Emotions are contagious. One depressed person can infect a whole household and become a pest even to comparative strangers. If, therefore, Ian Maclaren's admonition is justified, "Let us be kind to one another for most of us are fighting a hard battle," good cheer and good courage are among the most important kindnesses that we can show.

Lest anyone should avoid translating this fact into the practical terms of daily life, consider the picture of a familiar situation that Professor H. A. Overstreet has drawn:

X. comes home on a particular night, hangs his hat on the hat-rack with a sigh. His face is gloomy. That he is not always gloomy is evidenced by the fact that his children run to meet him. But this night he kisses them perfunctorily. "Don't bother me now." He greets his wife with a colorless "Hello." He takes his place at the dinner table with a creased brow and a lustreless eye. He sits absorbed in his soup. He has no lift, no encouraging glance for anyone. His wife, noting that the mood is on, serves him quickly and silently, hushing signs of disorder in the children. She has learned by experience not to ask the worried question: "John, dear, aren't you feeling well to-night?" The microdepressive does not like to be asked that question. He will glower. Best let him alone. Meanwhile the corners of his mouth sag; his shoulders sag; his coat sags; everything about him sags. After dinner he will slump into his armchair, smoke a cigar and bury himself in his newspaper. If he says anything at all, it may be a few sharp words about the cost of living or the generally unsatisfactory condition of the house or the children.

X., as we know, will recover from his depression and be properly ashamed of himself. To make up for his gloominess, he will probably, for a time, be kinder to his wife and children. But the black mood will be on him again —and yet again. The wife will sigh; the children will vaguely wonder what is the matter with dad; and dad will himself not really know what is the matter.

Such periodic sulkiness as X. exhibits is a definite abnormality. In children it is one of the most dangerous forms of emotional deformity. A young girl named Martha was so dull and stupid that the teacher thought her feeble-minded. "She only sits and looks." The physician, however, found her health sound and the psychologist found her I. Q. good. The trouble lay in the family background to which the child had tried in vain normally to adjust herself. Her father and mother had desired a boy, not a girl, and Martha knew from the time she knew anything that she was not wanted. Then a boy was born, and more than ever Martha was aware that he, not she, was the desire and joy of the family. Every way that she tried to meet this intolerable situation seemed blocked except one—sullenness. To retreat from life, to refuse to cope with it, to go down cellar within herself and stay there, to sit and look, seemed to this pathetic child the only strategy available in her distress.

X., without any such excuse as dispensed Martha from blame, should recognize his abnormality and take himself in hand. His sulkiness springs not from maltreatment but from maladjustment, and he may well incite himself to seek a cure by considering the vast mass of wretchedness in homes, friendships, business offices, and human relationships generally, caused by such recurrent sullenness. Indeed, one verbal relative of "sulkiness" suggests its inner nature. A sulky is a horse-drawn vehicle, consisting of a single seat on two wheels. The driver sits alone; no one can ride with him; he is essentially a solitary egoist. By a happy stroke of etymological common sense, "sulky" interprets the real meaning of "sulkiness." The sulky man is egocentric, self-absorbed, meeting unpleasant situations with a type of emotional retreat into himself that makes him one of the major curses of ordinary life. Few people need more to take to themselves the words of the penitent sinner in Masefield's poem: "The harm I done by being me."

The positive cure of such moods is to forget oneself and do something for somebody. William James' principle that the physical expression of emotion deepens and reinforces it, while the refusal of physical expression diminishes and may at last extinguish it, holds true of many forms of depression. If an angry man scowls, clenches his fists, and speaks irately, he grows angrier still; if he physically relaxes, slackens his muscular tension and keeps still, his anger cools. If a depressed man slumps, lets his body sag, pulls a long face, behaves like X., his low mood gets still lower; if he spruces up, walks as though he felt better than he does, speaks more cheerfully than his mood warrants, and especially if he thinks of others and tries to save the day for them, his own moroseness is mitigated. For the sulky man unselfishness is good medicine.

V

The fifth suggestion is: *In any depressing situation look for the possibilities.* Despondency is chronically associated with negative thinking. No discouraging situation into which we commonly fall is entirely homogeneous, pure disaster with nothing to be done about it except succumb. We ourselves make our situations seem like that by our selective attention, our absorbed concern with their depressing elements.

What can be done with appalling circumstances by a positive rather than a negative attitude is illustrated in Gontran de Poncins' account of the polar Esquimaux: "Here was a people living in the most rigorous climate in the world, in the most depressing surroundings imaginable, haunted by famine in a grey and sombre landscape sullen with the absence of life; shivering in their tents in the autumn, fighting the recurrent blizzard in the winter, toiling and moiling fifteen hours a day merely in order to get food and stay alive. Huddling and motionless in their igloos through this interminable night, they ought to have been melancholy men, men despondent and suicidal; instead, they were a cheerful people, always laughing, never weary of laughter."

The first technique by which many naturally try to win satisfaction from untoward situations is will power. Facing depressing circumstance, they call upon themselves to play the man; but the emotional conquest of depression is no simple matter of direct volition. To be sure, in some crises of disheartenment a despondent man may with good effect be told to "snap out of it." George Bernard Shaw makes one of his characters say to a self-pitying woman: "Your native language is the language of Shakespeare and Milton and the Bible; and don't sit there crooning like a bilious pigeon."

When, however, such reliance on strength of will is the person's sole resource in dealing with some long-drawn-out, chronic tragedy of illness, handicap, or bereavement, its results can be deplorable. Such a person may refuse to crack up, but only at the cost of hard stoicism. He may be strong, but only by becoming flint-like and obdurate, defying life and in the end growing scornful of it. So a strong-willed woman said to the minister after the funeral of her son: "Thanks for the service! It was kind of you. But for myself I have no faith in life left. My son is well out of this damned world." Far from being weak, her will was inflexible, but reliance on it as a sole resource in deep trouble carried her straight into a hard imperturbability, which is a long way from positive, constructive, inner victory over depressing situations.

When circumstances are dispiriting we need not only will power but *insight*—the capacity positively to see the possibilities for good still resident in the situation. Booker T. Washington even used the phrase, "The advantage of disadvantages." He ought to know. Born a negro slave, allowed to carry the books of his white master's children to the schoolhouse door but never to enter, shut out from the areas of privilege he craved most, the advantage of his disadvantages was far from obvious. Yet out of that early slavery with its cruel deprivation he won an appreciation of education, a determination to get it for himself at any cost, a sympathy with the children of his people who were denied it, a devotion to the cause of open doors for negro youth, that never could have been his with such depth and poignancy had he not been spurred by his own privation. Booker Washington was what he was not despite his early handicaps but in large measure because of them. As Emerson said, "Whilst [man] sits on the cushion of advantages, he goes to sleep. When he is pushed, tormented, defeated, he has a chance to learn something; he has been put on his wits, on his manhood; he has gained facts; learns his ignorance; is cured of the insanity of conceit; has got moderation and real skill."

This insight into the "advantage of disadvantages," carrying one from a negative to a positive attitude toward disheartening situations, is of far-reaching therapeutic value in ordinary life. Toward minor irritations, broken plans, or unexpected handicaps, some people instinctively make a negative response. They have never acquired the habit of gathering up the broken threads of their cherished plans and weaving something else out of them. Rossini once had to write an opera for a company whose contralto had only one good note in her voice—middle B flat. He might have taken a negative attitude but instead he wrote for her one of his most successful arias. He made her sing recitative on middle B flat while the orchestra wove glorious harmony around it.

To be sure, there are situations in life that may properly be called hopeless. There are incurable diseases, irretrievable financial disasters, domestic tragedies that cannot be remedied, fatal accidents—dead-end streets where all hopeful expectations are brought to a full stop. Even in such situations, however, one can be a real person, displaying an undefeated spirit in desperate circumstances. It takes genius to serve mankind by doing some things that need to be done, but mankind is also served by those who simply do not crack up when all expect them to. They make a stimulating company. Captain Scott faced a hopeless situation amid the blizzards of the antarctic ice-pack, but he was a real person to the end, and when what he could do was finished, what he did not do made a greater contribution than any successful polar exploration could possibly have made. He might have caved in, but he did not. This final possibility, even when circumstances present a cul de sac, is never closed. Even then there is, as Shakespeare said,

> . . . some soul of goodness in things evil,
> Would men observingly distil it out.

VI

The sixth suggestion also calls for deep resources of character: *Remember that some tasks are so important that they must be gone through with whether we are depressed or not.* Strong personalities commonly solve the problem of their despondency not by eliminating but by sidetracking it. They have a task on hand, a purpose to fulfill, and to *that*, whether or not they feel dejected, the main trunk-line of their lives belongs. We were made for tasks and duties; our personalities were meant to produce something, and, like eggs, if we do not hatch we go stale. Many are "fed up" with living, not because they have been badly battered by it but because they have never given themselves to any engrossing aims and obligations so demanding that no matter how they chance to feel, these major matters must be got on with.

The truth of this is manifest in those greater servants of mankind who have passed unswervingly through hells of depression in loyalty to their chosen aims, like Jesus in Gethsemane, sweating blood but for all that accepting a task that, whether or no, must be gone through with. Therapy directed merely toward a happy adjustment to life is by itself alone superficial, missing the deeper levels of experience that even ordinary men and women must sometimes face. John Bunyan, a prisoner in Bedford Jail

[204]

for conscience' sake, did not escape depression, but he had to hold an unswerving course whether he was depressed or not. So he wrote:

I found myself a man encompassed with infirmities. The parting with my wife and poor children hath often been to me, in this place, as the pulling the flesh from my bones; and that not only because I am somewhat too fond of these mercies; but also because I should have often brought to my mind the many hardships, miseries and wants that my poor family was likewise to meet with; *especially my poor blind child,* who lay nearer my heart than all I had beside. Oh, the thoughts of the hardships I thought my blind one might go under, would break my heart to pieces. Poor child, thought I, what sorrow art thou like to have for thy portion in this world! Thou must be beaten, must beg, suffer hunger, cold, nakedness, and a thousand calamities, though I cannot now endure the wind shall blow upon thee! But yet, recalling myself, thought I, I must venture you all with God, though it goeth to the quick to leave you. Oh, I saw in this condition I was as a man who is pulling down his house upon the head of his wife and children; yet, thought I, I must do it, I must do it.

Such an experience reveals the fallacy of too great contentment with the ideal of a well-adjusted life. Bunyan was not, and did not intend to be, well-adjusted to a state of society that denied such elemental rights as religious liberty. He was deliberately maladjusted to that. Though it cost him infinite dejection, he proposed to go on being undiscourageably maladjusted. No one, whose conscience has serious social significance, altogether escapes this summons.

Too exclusive an emphasis has been put in modern psychology on the problem a personality faces when he finds his wayward, primitive impulses and passions inhibited by the more orderly customs of society. This aspect of the matter, taken by itself alone, suggests the picture of an individual unruly with aboriginal instincts facing a society of superior orderliness and feeling himself cramped and suppressed. This picture has important truth in it but it does not tell the whole story. It is also true that fine-grained, socially-minded, well-integrated personalities face a society that is unjust and cruel. They do not so much find their primitive impulses inhibited by social order as they find their best ethical values and insights outraged by social disorder. To this unethical and inhuman state of affairs they refuse to become well adjusted. To war, to the evils of predatory economics, to racial prejudice, totalitarian dictatorship, or whatever other social ill confronts them, they refuse comfortably to adjust themselves. In such a case despondency cannot be lightly avoided, nor can it be exorcized by any psychiatric formula. It is a natural part of a total experience which the personality as a whole deliberately chooses, because, depression or no depression, it must be gone through with for conscience' sake. In comparison with that total experience, anything less would seem to the person a wretched surrender of his human dignity, so that in terms even of his own personal satisfaction he would choose it along with its accompanying despondencies rather than any easier way. Here is the basic psychological experience involved in the saying about Jesus: "Who for the joy that was set before him endured the cross, despising shame."

This technique of sidetracking low spirits operates less dramatically in ordinary living. If a man has a real vocation, he can make that essential and his off moods incidental. Millet's personal circumstances were at times depressing in the extreme. "We have only enough fuel to last us for two or three days," he wrote, "and we don't know how we are going to get any more; for they won't let us have any without money . . ." In such deplorable poverty he painted the "Angelus," and was at one time so despondent that he contemplated suicide. Had he not been painting the "Angelus" he might have committed suicide. But there it was, his work that ought to be carried through whether he was despondent or not. His work saved him not by eliminating low spirits but by preventing their dominance over him. Now he is remembered by his work, not by the incidental dejections he pushed aside in order to do it.

Whoever has a task that dignifies his days, so that, depression or no depression, he proposes to see it through, has one of the major prerequisites of mental and emotional health. Speaking of ills such as neurasthenia, psychasthenia, obsessions, hysteria, and mental disorder generally, Dr. William H. Burnham says: "We find . . . the same sovereign method for developing integration of the personality or checking the mental disintegration, in the doing of worth-while tasks with a maximum of freedom in the choice and the doing. . . . Thus in all conditions of life and all the varied situations in which an individual may be placed, in periods of monotony and boredom, or in times of storm and stress, in all the varied fortunes and misfortunes that meet the individual, when opportunity is lost, when disheartened by failure, even

[207]

in conditions of distress and despair, the day's work is the one consolation; and with habits of coordinated activity, of mental and physical work developed from childhood, one has always an anchor of safety whatever the mental chaos and distraction."

VII

Such suggestions, directed to the relief of depression, and assuming that its origin is in wrong mental and emotional attitudes, do not, of course, meet the whole issue. Some despondency is physically caused. Glandular maladies can poison the system and issue in melancholy moods beyond the power of anyone's satisfactory control. To the victims of such depressive states the best-intentioned counsel, putting upon their minds and wills responsibility for their melancholia and bidding them rise above it, may easily do more harm than good. To the black moods they suffer because of bodily dysfunctioning, further dejection is added when they, in their powerlessness, are held accountable.

In such cases the wise physician is an indispensable resource. The vast majority of us, however, who fall victim to occasional or settled moodiness and gloom have no such justification. Not only is it in our power to correct our despondency, but better yet to undertake a way of thought and life that will prevent it. The ideal is not to fall into blue moods and then escape them, but to forestall them with a life that keeps its zest and savor. This achievement involves the whole process of healthy living, from holding great faiths about life's meaning to enjoying varied hobbies and recreations that diversify life's interests. Much of the depression we struggle with downstream could have been prevented upstream if we had been wise. Great convictions to live by, great resources to live from, great purposes to live for, the love of nature, the companionship of books, the nurture of friendship, the fine uses of play, the satisfactions of an unashamed conscience—such factors enter into a life that keeps its savor, and furnish an immunity to despondency which makes cure needless.

CHAPTER IX

The Principle of Released Power

I

THE sense of inner inadequacy to meet life's demands is one of the commonest causes of personal disintegration. Nothing crumbles one up more quickly than the feeling of helplessness. Anyone feeling about his trouble, *I cannot stand it,* or about his work, *I cannot do it,* and so facing the danger of going to pieces, must see that the attainment of a strongly-knit, coherent personality presents a power-question.

Every truth we have so far faced about shouldering responsibility, accepting ourselves, conquering egocentricity, rising superior to fear and depression, and utilizing for good ends our native drives and impulses, raises this central question concerning resources of interior strength. It takes more than a knowledge of psychiatry to pull a personality together, else some of the psychiatrists themselves would be better integrated than they are. It takes inner reserves of power, available for daily use, the consciousness of which brings confidence, security, and courage. People come to the minister who have consulted so many psychiatrists already that they know their diagnosis by heart, but for all that are shaken and disorganized. Under the stress of their problems they feel like trees in a high wind with thin rootage, like cisterns that are going dry, like armies with all their troops in the front line and no reserves. They have no interior backing and do not know where to find it; and this sense of basic inadequacy renders futile whatever good advice can be given them.

The disorganizing effect of powerlessness is illustrated in the physical realm by the results of overfatigue. When our nervous strength is exhausted we fly off the handle and lose our self-control. Depletion of resources reveals itself at once in a break-up of personal cohesion. A young man is brought to the minister by an anxious family. Gifted with a brilliant mind, he graduated from college at the head of his class at the age of nineteen, but now in his second year of postgraduate study is facing a devastating experience which he does not understand. His personality seems suddenly and completely to have changed. He cannot concentrate. He has no interest in his work. His mind has started circular brooding, as though a few wretched victrola records, beyond his power to prevent, played the same unhappy tunes over and over again. He has lost all faith in God and in himself. He feels every morning that he cannot endure the day, and every evening that he cannot face the night. He thinks he is on the verge of insanity. He is toying with the idea of suicide. The counselor, however, knows that this horrid hell is not half as serious as it feels. This is typical neurasthenia brought on by overfatigue, and three months on a ranch will probably put that youth in fighting trim again. So it turned out.

The shattering effect of depleted nervous resources

may be thus a transient episode in the life of a person who on the whole is well organized, but the absence of spiritual resources is likely to present a more constant problem. A man feels chronically insufficient. He has no access to reserves of personal power that he can count upon. His typical reaction in the presence of a difficult task is that he cannot do it, and in the presence of heavy trouble that he cannot stand it. Wise and careful diagnosis of his various maladjustments gets him nowhere. It only presents him with another series of decisions he feels powerless to make and of endeavors he has no strength to sustain. Listening to sermons wears him out. They present him with ideals he cannot reach and duties he cannot do, and when they call for courage instead of fear, radiance instead of depression, taking the offensive toward life instead of letting it drive one to the defensive, he feels rightly, and often despairingly, that this raises a prior problem he has not solved—the power-question.

II

In dealing with this need of interior resources we face a major problem of all living organisms. Power to sustain existence amid hazard and difficulty is a universal need in the organic realm, and from the Infusoria up no organism successfully meets it by volition alone. Every living creature exists by assimilating and releasing power from beyond itself. The most ephemeral insect must thus appropriate energy, and for the few hours of its existence must become a focus where cosmic forces are concentrated and set free.

That the human body illustrates this principle is obvious. As truly as a tree exists by means of chemical assimilation through roots and leaves, our physical organisms sustain themselves by appropriated power, their energies absorbed from sunshine, air, and food. Our available physical resources are not self-contained, as though a human body could be marked off from the rest of the universe by a sharp line; rather, the entire cosmos is part of our physical constitution, furnishing the indispensable means by which we live at all. We are pensioners on universal energy, and our power is not fabricated in us but released through us.

That this principle of released power which operates throughout the entire organic realm stops abruptly at any supposed line separating man's physical from his spiritual experience, is difficult to think, and the testimony of the greatest souls of the race denies such limitation of its scope. That our spirits are continuous with a larger spiritual life, that in this realm also, as everywhere else, our power is not self-produced but assimilated, is the affirmation of all profound religious experience. Many psychologists leave this aspect of personal resource untouched as being beyond the range of science. Others, aware of those indubitable experiences that indicate its reality, are perplexed by them. An increasing number of others, however, deal seriously with them. In powerful personality on its deeper levels man's spirit does not seem like a self-contained, landlocked pool, but like a bay, open to the tides. In hours of receptivity man's reserves can be renewed. His spiritual power is not self-generated by forceful strokes of his volition but is welcomed and assimilated; and the consciousness that just as the scientist does not create cosmic energy but liberates, concentrates, and uses it, so man's personality as a whole can release power from unfailing reservoirs, brings confidence, stability, and courage. As William James put it: "We have in *the fact that the conscious person is continuous with a wider self through which saving experiences come,* a positive content of religious experience which, it seems to me, *is literally and objectively true as far as it goes.* . . . God is the natural appellation, for us Christians at least, for the supreme reality, so I will call this higher part of the universe by the name of God. We and God have business with each other; and in opening ourselves to his influence our deepest destiny is fulfilled."

At this point theism and atheism work themselves out to a practical collision. On the one side atheism, as one exponent of it says, holds that in his spiritual aspects "man is left more and more alone in a universe to which he is completely alien." On the other side theism holds that man's conscious self is coterminous with a wider spiritual reality, *"a MORE of the same quality, which is operative in the universe outside of him, and which he can keep in working touch with."* That this difference is of far-reaching importance in dealing with the power-question is clear.

Some people are like self-contained pools. They have so much resource and no more. Expenditure threatens depletion. They may easily dry up. Others are like rivers. There is plenty of water available. Their power does not originate in them but flows through them. If they keep the channels open their strength need not fail, for output can be matched by intake. They carry over into their daily personal experience the process by which all living organisms survive and thrive—the appropriation and release of power greater than their own.

III

Whether or not one accepts the full religious implications of this view of life, the need of some such solution of the power-question is imperative. No more pathetic cases present themselves to the personal counselor than those whose only technique in handling their problems is to trust in the strength of their volition. Into the tackling of any difficult situation they put their wills; determination and aggressiveness are their only resource. Soon or late, however, they face problems to which such a technique is utterly inapplicable. One cannot blow on one's hands, put one's back into it, and *will* peace of mind, purity of heart, freedom from bitterness under abuse or from despondency under misfortune. Dealing with stormy emotions by will alone is like hammering on water—it does not still the waves. When bereavement comes, bringing with it profound sorrow, all volitional appeals, calling on the will to arouse itself and solve the problem, are an impertinence. When a habit such as alcoholism has run its course into seemingly hopeless slavery, to tell a man to try hard gets nowhere; he has been trying hard for years. When a passionate infatuation obsesses a man or a woman, volition alone is a lame reliance. When emotional disorder comes, as in neurasthenia or melancholia, the harder one tries, the worse off one is, like a kitten in a skein of yarn, who is the more entangled the more it struggles. As for more ordinary

[215]

occasions, when one's responsibilities seem utterly to overpass one's competence, the sense of powerlessness cannot be resolved by calls for a lusty will. Such situations reveal the limitations of volition and raise the deeper question, whether or not there are available resources of power which one can tap.

Here is a typical youth who has always succeeded in getting what he wanted by strength of will. He has won his way with distinction through college and is fortunately launched on his professional career. He has pounced on what he wanted like a leopard, and seized it, and so effective has his combination of native ability and strenuous volition proved to be that it has not occurred to him that life requires any other technique. Now, however, he has crashed. Insomnia, melancholia, obsessive anxiety, serious nervous disorganization afflict him. To this problem also he naturally addresses the only method of handling life he knows. He puts his aggressive will to work, only to discover that the harder he struggles, the worse off he is. It is a baffling experience when the only technique for living one knows lets one down. Even an irreligious psychiatrist would tell that man to stop struggling, to substitute healing receptivity for strenuous activity, and would endeavor to supply such reassuring resources of hope and courage as he could bring within reach. The religious counselor goes deeper. The only adequate method of handling those areas of experience where volition is inapplicable is the use of another technique altogether. Power is primarily a matter not of self-generation but of appropriation. Not strenuous activity but hospitable receptivity is the ultimate source of energy. The Psalmist is right about the blessed man

[216]

being "like a tree planted by the rivers of water." Says Dr. Hadfield: "Speaking as a student of psychotherapy, who, as such, has no concern with theology, I am convinced that the Christian religion is one of the most valuable and potent influences that we possess for producing that harmony and peace of mind and that confidence of soul which is needed to bring health and power to a large proportion of nervous patients."

Into the minister's office comes a typical woman, vigorous, able, practically successful, who has always handled her tasks with competence by the volitional technique. Now, however, disappointed in a love on which she had set her heart, she has collapsed. One cannot capture a lover merely by willing it, or handle well the hopeless heartbreak of frustrated love by strenuous volition. The breakdown of the only technique she knows has left her flat. For the first time in her life she is completely baffled, determined to deal well even with this new difficulty but having no effective implementation by which her determination can take hold on it. Like one in quicksand, the harder she struggles, the more deeply she is mired. She cannot lift herself out; she must be lifted. In all such situations a non-volitional technique is called for, centered not in self-produced but in appropriated power. Says Dr. Alexis Carrel: "As a physician, I have seen men, after all other therapy had failed, lifted out of disease and melancholy by the serene effort of prayer. It is the only power in the world that seems to overcome the so-called 'laws of nature'; the occasions on which prayer has dramatically done this have been termed 'miracles.' But a constant, quieter miracle takes place hourly in the hearts of men and women who have discovered that prayer supplies them with a steady flow of sustaining power in their daily lives."

IV

Whether one calls it prayer or not, some such consciousness of assimilated power is present in all effective personalities. As Ruskin said of the great artists, their power is not so much *"in* them, but *through* them." All geniuses have a common characteristic—they are extraordinarily sensitive, impressionable, absorbent, hospitable, assimilative. They feel not so much that they are doing something as that something is being done through them. All great work in art, music, literature, and in character as well, is associated with this consciousness of released power. George Eliot said of her work: "My predominant feeling is—not that I have achieved anything, but—that great, great facts have struggled to find a voice through me, and have only been able to speak brokenly." So Ralph Waldo Emerson said: "When I watch that flowing river, which, out of regions I see not, pours for a season its streams into me, I see that I am a pensioner; not a cause, but a surprised spectator of this ethereal water; that I desire and look up, and put myself in the attitude of reception, but from some alien energy the visions come."

A young boy once went with his family to church on Sunday morning. He was not trying hard about anything. His will was unharnessed and it did not dawn on him that anything important was afoot. He can now recall nothing about the service until the minister was well on in his sermon concerning the high use of life to meet human needs. Then doors began to open in that boy's mind; there came visions of possibility not there before and a new sense of direction and purpose. That was nearly sixty years ago, and the boy has never escaped the influence of those few moments. This is a typical human experience—a single hour of inspiration when we are not trying can determine the meaning of many subsequent years when we are trying.

Certain types of work such as authorship plainly depend for their effectiveness upon this kind of experience. In all worth-while writing there is a sense in which, as Anthony Trollope said, "It's dogged as does it," but if that is the writer's sole resource, how little his work will amount to! The ultimate quality and significance of any author's output depend on hours of insight, intuition, inspiration. If one has no such hours one is a drudge, and little will come of the drudgery. One cannot explain Shakespeare, Beethoven, Raphael, merely by saying, How hard they tried! As for the realm of personal character, to attempt such an explanation of Jesus is futile. Of course he tried; his volitional attack on life was powerful and sustained. But his deeper secret was not so much activity as receptivity, not so much aggressiveness as inner hospitality, and to account for his quality without this use of impressionable, assimilative hours, is impossible. To use his own figure of speech, his life was like a well, and from deeper sources than his own came a constant supply of appropriated power.

In this regard the geniuses tell in capital letters the same story that in common folk appears in ordinary type. There are two techniques in living, not one, and to neglect the second is a familiar cause of personal disintegration. This is often displayed the more tragically in personalities of the stronger sort. They are not loose and disjointed, but determined and courageous; they propose to handle life effectively; they put their best effort into it; they develop volitional potency of a high order. But the more strong-willed they are, if that is their sole reliance, the less adequate they may become to face life as a whole. The very aggressiveness they rely upon misleads them. They grow hard and domineering; they are self-willed; they ride a high horse; they become dictators, national or domestic; they miss those finer and, in the end, more enduring qualities that come from spiritual openness and hospitality; they have no humility, no consciousness of being indebted to, and dependent on, resources greater than their own. Such self-sufficient wills produce pride, obduracy, insensibility. Their owners may be forceful and hard-driving but they become intolerable. This is the will-technique come to its extreme consequence.

One sometimes meets such persons at the end of their road. Some things they have been able to do, but not to keep loyal friends, have happy families, win genuine esteem, develop well-rounded, gracious, understanding character. Their high-handed dealing may even have overreached itself and brought public humiliation and disgrace. The pride that goes before destruction may have ruined the very achievements they gloried in. They have tried to outwit one of the elemental facts of all organic life and it cannot be done.

It is one of the specialties of religion not only to insist

on the necessity of both techniques—a dedicated will and a superior source of assimilated power—but to furnish means and occasions so that this experience of intake may be real and operative. Many people who would not deny the theory that life thus presents a dual requirement leave to haphazard the appropriation of resources deeper than their own. Then in extremities they seek suddenly to discover the secret of released power. They clamor for help in prayer and often are disillusioned because they cannot get it. They carry over, even into their search for Divine assistance, the same aggressive methods they have used everywhere else. They explode themselves toward God in their demand for help, so obsessed by the will-technique that they use it even when seeking resources that come by another route altogether. They have never made receptivity a habitual resort in daily living, nor organized their lives so that periods of inspiration are as much a part of the spirit's regimen as times of eating are for the body. They have never learned the day-by-day secret of interior reinforcement, concerning which Dr. Alexis Carrel says, "When we pray, we link ourselves with the inexhaustible motive power that spins the universe. We ask that a part of this power be apportioned to our needs. Even in asking, our human deficiencies are filled and we arise strengthened and repaired." It is not to be wondered at if turning to prayer in crises only, with frantic and spasmodic outbursts of supplication, we get nowhere. This is not really using the technique of released power; it is merely endeavoring to use the aggressive will-technique in a realm where it is irrelevant. To become a river instead of a pool, a well instead of a cistern, is a far profounder matter. That is a day-by-day, habitual way of living.

Professor Bliss Perry, lately of Harvard University, writes that when a student at Williams College, he once complained to his father, a professor there, about the waste of time that the chapel services involved. "Father's reply," he says, "was very fine: 'If you are turning a grindstone, every moment is precious; but if you are doing a man's work, the inspired moments are precious.'"

V

The power-question is critically raised in human life by two major experiences, the first of which springs from the difference between real and bogus integration. Many people are so favorably situated, are so propped and held together by supporting circumstances, that neither they nor those who externally observe them are aware of a disunited and fragmentary life. When in Stevenson's *Dr. Jekyll and Mr. Hyde* they read, "I hazard the guess that man will be ultimately known for a mere polity of multifarious, incongruous and independent denizens," it does not seem to apply to them. They appear to hold together very well. This semblance of integration, however, is externally caused; they are shored up by an established social position, a secure family, a fortunate and assured environment. They are like a sheaf of wheat tied together, like a collection of iron filings clustered on a magnet, like a mosaic of separate pieces held in place by cement. Their seeming integration is not inherent but is dependent on the continuance of their outward situation.

Could they see themselves as they really are, they might well say with Thoreau,

> I am a parcel of vain strivings tied
> By a chance bond together.

The personal counselor commonly sees them when the "chance bond" has broken. Death or divorce dissolves the family; economic misfortune destroys the social position; personal trouble, such as illness or disappointed love, makes external props an inadequate reliance, throwing the individual back upon himself; the youth, braced and buttressed at home by a strong nexus of traditions and social habits, moves to another community where he is on his own. One way or another, the outward supports that held the life together are taken away. We say that such experiences *cause* the subsequent disintegration, but the truth commonly is that they *reveal* the disintegration that was already there. The person never had been inwardly well organized. His seeming coherence was the transient result of a "chance bond."

Here is a man who had always appeared poised and well articulated. Blessed with an unusually steady family background, born into an assured social position and into a business opportunity fitted to his abilities and his desires, he might have continued to seem poised and whole had the situation remained unchanged. Disgrace, however, now has fallen on the family. His father, caught in defalcation, has gone to prison. The entire setup of the man's life—the cement that held the mosaic together—has crumbled, and the man has fallen to pieces with it. Going deeply into his problem one discovers that he never had been well integrated. The outward disaster did not so much cause his inner disunity as reveal it. He never had possessed for himself an inner core of personal life sustained by strong faiths, adequate resources, worthwhile purposes that were his very own. He had been not a real person but an assemblage of personal elements held together by an external situation, and when now he faces the transition from sham to real integration, he runs headlong into the power-question.

This profound inwardness of all great living must be faced if the deepest problems of personality are to be solved. The world is full of people who are merely tied together. Let the binding cord of circumstance remain unbroken, and their coherence will continue, but the chances of that are small. Not only are world conditions chaotic, and revolutionary changes in thought and life certain, not only are more and more people torn from accustomed settings and tossed into situations where old supports are gone, but in the very nature of human life "chance bonds" are essentially inconstant. No wonder the statistics of insanity mount so that at any one time there are more hospitalized cases of mental disease than of all physical diseases put together, and if admissions to institutions for mental diseases continue at the present rate a million of our boys and girls now in American schools and colleges will for a time at least in their lives be hospitalized. To remedy such social evils as shatter personality is imperative, but no remedy can ever make a merely propped up person immune to the shocks and changes that knock the props away and reveal that his coherence was a sham.

All great living must spring, like a fountain, from

within. The genuine artist is not merely held together from without; the secret of his life is an inner criterion—

> Antonio Stradivari has an eye
> That winces at false work and loves the true.

The man of honor is not merely shored up by external supports; he lives by an interior scale of values that are his very own, like William Penn in London Tower, saying, "My prison shall be my grave before I will budge a jot; for I owe my conscience to no mortal man." The genuine Christian is not merely the inheritor of a creedal tradition, or the passive servant of an accepted code; his motive power is inward and dynamic—"I live; yet not I, but Christ liveth in me."

The acceptance of such an idea of what being a real person means puts upon life a serious demand. The first effect of the demand is to stand us off one from another, each of us an independent character with distinctive rootage of his own. As Thomas Mann puts it, "The world hath many centres, one for each created being, and about each one it lieth in its own circle. Thou standest but half an ell from me, yet about thee lieth a universe whose centre I am not but thou art." Its second effect is to require resources of power adequate for handling a life so conceived.

Many a youth experiments with doing in Rome as the Romans do; like a chameleon, he takes the moral color of his various social environments and so manages to feel at home in diverse ways of living, from unrestrained looseness to formal respectability. He defends this by a theory in accordance with which, as one modern writer expresses it, morality "is really nothing but a fashion, which changes from one year to another, from one country to another, from one place to another, and more especially from one person to another, as surely as the fashion and taste in hats or furniture." Accommodating himself thus to the various social groups he travels with, the youth feels supported by their concurrence, and at first experiences no inner distraction and disunion. Soon or late, however, he runs upon a stubborn fact. Conduct tends, one way or another, to develop a pattern; it becomes set and habitual; there are rigorous limits to the possibility of switching from one moral style to another, as though only a change of fashion were involved. One cannot be a night-club habitué, a devoted husband and father, a drunkard, a good citizen, a debauchee, a trusted businessman and a spendthrift all at once—or even in succession, turning at will from one to the other. As William James said, "The philosopher and the lady-killer could not well keep house in the same tenement of clay." A settled style of behavior is a forced issue; if one does not decide it for oneself it will be decided by the steady deepening of habit; one has to live, in the end, one way or another.

Facing this fact, the youth sees as an alternative to his present course the uninviting prospect of surrender to conventional codes. This he resents and resists. Are not moral customs mere fashions, like the style of hats? Why should he accept this special pattern of behavior demanded by current respectability, just because it happens to be current? Many modern people live in this state of ethical confusion, satisfied neither with trying to live all kinds of moral life at once nor with surrender to conventional respectabilities.

Their fallacy lies in the fact that both alternatives, as they conceive them, are external. Neither the attempt to live all sorts of ways, nor the attempt to copy the conventionally respectable, reaches far into the depths of personality. Serious ethics involves a third type of living which St. Augustine enjoined when he said, "Love God and do as you please." That is to say, goodness, to be genuine and dependable, must spring from within, from insights, loves, and devotions personally possessed. Let these interior tastes and affections be right and one can do as one pleases to the profit of the world. As Jesus said, "A good tree cannot bring forth evil fruit." There are thus not two, but three major types of ethical living: trying all the moral fashions there are; accepting the conventional code; opening oneself in the depths of one's personality to such faiths, loves, and loyalties, that one's ethical quality inevitably comes from living up to them and out from them.

Far from being super-idealistic, the practical importance of this third type of character is continually illustrated in ordinary experience. A boy growing up in a good home amid the sustaining support of decent traditions in his community may present the appearance of well-ordered, moral living, but his goodness may be illusory. He may be merely held in place by his bracing environment. When, therefore, change of scene or loss of family removes the accustomed support, he goes to pieces. His supposed goodness sprang from no inner criterion; it was nourished and maintained by no faiths and loves that had become so integral with his personality that wherever he went—even ". . . east of Suez, where the best is like the worst"—those interior resources went with him. The injunction to love God and do as you please, far from being visionary, represents the only type of moral living that confers on its possessor at one and the same time the highest quality of character and the maximum of personal stability and independence.

These three major types of moral living are illustrated in the historic experience of mariners. In the early days seamen faced a disagreeable choice, either to risk unguided adventure on the high seas, with no help of chart or compass, or else to restrict themselves to the coastline and beat up and down the shore. Either alternative was unsatisfactory; loose sailing of uncharted seas with no means of guidance was perilous and generally pointless, and holding themselves to the coastline was inhibiting. The solution of their problem came with the mariner's compass, and what that did was to *put inside each ship something to sail by*. This worked a complete transformation of seamanship; it brought liberation from the coastline and it made wide sailing of the seas no mere dash of self-expression but a well-directed venture. Something inside to sail by is essential to real personality, and nowhere more evidently than in ethical living.

Every significant ethical system, one way or another, has recognized this fact, and it is the essential element in Jesus' teaching. All his emphases strike inward to the quality of life from which outward conduct comes. Freedom from hate, not simply from the act of murder; from lust, not simply from adultery; from insincerity, not simply from perjury—such inwardness is characteristic of his ethical message. To him a real person must *be*

[228]

...de of the cup and of the platter" must be

...ver, any man faces this demand seriously,
...ed the limits of volition. No man can, out
... *be* this kind of person. Just as a scientist
... result, such as the use of electricity for
...ot by a forceful stroke of will alone but by
... fulfilling the conditions that make that
...ssible, so a personality, to be right within
... conduct, naturally tinctured with his own
..., flows from him, must fulfill the law-abiding re-
...rements of such living. To do that without the recep-
tive technique, without hours of intake and inspiration
and the experience of appropriated power, is impossible.
We are made what we are, not alone or chiefly by our
deliberate acts but by what we are hospitable to, what we
trust and love, are loyal to and guided by. Such inner
quality necessarily raises the power-question.

VI

The second critical experience calling for appropriated
power appears when the problem a man confronts is not
simply the organization of his personality but its reorganization. Integration, as we have noted, can take place
around low centers. Life can become wrongly, as well as
rightly, patterned, gaining coherence indeed, but to evil
ends. When the problem of integration is presented
solely in terms of putting together a personality that has
never been together or that has fallen apart, it is over-
simplified. Many a personality has been so powerfully

put together that, far from being crum
tered, it is strongly centralized and one-di
on the basis of a mistaken pattern. Such pers
it were, to be un-made before they can be re-m
the New Testament says, they need to be transfo
the renewing of their minds.

Personality insistently tends to become set, an
endeavor afterwards to remodel it is often desper
difficult. Prevention, therefore, forestalling in childh
the need of restyling a life that has been styled mistakenl
is supremely to be desired. No one of us, however, ever
yet solved all his problems by prevention. Some do it
better than others, but none altogether avoids the need
of re-patterning a life that has been wrongly put together.
Conversion was once almost exclusively a matter of religious emphasis; now it is the daily problem of psychiatrists.

When Brahms said, "On the whole, my pieces are nicer
than myself, and need less setting to rights," he struck a
profoundly human note. It is we ourselves who need re-
construction, not alone because we are at loose ends and
unorganized, but because we *are organized,* our lives set,
sometimes, like plaster in a mold we cannot break. Years
ago a young man hard held by a habit that was determining the entire system of his living came to the minister,
saying, "I do not believe in God, but if you do, for God's
sake pray for me, for I need him." The fact that today he
is a good citizen and a good Christian, re-patterned on
another basis altogether, is evidence both that the re-
modeling of personality is possible and also that it commonly involves a problem so far beyond the range of
volition that it imperatively raises the power-question.

Psychiatry, even in the hands of those who have no use for religion, has confirmed many of religion's insights regarding the necessity and possibility of such radical conversion, and as well has described in detail the processes that are involved when it occurs. Sometimes *sublimation* is involved. One of the primary emotional urges of human nature—ambition, for example—can be redirected so that the entire quality and significance of life are changed. Sometimes *readjustment* is involved. One who has been trying to solve the problem of difficult situations by a series of defense-mechanisms, such as shyness and seclusiveness, can be shown a better technique until, emerging from his shell with a profoundly altered personality, he becomes an outgoing, effective man. Sometimes *re-motivation* is involved. Motives, says Professor Gordon Allport, are "completely alterable." New interests can take possession of a personality, a new philosophy can reorient his life. Even egoism can so change its quality, as the "ego" finds itself not so much within itself as in other people and in public causes, that the New Testament's exclamation, "Old things are passed away; behold, they are become new," is applicable to the result.

Through these and other kindred processes psychiatry sees the radical transformation of personality taking place, and whether intentionally or not confirms the age-long affirmation of religion that human nature is plastic, that no man need stay the way he is, that as a desert, irrigated, can become fertile, so seemingly hopeless cases of personal failure can be remedied. The minister pleading the need and possibility of spiritual rebirth is not nearly as lonely as he used to be.

Even sudden conversion, once commonly regarded by

the intelligentsia as an emotional abnormality, is now psychologically established. Crisis is as real a fact in personal life as is gradualness, especially during adolescence. It is not a minister but a psychologist who now rebukes the "error of underestimating the frequency with which radical alterations of personality do occur in the period of *Sturm und Drang*." One of the most powerfully transforming influences that can affect anyone is the impact of another personality. One may date the beginning of a new era in one's life from a personal encounter, such as Dante's with Beatrice, or Simon Peter's with Christ. Such encounters, however, are often not gradual but sudden; they precipitate a crisis and occasion a profound change. Moreover, whether personally incarnate or not, a new idea may come upon the mind suddenly. Granted, that such transforming occasions must be consciously or unconsciously prepared for, as Newton's mind was ready for the falling apple! When the occasion comes, however, it may come suddenly, as when Keats picked up Spenser's *Faerie Queene* for the first time and decided straightway the dedication of his life to poetry.

Conversion can now no longer be thought of as an ecclesiastical specialty. It is a profound human necessity, and far beyond the range of organized religion it is continually occurring as an indispensable prelude to the achievement of healthy personality. In its most typical exhibitions, as in the illustrations we just have used, this experience is not achieved by any mere stroke of our wills but has the aspect of an invasion from beyond ourselves. A new personality impinges on us, a new idea dawns on our thinking, a fresh interest captures us, and the crux of the experience's effectiveness lies in our receptivity rather than in our aggressiveness.

If this is true of those aspects of conversion that lie within the range of psychology's technical descriptions, it is even more true of the total experience in its more serious forms. Nothing brings down on a personality a more shattering sense of powerlessness than a wrongly systematized life, set in its ways and rigidly resistant to change. A life still unassembled, that never has been organized, presents to the endeavor after integration a problem serious enough, but a life wrongly assembled and now hardened in habit, commonly seems hopeless. Nowhere is the tragic contrast between saying "I will" and saying "I can" more evident than here. The alcoholic, the chronic depressive, the habitual worrier, the slave of hypersensitiveness, the victim of jealousy or vindictiveness, however stoutly he says "I will," finds saying "I can" beyond his power. Paul's words, "The good which I would I do not: but the evil which I would not, that I practise," express the perennial experience of a life for whose deepest need volition alone is inadequate.

Whatever else religion has done or left undone, it has brought to those who genuinely have known it a transforming access of power. As Paul said, "In Him who strengthens me, I am able for anything." That kind of experience springs not so much from a strengthened will as from the discovery and utilization of another principle of living altogether. A man can cease being a pond and become a channel, with his power not static in him but streaming through him. In Professor Henry Wieman's figure, he can inwardly complete the circuit, so that energy greater than his own is released. When the baffled struggler with a misorganized self begins even a little to apprehend this fact, the results are often startling. The very idea that his impoverished will is not his only resource is tonic. Even a first, fleeting, tentative experience of energy, not so much self-induced as assimilated, opens new vistas of hitherto incredible possibilities. One of our modern psychiatrists says that "the doctrine that the will alone is the way to power is a most woe-begone theory for the relief of the morally sick." When, then, a way to power is opened by another process altogether, so that life has available backing and resource, the very idea that such a manner of living is possible radically changes the entire situation.

A contemporary illustration of this is seen in the growing work of Alcoholics Anonymous—groups of men and women in American communities, all of whom were once regarded as hopeless victims of the drink habit, who now, completely cured, have banded together to help their fellow-addicts. So long as a man thinks he can escape his slavery by trying, they will not take him on. Let him try! When, however, he confesses that he is whipped and his volition ineffectual to save him, he is eligible. Then, when he knows he needs it, they will introduce him to the technique of released power as it operates in the experience of drink-enslaved people. They have no sectarian partialities—they are Jews, Catholics, and Protestants. They have no dogmatic theological theories —some of them were formerly agnostics and atheists. But all of them have discovered that they can complete the circuit, and that what volition alone cannot do, appropriated power furnishes resource for doing. The psychiatrist in charge of a large New York sanitarium for victims of drink and drugs says that before Alcoholics Anonymous began operating among the patients, the percentage of cures among drink's victims was three per cent, but that since that time it has risen to twenty-five per cent. Let the skeptic explain this as he will, the ex-alcoholics themselves are sure they know the reason. Over the fireplace in one of their club rooms hangs the motto of their rapidly growing fellowship: "But for the grace of God!"

The need of personal reorganization in any realm imperatively raises this power-question, and the endless list of changed lives whose self-explanation centers in being "strengthened with might by his Spirit in the inner man," suggests that, far from being outmoded, this experience has in it unguessed possibilities. Modern psychology on its profounder levels has not eliminated but illumined it, and sometimes most interestingly when the psychologist himself would have professed neither concern with, nor belief in, religion. Far from being unscientific, the experience of released power finds in science its most impressive, large-scale illustration. Miraculous events involving suspended or violated natural law are incredible to modern minds, but the word "miracle" still retains its place in our vocabulary. Science does work miracles—achievements hitherto incredible—and all of them are exhibitions of released power. There is no telling what may yet be done on earth as this scientific process goes on, putting more and more cosmic energy at man's disposal. Such miracles of science one must believe in, and not less real are those miracles in personal life where transformations of character, gradual or sudden, utterly impossible to the unaided will, are wrought by the appropriation of Divine power.

VII

Not only in these two profoundly searching experiences—the demand for real rather than sham integration, and the need of radical reorganization of character—but in the more ordinary wants of daily life, the power-question is insistent. In many cases of emotional disorder, activity is a major means of therapy, but in many others, overactivity, so exclusively indulged in that the person has no other way of meeting life, is the main cause of the disease. A restless, hectic, feverish individual, forever on the go, is emotionally sick. However extended in length and breadth of action such a life may be, it lacks the dimension of depth.

Peace is fundamentally a matter of power. Plenty of people who do not need to worry about finances do worry about them. Plenty of people with average health are hypochondriacs, worrying over imaginary illnesses. Such folk constantly suffer from a feeling of skating on thin ice and expecting to go through, and the real reason is within themselves. They have no interior resources of power, no margin of reserve around their daily needs, no sense of available backing that sends them into each day's tasks and difficulties *sure that what they ought to do they can do and what they must endure they can stand.* No mere techniques of psychiatric readjustment can meet this situation. Ultimately this is a religious question.

Into the minister's home one night came a man who

[236]

had just tried to commit suicide by hanging. The strap broke, and before he tried it again, he decided to seek personal counsel. Psychologically speaking, it took only a short time roughly to diagnose his trouble—an "inferiority complex," with a definite history that could be easily traced, ending in a debilitating sense of inadequacy to face life. This analysis of his problem was in itself encouraging. "Do you mean to say," exclaimed the man, "that *that* is all the matter with me?" But even so, while his circumstances were not abnormally difficult, and while he could see the long course of mistaken thinking that had brought him to his present pass, this alone was no full solution. Only when out of the deeper levels of his memory and experience his awareness of Divine resources was brought into the forefront of his thought, and he began to face life, not in his own strength alone but with the consciousness of appropriated power at his daily disposal, did he reach the place where he could say at last to the minister, "I am on top of the world."

Many so-called Christians critically need to learn this lesson. One side of Christianity they have tried to take in earnest, its ethical demands. To be unselfish, to care and work for others, to be busily engaged in philanthropic causes—this they have accepted as good religion, as indeed it is. But taken alone it is all output. It exhausts its meaning in demands for activity. Moreover, when Christianity's ethical requirements are taken seriously they are the most exacting human life has ever faced. They call out such descriptions as "impossible possibilities." No one can fulfill such demands as Christian ethics impose merely by trying hard. Christians feverishly absorbed in activity, with no corresponding intake of power, can be just as restless and hectic in their "religious work" as any worldling is in his secular pursuits. If to be a Christian means to be Christlike, such persons have missed its deepest secret. Some hymns they understand, such as, "Awake, my soul, stretch every nerve," but others they have never fathomed the meaning of, such as, "Spirit of God, descend upon my heart."

In whatever way life is approached the power-question is central. Output without intake in any realm is fatal. The longer an orchestra plays, the more it needs to be tuned. The farther an airplane flies, the more it requires ground-service. The more strenuous a prophet has been, the more he needs the secluded hour and the "still small voice." The more busy and laborious modern life becomes, the more modern men and women need those inner resources that, as the Psalmist says, restore the soul.

CHAPTER X

The Practical Use of Faith

I

EVEN a little introspection reveals that if a strong, one-directional drive takes possession of our lives, it is associated with faith in something or someone. Faith is an inner act of confidence and self-committal that naturally draws one together around its object. If "Mr. Facing-both-ways" ever becomes Mr. Facing-one-way, faith in some person, cause, idea, or possibility, believed in as worth while and surrendered to as worth serving, has inevitably played a part in bringing the blurred life to focus.

Unfocused people, however, who want this experience, are commonly baffled in attaining it. Surely, a man cannot honestly and intelligently *will* to have faith. How, they ask, does one get faith if one does not have it? It is of first-rate importance, therefore, to see that faith is not something we *get,* but something we *have.* It is inherent in our psychological constitution just as truly as affection is, and is sure to be used one way or another. None of us ever escapes this capacity to believe in persons, ideas, and causes, and confide ourselves to them. Far from lacking faith, man has a surplus of it, associated with more curious

and diverse objects than tongue can tell—faith in dictatorship or democracy, in astrology or rabbits' feet, in endless
policies concerning war and peace, in one economic
nostrum or another, in our own possibilities or in the
power of our circumstances to crush them, in unselfishness or self-indulgence as the way to happiness, in God or
in materialism. Faith is a drug on the market. "The
capacity of modern man to believe," said Mussolini, "is
unbelievable." That we have more faith than we know
what to do with is shown by the way we give it to every
odd and end that comes along. A man can no more run
away from his faith-faculty than he can run away from
his own legs; they are what he does his running away
with. If a man says he will have no faith, then the policy
of no-faith is what he has faith in.

When, therefore, an exhorter urges us to have faith, he
mistakes the state of the case. We have faith already; we
never have existed an hour without exercising it. Just as
we have a love-life, we have a faith-faculty; our need is to
learn how to handle it. Of all mad faiths the maddest is
the faith that we can get rid of faith.

To be sure, a man may lose faith in his wife, in the
possibility of achieving peaceful world organization, in
any specific religious doctrine, or in God, but a man thus
surrendering faith has not ceased to exercise his faith-
faculty. Our trick of words—"belief" vs. "unbelief"—
obscures this significant matter. No man can really become an unbeliever; he is psychologically shut up to the
necessity of believing—in God, for example, or else in no
God, or else in the impossibility of deciding. One way or
another, in every realm, man is inherently a believer in

[240]

something or other, positive or negative, good, bad, or indifferent.

This psychological capacity ill-used tears life to shreds, while well-used it brings, as the New Testament says, the "victory that overcometh the world"; and without its constructive exercise the achievement of unified and satisfying personality is impossible. When positive faiths die out, their place is always taken by negative faiths— in our impossibilities rather than our possibilities, in ideas that make us victims rather than masters of life, and in total philosophies that plunge us into Rabelais' dying mood, "Draw the curtain; the farce is played." Many try to dodge this fundamental fact, but do not succeed.

> She set a rose to blossom in her hair,
>   The day faith died;
> "Now glad," she said, "and free I go,
>   And life is wide" . . .
> But through long nights she stared into the dark,
>   And knew she lied.

II

Among the typical people whose problems cannot be solved without the constructive use of faith the following are familiar.

The youth whose mind has never waked up. Nothing is the matter with his I.Q. Far from being outwardly handi-capped, hard-bestead, or emotionally warped and crushed, he is comfortable, secure, and easygoing. But he is also aimless and apathetic. The latent powers of his mind are sound asleep.

The arousal of such a youth from his lethargy is always associated with the awakening of faith. Only when some person, idea, or vocation that he believes in comes up over his horizon will he bestir himself. Conversion is commonly described in terms of transformation from sin to goodness, but some of its most startling examples are the awakening of listless minds by the impact of a compelling faith that becomes the center of their interest, the object of their trust, and the impetus to their self-dedication. At that point their life really begins, for as Oliver Wendell Holmes said, "It's faith in something and enthusiasm for something that makes life worth looking at."

To one, therefore, who thinks of faith as an inherent power in human nature, faith, far from being hostile to intellect, is indispensable to its arousal. Wherever man's intelligence is focused on objectives it is determined to achieve, the inspiration of such intellectual endeavor is always faith in something. Faith in aviation's possibility came first, then intellect was concentrated on it. As President Pritchett of the Massachusetts Institute of Technology used to say, "Science is grounded in faith just as is religion." In all scientific experimentation faith blazes trails that intelligence converts into highways, believes in possibilities that intelligence makes into actualities. No faith in anything, no marshaling of intelligence around it!

Faith, conceived *theoretically* in terms of the false opinions it can be credulous of, can be the foe of intelligence, but conceived *psychologically* as an inherent capacity of our nature, it is indispensable to the arousal and concentration of intelligence. Dealing with the faith-function is often as delicate and difficult as dealing with the love-life. To bring the right girl within range of the youth's affection so that he will fall in love with her is not easy. To bring the right idea, vocation, or personal possibility so within range of the youth's faith that he will believe in it, be aroused by it, and give himself to it, is difficult. But failing that many a mind never wakes up.

A man can deal with himself in this regard more effectively than anyone else can deal with him. His friends may think him by nature stupid, and he may have accepted this picture of himself as true, whereas the real trouble may be not that his mind is dull but that his faith-faculty is dormant. Charles Darwin tells us that his father at one time was discouraged about him and thought he would amount to nothing: "My father once said to me, 'You care for nothing but shooting, dogs, and rat-catching, and you will be a disgrace to yourself and all your family.' " Who could have guessed what would happen when faith in an idea dawned on that mind, marshaling its latent powers for a lifetime's work?

The person who is being disorganized by negative attitudes. William James' saying that "the sovereign cure for worry is religious faith" illustrates the effect of any positive use of the faith-function upon a soul harassed by fearful and self-pitying moods. Anxiety, loss of confidence, self-depreciation, the lonely sense of being shut up

[243]

within oneself, powerlessness, misgiving, apathy, pessimism, fearfulness—such negative moods take from the person his power of attack on life, and the corrective attitude is confidence in life, belief in its possibilities, trust in its available resources, assurance of its worthwhileness— that is to say, a positive faith.

Many psychological roadways lead into the morass of negative moods, but only one leads out—faith. With the debilitating sense of inferiority we have dealt already, but the sense of superiority can be equally enfeebling. The perfectionists make up a sad company. One man with an utterly negative attitude toward life sought the minister's help. He thought very highly of himself. He was proud of his fine, uncompromising principles; he was an overscrupulous idealist; and he could do nothing with the world. He tried to go to church, but the church was not good enough for him—he despised it. He tried business, but business was all wrong—he could not endure it. He undertook a profession, but what he met there shocked him—he left it. As for the world at large, it was too evil for a man like him—he shrank from sullying his pure soul by contact with it. His perfectionist idealism unfitted him to step up to any imperfect, unfinished, disliked situation, to perceive its possibilities, believe in its worth-while aspects and so with a stimulating faith attack it as a sensible and courageous man should.

By whatever road one gets into this swamp of negation, it is only by the constructive use of the faith-function that one gets out. If in any disagreeable, morally deplorable, or tragic situation a victim of negative moods can be persuaded that any shred of goodness or any valuable possibility is still there to believe in, the hope of cure has dawned.

The individual whose personal energies have petered out. "Every sort of energy and endurance," said William James, "of courage and capacity for handling life's evils, is set free in those who have religious faith." This statement, to be sure, one may not use indiscriminately as an argument for "religion." Religious faith does indeed release every sort of energy; it can mass its powerful drive on the wrong side of great issues as well as on the right; it has backed idolatry, human sacrifice, and war; it familiarly issues in bigotry and persecution, and has repeatedly made credulity of false and harmful creeds a sacred duty. That is to say, whether intellectually true or false, whether ethically good or bad, religious faith is powerful, and in this potency it exhibits the characteristic psychological effect of all positive faith as a releaser of personal energy.

A friend once wrote to Turgenev: "It seems to me that to put oneself in the second place is the whole significance of life." To this Turgenev replied: "It seems to me to discover what to put before oneself, in the first place, is the whole problem of life." Whatever one does put thus before oneself is always the object of one's faith; one believes in it and belongs to it; and whether it be Christ or Hitler, a chosen vocation or a personal friend, when such committal of faith is heartily made, it pulls the trigger of human energy.

An individual habitually feeling fed up with life, tired out and done in, seeks a physician who assures him that

[245]

there is nothing the matter with his body in general or his nerves in particular. He is an illustration of the saying that "Tiredness . . . begins in the mind." First he tried to use his intellect to solve his problem, but the more he analyzed his situation the worse he felt about it and the less he could do with it. Then he tried using his will, but that was like blowing with full cheeks upon his own sails to make the ship go—it got him nowhere. As one physician put it: "The patient says, 'I cannot'; his friends say, 'He will not'; the doctor says, 'He cannot will.' " The liberation of such a life from its tiredness and feebleness into the experience of released energy commonly waits upon the awakening of the faith-faculty. An idea, cause, possibility, or person captures the man so that something in which he positively believes is put before himself, in the first place, and when this happens, startling releases of energy may follow as though a seeming atomizer had become a fire-hose.

One of the tragedies of personal life is its unutilized energy, and it is faith in something or someone that taps these unused reserves of power. Dr. T. R. Glover, an English scholar, in a study of Marcus Aurelius, the Roman emperor, pays high tribute to his character, but turning to his total philosophy, that made the heavily burdened ruler feel life's ultimate futility so that even his best effort was like pouring water into a sieve, Dr. Glover passes a judgment that applies to multitudes: "He does not believe enough to be great."

The lonely individual, poor in personal relationships, who feels all shut up within himself. The cure of such socially impoverished people is commonly thought of in terms of the tenderer emotions—affection, friendship, love—which certainly are indispensable. Nevertheless, alike in the circle of our homes and in the world at large, our experience of personal relationship is primarily enriched by the people in whom we have faith. Faith is the basic builder of personal fellowships.

In breaking through the isolating walls of lonely individualism into a vital and kindling experience of interpersonal kinship and unity, love is habitually overemphasized. Even in passionate romance, and in all dependable marriage, family life, and friendship, faith in the people concerned is, in the long run, the heart of success. One cannot ultimately be happy in loving a person in whom one lacks faith, so that while romantic love may launch a home, and strong, continuing love may be its driving power, its very hull and keel are the faith we have in one another. Nathaniel Hawthorne once wrote to his fiancée, with whom he later set up an abiding and beautiful home: "It is very singular . . . that, while I love you dearly, and while I am so conscious of the deep embrace of our spirits, still I have an awe of you that I never felt for anybody else . . . it converts my love into religion." He not only loved her, but believed in her.

As for the wider circle of persons, the "noble living and the noble dead," faith in those whom we vividly apprehend and cordially believe in carries us out of ourselves, incorporates and blends our lives with theirs, and transforms the impoverished and solitary *I* into the enriched and commingled *We*. No man is the whole of himself; those to whom he has given his faith are the rest of him.

Lack of this experience leaves one a sequestered, isolated self. As Thackeray said, "How lonely we are in the world! how selfish and secret, everybody! . . . Ah, sir,— a distinct universe walks about under your hat and under mine—all things in nature are different to each—the woman we look at has not the same features, the dish we eat from has not the same taste to the one and the other—you and I are but a pair of infinite isolations, with some fellow-islands a little more or less near to us." Anyone, however, who is thus isolated is not a real person. Full-grown personality involves the blending of lives, and this is possible only because we have the capacity to believe in others until they become an integral part of us. To the theologian, Paul's characteristic saying, "That Christ may dwell in your hearts by faith," has important doctrinal significance; to the psychologist it is an arresting statement of indubitable experience. When faith is strongly reposed in another person, it does issue in a blended life, so merged that the one is indwelt, enriched, and empowered by the other.

Many people who are thinking of themselves as starved for love and so are waiting for some lucky romance or redeeming friendship to come around the corner, could nonetheless enrich their world of interpersonal relationships by a constructive use of their faith-faculty. This world has some great people in it to believe in. Instead of being unhappy, isolated selves, we can by faith become effective, positive, conjunct personalities in whom the best souls of the race live again.

The person who is inwardly unstable and insecure. Nothing more effectively steadies a shaken life than positive faith. The word "confidence" has the Latin root meaning "faith" at the heart of it. Let faith in something or someone rise strongly, even amid deplorable situations, and in the people affected panic dies down, assurance returns, and they pull themselves together.

This notably is the effect of a genuine religious faith. To be sure, in the religious realm as in any other the faith-function can be grievously misused. John Burroughs was reared in a wretched type of sectarian bigotry. His father, a fanatical Baptist, said he would as soon be found in a liquor saloon as in a Methodist church, and for a time was angrily afraid that his son might become a minister in that dangerous denomination. Against this sectarian narrowness John Burroughs rebelled; he became a lover of nature, a lover of his fellowmen, a rare soul of singular depth and serenity, but commonly counting himself, and regarded by others, as irreligious. Yet, agnostic as he was in theory, his inner coherence and stability were rooted in something more positive than that. "As the poet hungers for the beautiful," he wrote, "so the religious nature hungers for the divine—that which Jesus exemplified more fully than any other man —the humanization of the eternal power of the universe, or the fatherhood and brotherhood of God." Agnostic or no agnostic in theory, he lived by positive faiths:

> The stars come nightly to the sky,
>   The tidal wave comes to the sea;
> Nor time, nor space, nor deep, nor high,
>   Can keep my own away from me.

Interior steadiness is the natural effect of a confident faith, and multitudes of insecure lives will never find coherence and poise without it. When, therefore, religious faith collapses, as it has in multitudes today, the nervous results are unmistakable. An atheist, says John Buchan, is "a man who has no invisible means of support." The old idea that without religious faith a man would go to hell has taken on contemporary meaning, for many nervous hells are being arrived at by precisely that route, and not preachers so much as psychiatrists are saying it. Thus Jung criticizes Freud for expecting man to handle by unaided will the disruptive forces of his subconscious life: "Freud has unfortunately overlooked the fact that man has never yet been able single-handed to hold his own against the powers of darkness—that is, of the unconscious. Man has always stood in need of the spiritual help which each individual's own religion held out to him. . . . It is this which lifts him out of his distress."

Faith in divine backing and resource when practically utilized in daily life is incalculably reassuring. Bishop William Quayle, awake at night, fruitlessly worrying, heard God say to him, "Quayle, you go to bed, I'll sit up the rest of the night." Whimsically put, that experience symbolizes a matter of major importance in the cure of anxious souls. Throughout this book we have urged the necessity of each man's shouldering responsibility for himself, but there is another side to the matter. One hardly knows who is more to be pitied, the man who refuses such responsibility, hiding behind rationalizations and alibis, or the man who takes responsibility for everything, shoulders the burdens of the world, worries about everyone else's business as well as his own, and so becomes a meddlesome, overstrained, distracted person. The sense of responsibility can be ruinously overworked until it wrecks both inner peace of mind and outer personal relationships. None of us is big enough to take responsibility for everything. Our accountability is limited by our ability, and that is small. Any man, then, who can handle his proper obligations that lie near at hand, doing the day's stint as best he can, sure that the larger load has under it Shoulders stronger than his and behind it a Mind wiser than his, has some chance of being an effective person with the inner calm and poise that are the mark of real strength. One way or another such unhurried, unstrained, composed, and confident living always involves a positive faith.

Professor Hocking of Harvard reports a conversation with one of his colleagues:

A short time ago as I was talking with a colleague, a psychiatrist, he said, "Something has been occurring to me recently which seems important, and yet it is so simple that I can hardly believe it very significant. It is a way of taking the miscellany of events which make up the day's impressions of the world. One sees no trend in them. But suppose there were a trend which we cannot define but can nevertheless have an inkling of. There is certainly some direction in evolution, why not in history? If there were such a trend, then we men could be either with it or against it. To be with it would give a certain peace and settlement; to be against it would involve a subtle inner restlessness. To have confidence in it would be a sort of commitment, for better or for worse. I wonder if that is what you mean by religion."

"Yes," I said. "I think that is the substance of it. The great religious ones seem to have had a certainty that they were going along with the trend of the world. They

have had a passion for right living which they conceived
of as a cosmic demand."

"There is nothing contrary to science in that."

"No, but it makes a difference, doesn't it?"

"Strange that such a simple thing should make so very
much difference."

III

When one thus considers the varied psychological effects of positive faith—how it awakens listless minds, ex-
pels negative moods, releases dormant energy, breaks
through the isolating walls of lonely selves, and creates
in insecure souls a basis for steadiness and poise—it becomes clear that the way we handle our faith-faculty is
predominantly important even to physical health.

In the ancient world, largely ignorant of what we now
call "scientific medicine," reliance for the cure of disease
rested mainly on nonphysical factors. Whether in the
New Testament or out of it, healing in the ancient world
was the most familiar kind of "miracle"; maladies both of
mind and body were cured by spiritual means, especially
by faith and prayer conceived as releasing divine help.
Around this concept gathered so great a mass of ignorant
and superstitious theory and practice that when scientific
medicine emerged it had to make its way against the dead
weight and active antagonism of this ancient, inveterate
competition. That conflict necessarily produced not cooperation but rivalry and hostility between physical and
psychic approaches to health. The new *materia medica*
faced its deadliest enemy in the old ideas of healing by

magic and miracle, and only when scientific medicine had won its case until the truth of its basic propositions was clear and its amazing achievements unquestionable, was the way open for the revolutionary change that now is taking place.

That change is indicated by the affirmation of one of our outstanding physicians: "It is not an overstatement to say that fully 50 per cent. of the problems of the acute stages of an illness and 75 per cent. of the difficulties of convalescence have their primary origin not in the body, but in the mind of the patient." With such recognition of the importance of nonphysical factors in causing and curing disease, a new day has dawned: the material and spiritual approaches to the problem of health can now become cooperative instead of competitive.

A young woman came to the counselor obsessed with abnormal anxiety about her mother. Her mother was in excellent health, but the daughter was devoured by worry concerning her imminent death. From her business office the young woman phoned repeatedly during the day to make sure that all was well. She thought that her love for her mother was so great that she could not endure her loss, and that she was distracted by the fear of it. Expert analysis revealed that the real state of the case was very different from the victim's interpretation. The fact was that the daughter hated her mother, and in her unconscious emotions deeply desired her death. Such an attitude, however, was so ethically repugnant that her conscious self could not acknowledge it, and the suppressed desire to be free of her mother's presence took the inverted form of obsessive solicitude about her health. Such a psychopathic situation is bound to have physical results—the whole organism is undermined and threatened by it—but no merely physical therapy can reach the root of the trouble. In some old shrine of healing, as at Epidaurus in Greece, such a young woman might have experienced an emotional release that would have restored her health, both physical and mental, so that her cure would have seemed a miracle to all who saw the change. A vast range of fact, of which such a case is a meager illustration, has forced scientific medicine to recognize that man is a psychosomatic organism whose health depends on spiritual, as well as physical, factors.

The personal counselor is often unsure with which set of factors the disorder he confronts really began. Many people present moral and spiritual symptoms behind which one suspects a physical cause; the loss of inward peace and of the power to pray may spring from hyperthyroid. Many others, however, crushed by physical ailments, seek spiritual resources to endure them when one suspects that the bodily ills themselves are emotionally caused. The scientific evidence to this effect is mounting steadily. It is altogether typical to find two physicians—Dr. Daniel T. Davies and Dr. A. T. M. Wilson—after studying 205 cases of peptic ulcer concluding that in 84 per cent of the cases the symptoms began after some occasion of acute anxiety and that "chronic peptic ulcer is an example of the influence of the mind in producing structural change."

The common sense of mankind has always known that a sick mind can cause a sick body. Moral disgust readily expresses itself in physical nausea; a fatigued spirit makes an exhausted physique; a hated task or endurance, for which one has "no stomach," causes loss of appetite;

paralysis may be due to bodily lesion, but it may be a psychological alibi, seeming entirely real and insurmountable to the victim, by which he escapes the facing of a dreaded situation. As for "nervousness" in all its distressing forms, much of that clearly springs from nonphysical sources. As one physician says: "Paradoxical as it may sound, there is nothing the matter with a nervous person's nerves." And now, giving to this whole range of fact both horizon and detail, scientific research is opening up, with regard to one disease after another, the importance of the nonphysical factors.

The gist of the matter is that we can no longer split apart the physical and psychic in the diagnosis and treatment of disease, much less split up the physical into neat specialties and deal atomically with man's ailments as though that were adequate. The whole person is involved in illness and its cure, and in facing that fact the constructive use of the faith-function assumes immense importance. The entire tone of a person's life commonly depends on it. "Miracles" of healing are once more familiar occurrences. They involve no magic, no neglect of scientific medicine, no absurd claim that the material is not real, no substitution of spiritual therapy for expert, detailed diagnosis, but they do involve recognition of the fact that to have the person *as a whole,* strong, hale, and hearty in mind and emotion is one of the decisive ingredients of health. Scientific medicine in its early stages centered its attention on the fact that if the ailing part can be cured, the whole man will have a chance at health; now, the complementary emphasis is coming to its own, that if the whole man is spiritually master over fear, anxiety, hatred, resentment, shame, and guilt, every part of him will have a stronger guarantee of being well.

Increasingly, therefore, faith as a minister of health is recognized, not simply in healing cults, with their frequently unbalanced ideas and methods, but in the medical profession itself. A new day has dawned for co-operation between the minister and the doctor. One physician writes even about typhoid fever that while the *bacillus typhosus* "certainly is the only known specific cause," nevertheless there are other factors, commonly called " 'immunity,' 'resistance,' 'susceptibility,' etc.," that "the affective psychical states of the patients can easily modify." Another physician writes concerning such maladies as tuberculosis, asthma, and pneumonia, that specific infections are not their complete explanation; that "there is now a growing body of evidence which leads to the belief that psychic influences as well play an important part in the process of falling ill." Still another physician says concerning angina pectoris, "The spiritual side of the case must not be neglected in this disease in which the emotions play so important a rôle," and among other spiritual factors he notes "the development of a philosophy of life" as "of real medical benefit."

IV

The need of a constructive philosophy of life if one is to have total health is an inescapable experience in mature and thoughtful people. To be sure, a man's creed and his character may be utterly incongruous. A creed can be inherited, or borrowed from one's associates, or lightly acquired by superficial thinking. In such cases the effective forces that mold and color the personality may be quite mundane, and one's creed may be merely excess baggage. A man fortunate in his emotional relationships may be happy and well co-ordinated, while his creed about life's total meaning ought logically to leave him hopeless; and another man with the most optimistic and stimulating of creeds may be distracted and wretched.

One must break through the crust of such superficial creedalism before one reaches the real situation. Underneath our inherited, borrowed, or casually argued beliefs there is always, in some degree and form, a man's underlying attitude toward, and idea about, life's basic meaning. We cannot live with anyone or anything decade after decade without accumulating a general impression; much less can we live with life itself and the world that encompasses it, without taking on, whether we want to or not, habitual attitudes toward it, and so acquiring characteristic conceptions of it. The result of this unavoidable psychological process is a man's real faith about life, often widely different from his formally held beliefs. This vitally acquired "philosophy" may be well defined or inchoate, clearly held or largely unconscious, but in maturity it is inevitably there, and it is one of the most powerful influences in personal life.

Sometimes a crisis occurs when under the impact of shock the individual becomes aware that the beliefs he supposed he held are not his real beliefs at all; that life has long been making on him another impression altogether; that this underlying, gradually accumulated attitude toward, and concept of, life, cannot longer be suppressed; that at the center of his personality is now a faith—a total view of the meaning of existence in this universe—which is profoundly affecting him and with which, one way or another, he must deal. This crisis is also an opportunity. The man is facing one of the most significant facts in human experience: the power of one's actually operative faith concerning life's meaning either to help or hinder the making of a real person.

The most impressive statements of life-philosophies are not formal creeds but unconventional affirmations of the way life has come to look to different individuals. Every year, says Mark Twain, millions of people die who, as they come to life's end, scoff at it in their hearts—"scoff at the pitiful world, and the useless universe and violent, contemptible human race," deriding "the whole paltry scheme." To say that such a negative faith concerning life's ultimate meaning has nothing to do with being or not being an adequate and satisfactory person, is, of course, fantastic.

"Side by side with the decline of religious life," writes Jung, "the neuroses grow noticeably more frequent." The reason for this consequence becomes the more apparent when one considers that in the gradual accumulation of one's actual and operative faith concerning life as a whole, we are dealing with a two-way process: Our ruling emotions express themselves conceptually in our theories about life, and our theories about life react with powerful effect upon our emotions. Professor Gordon Allport says that "according to Lotze, a man's philosophical creed is more often than not merely an attempt to justify a fundamental view of things adopted once for all early in life." The large measure of truth in this is apparent to anyone who reads not only the theories of the

[258]

philosophers but their biographies as well, or who examines with careful introspection the growth of his own major ideas about life's meaning. Far from invalidating the process of developing a life-philosophy, it makes the whole matter vital and transcendently important. One's dominant faith about life's meaning is no merely theoretical affair; it is rooted in day-by-day attitudes and emotional responses, and it reacts with potent effect upon them.

A philosophy, commonly thought of as altogether "intellectual," really involves the whole inner life. When Macbeth launched on his career of ruthless ambition, he did not suppose he was constructing a theory of life, but Shakespeare rightly saw that he was. When Macbeth had entangled himself in a hopeless situation, when his cruel emotions brought their aftermath, and the consequences of his self-centeredness were closing in, the appropriate "philosophy" emerged from his emotional conflict. It was then that he railed at life as

> ". . . a tale
> Told by an idiot, full of sound and fury,
> Signifying nothing."

Out of his actual living that total impression of life's meaning came, and on his actual living it reacted with fatal effect.

This process of developing a dominant faith goes on willy-nilly, and when faith thus vitally acquired is negative and cynical, the results are tragic. "I am convinced," wrote Edith Wharton, "that no storyteller, however great his gifts, can do great work unbased on some philosophy of life. Only the author's own convictions can give that underlying sense of values which lifts anecdote to drama." If without an undergirding faith it is impossible even to write a great story, much less is it possible to construct a coherent personality.

The failure to achieve, or the loss of, a positive, constructive religious faith, is today having ruinous personal results, and the reasons for this can be analyzed and defined.

Irreligion leaves wide areas of man's experience—and the best areas at that—unaccounted for. Every man has spiritual experiences that materialism cannot explain. On the basis of thoroughgoing irreligion, what made Plato Plato, Beethoven Beethoven, Christ Christ, is an accidental by-product of merely physical processes—an inexplicable fortuity in the experience of man, who is himself, as one materialist says, "a curious accident in a backwater." The entire spiritual life of man, then, involving whatever gives humanity such distinction and dignity as it possesses, is a misfit in the cosmos. As Joseph Wood Krutch, one of our most honest and logical atheists, puts it, "Ours is a lost cause and there is no place for us in the natural universe."

When any man's feeling about life and his thought concerning it have come to this conclusion, he faces distraction at the very center of his personality. His *best* is a cosmic mischance and misfit. He may decide to stand by his best and he may do well at it, but whenever he turns his thought to the total meaning of life, the sense of ultimate futility cannot be escaped. A deep fissure

[260]

splits such a life in two, and the psychological results are often evident.

This disintegrating effect of irreligion becomes more manifest when its ethical results appear. A man of sensitive spiritual life may pass, by some combined emotional and intellectual route, into a materialistic philosophy, but there he finds himself facing a profound personal schism. What in his idealism he thinks *ought to be* pulls in one direction; what in his philosophy he thinks *really is* pulls in another. He thinks man ought to be a high-minded, spiritual being, but he thinks man basically is an animal, accidentally produced. He thinks that human society ought to be a family of brothers, but he thinks that man's history is really under the ultimate dominance of completely nonmoral, unspiritual forces. He thinks this earth ought to be the scene of an ascending series of ethical victories, but he thinks that it is really a fortuitous "sport" of protons and electrons. He is, then, an intellectual animal in a universe where there is ultimately no intellectual element, and an ethical animal in a universe where there is ultimately no ethical element.

Such a situation involves theoretical problems which the philosophers endlessly discuss, but it is also the fertile source of serious psychological problems. When a man's *ought* and his *is* are thus at loggerheads, the difficulty of personal integration is incalculably increased.

This disintegrating effect of irreligion is apparent when attention is centered on a man's opinion of himself. Schopenhauer, so runs the story, walking down the street, accidentally bumped into a stranger. The stranger, irritated, turned on the philosopher and exclaimed, "Who are you anyway?" to which Schopenhauer, lost in meditation, answered, "Who am I? How I wish I knew!"

The essence of every philosophy appears in its reply to that question, and in view of this fact the relevance of one's total faith to one's psychological health is obvious. A student's editorial in the *Yale News* says that atheism makes us seem like "ridiculous parasites on a dying speck of matter in infinite space and infinite cold." Any philosophy with that effect is of momentous psychological concern.

To be sure, man has many ways of sustaining his self-esteem. His need of thinking highly of himself is so urgent that, even when his total faith would logically picture him as a ridiculous parasite, he manages to make the most of every minor justification he can find for self-appreciation. The chaplain's prayer before a genealogical society, where all were congratulating themselves on being the descendants of their ancestors, expresses one of man's deep desires: "Justify, O Lord, if it be possible, the high esteem in which we hold ourselves." In seeking satisfaction for that desire man uses any support for self-approbation he can find, but the more thoughtful a person is, the more his ultimate answer to the question, *Who am I?* springs from and shares the quality of his total philosophy. To call man a "child of God" is doubtless a metaphor, but so too is the statement that man is "a bundle of cellular matter upon its way to becoming manure," and both affirmations illustrate the necessary impact of one's basic faith, not simply on one's thought about the universe, but on one's thought about oneself.

Any personality trying to live a high life on the basis of a low idea as to who he is, faces distraction at the center of his endeavor. Whatever else religious faith does, it sees man as essentially spirit and not matter; it regards him as a soul with a body and not as a body with accidental mental and spiritual functions; it grounds his best in eternal reality and teaches him to esteem himself as a being of divine origin, nature, and destiny. Great religion furnishes the most stimulating answer ever given to the question, Who am I? and the history of religious experience at its best is rich in illustrations of Adler's statement, "By changing our opinion of ourselves we can also change ourselves."

v

George Bernard Shaw describes an experience of his that took "a mob of appetites and organised them into an army of purposes and principles." This process of organization, essential to personal wholeness, always involves two elements, *discrimination* and *renunciation*. Amid the miscellany of life the person who is to achieve integration must get his eye upon, and commit himself to, those values and aims which he chooses as supremely worth while. He cannot put all values first; integrated living begins with selection; "the seeker of his truest, strongest, deepest self," as William James said, "must review the list carefully, and pick out the one on which to stake his salvation." And along with this primary act of discrimination goes of necessity the accompanying act of renunciation. Every center of integrated living involves not only inclusions but exclusions, and he who

[263]

seriously says *Yes* to any self-committal must say *No* to its contradictions.

This dual process of discrimination and renunciation, however, is never self-produced. It takes a positive faith to get it started. Some idea, cause, or person captures our confidence and devotion; we believe in some value and give ourselves to it; and in that act of faith we practice discrimination in its most profoundly satisfying form, and renunciation of our faith's opposites follows with a minimum of strain. A constructive faith is thus the supreme organizer of life, and, lacking it, like Humpty Dumpty we fall and break to pieces, and the wonder is whether all the king's horses and all the king's men can ever put us together again.

References

Unless otherwise noted Biblical references are to the American Revised Version of the Bible, copyrighted 1919 by the International Council of Religious Education and used with their permission.

INTRODUCTION

PAGE	LINE	
xi	32	In the Preface to the 1743 edition of *Histoire de mon temps,* as quoted in Friedrich Meinecke, *Die Idee der Staatsräson* (Berlin, 1925), p. 377.
xii	5	*The Autobiography of Benjamin Franklin,* edited by John Bigelow (New York, 1909), p. 80.
xii	9	Gustave Flaubert, *Correspondence* (Paris, 1907), III, 324, to George Sand, 1867.
xii	14	"The Enchiridion," XLVIII, as quoted in Bonaro W. Overstreet, *Brave Enough for Life* (New York, 1941), p. 19.
xiii	10	*Medicine, Magic, and Religion* (New York, 1924), p. 144.

CHAPTER I
SHOULDERING RESPONSIBILITY FOR OURSELVES

1	9	Samuel W. McCall, *Daniel Webster* (Boston, 1902), p. 55.
2	20	*The Principles of Psychology* (New York, 1890), I, 488.
2	23	From a London newspaper, as quoted in Gordon W. Allport, *Personality; A Psychological Interpretation* (New York, 1938), p. 147.

REFERENCES

PAGE	LINE	
2	28	"The Excursion," Book IV, l. 1264, *The Poetical Works of William Wordsworth,* edited by William Knight (New York, 1896), V, 192.
2	29	William Ernest Hocking, *Human Nature and Its Remaking* (New Haven, 1918), pp. 9-10.
4	23	*If You Don't Weaken* (New York, 1940), p. xi.
5	6	CXIV, *The Complete Poems of Emily Dickinson* (Boston, 1924), p. 60.
6	14	Patrick Fraser Tytler, *Life of Sir Walter Raleigh* (Edinburgh, 1840), p. 359.
6	19	*The Life and Letters of Charles Darwin,* edited by his son Francis Darwin (New York, 1887), I, 320.
6	22	*Shut-In* (New York, 1936), p. 107.
7	5	(New York, 1942), p. 203. See also Allport, *op. cit.,* p. 120. For an excellent treatment of the influence of the glands see R. G. Hoskins, *The Tides of Life; the Endocrine Glands in Bodily Adjustment* (New York, 1933).
8	1	Edward John Trelawny, *Records of Shelley, Byron, and the Author* (London, 1878), I, 27-28.
8	22	Luke 10:29.
9	19	"Hamlet," Act III, Sc. II, *The Complete Works of William Shakespeare,* edited by William George Clark and William Aldis Wright (New York, 1911), p. 1028.
10	18	*Studies of Good and Evil* (New York, 1902), p. 208.
10	20	R. M. MacIver, *Society; A Textbook of Sociology* (New York, 1937), p. 40.
10	28	Rufus M. Jones, *Social Law in the Spiritual World* (Philadelphia, 1904), p. 58.
11	22	Vernon Louis Parrington, *The Beginnings of Critical Realism in America* (New York, 1931), p. 324.
11	23	Sherwood Anderson, *Winesburg, Ohio* (New York, 1919), p. 247.

REFERENCES

PAGE	LINE	
12	14	*The Issues of Life* (New York, 1930), p. 98.
14	12	*Journals of Ralph Waldo Emerson* (New York, 1911), VI, 298, October, 1842.
14	19	*Rubáiyát*, LXIX (London, 1929), p. 50.
15	6	Lyman Beecher Stowe, *Saints Sinners and Beechers* (Indianapolis, 1934), p. 52.
15	22	Shakespeare, "Julius Caesar," Act I, Sc. II, *op. cit.*, p. 951.
16	14	*Letters From the Underworld,* as quoted in Nicholas Berdyaev, *Dostoievsky; An Interpretation,* translated by Donald Attwater (New York, 1934), p. 53.
16	25	*Op. cit.,* p. 1.
18	6	*Philosophische Studien,* 1886, p. 204.
19	22	*The Rediscovery of Man* (New York, 1938), p. 14.
20	10	Hocking, *The Self; Its Body and Freedom* (New Haven, 1930), p. 45.
21	24	William Lawrence, *Life of Phillips Brooks* (New York, 1930), pp. 19-20.
25	16	Mrs. John Charles Frémont, as quoted in Allan Nevins, *Frémont, Pathmarker of the West* (New York, 1939), p. 602.
26	7	Jones, *op. cit.,* p. 71.
26	23	Luke 15:17.

CHAPTER II
WHAT BEING A REAL PERSON MEANS

27	14	"A Death in the Desert," *The Complete Poetic and Dramatic Works of Robert Browning* (New York, 1895), p. 391.
30	1	*Psychology, Briefer Course* (New York, 1900), p. 179.
30	8	"The Pirates of Penzance," Act II, *Plays and Poems of W. S. Gilbert* (New York, 1935), p. 175.

PAGE	LINE	
30	18	J. C. Smuts, *Holism and Evolution* (New York, 1926), p. 263.
30	26	As quoted in William H. Burnham, *The Wholesome Personality* (New York, 1932), p. xii.
32	14	*Psychology and the Promethean Will* (New York, 1936), p. 9.
35	27	Arthur Conan Doyle, "The Last Bow," *The Complete Sherlock Holmes* (Garden City, 1936), p. 1155.
37	13	Francis Arthur Jones, *Thomas Alva Edison; Sixty Years of an Inventor's Life* (New York, 1908), p. 7.
37	30	"Antony and Cleopatra," Act II, Sc. II, *The Complete Works of William Shakespeare,* edited by William George Clark and William Aldis Wright (New York, 1911), p. 1143.
38	6	*Courage* (New York, 1922), pp. 4, 17.
38	9	*Trivia* (Garden City, 1922), p. 101.
39	32	CI, *The Complete Poems of Emily Dickinson* (Boston, 1924), p. 54.
41	9	Edwin Ewart Aubrey, *Man's Search for Himself* (Nashville, 1940), p. 130.
42	24	As quoted in John Buchan (Lord Tweedsmuir), *Pilgrim's Way* (Cambridge, 1940), p. 236.
43	1	Townsend Scudder, *Jane Welsh Carlyle* (New York, 1939), p. 283.
43	6	Edwina Booth Grossmann, *Edwin Booth* (New York, 1894), p. 42.
43	11	Lytton Strachey, *Eminent Victorians* (New York), p. 141.
43	17	Robert Haven Schauffler, *Beethoven; The Man Who Freed Music* (Garden City, 1929), I, 87.
43	21	Romans 7:19, 24.
44	3	*The Novels, Tales and Sketches of J. M. Barrie* (New York, 1927), VII, 422.
44	17	"Of vaine Subtilties," *The Essays of Montaigne,*

PAGE	LINE	
		translated by John Florio (London, 1892), I, 360.
45	14	Burnham, *op. cit.*, p. 279.
45	18	George Ross Wells, *The Art of Being a Person* (New York, 1939), p. 94.
45	23	Burnham, *op. cit.*, p. 278.
46	24	William G. Blaikie, *The Personal Life of David Livingstone* (London, 1917), pp. 190, 252.
46	30	John 12:27.
46	31	Mark 14:34.
46	32	Luke 22:44.
47	12	Gamaliel Bradford, *Biography and the Human Heart* (Boston, 1932), p. 11.
47	28	*The Varieties of Religious Experience* (New York, 1914), p. 189.
48	7	Henry Thomas and Dana Lee Thomas, *Living Biographies of Great Philosophers* (Garden City, 1941), p. 300.
49	17	"Address on University Education," *Collected Essays* (New York, 1902), III, 236.
49	23	Sören Kierkegaard, *Begriff der Angst* (Leipzig, 1844), p. 57.
49	29	Louis I. Dublin and Bessie Bunzel, *To Be or Not to Be; A Study of Suicide* (New York, 1933), pp. 96-97.
50	7	See, for example, Dr. Karen Horney, *The Neurotic Personality of Our Time* (New York, 1937).
50	13	"Epistle to Davie, A Brother Poet," *Poems by Robert Burns* (Edinburgh, 1811), I, 166.
50	20	Thomas R. Kelly, *A Testament of Devotion* (New York, 1941), pp. 115-116.

REFERENCES

CHAPTER III
THE PRINCIPLE OF SELF-ACCEPTANCE

PAGE	LINE	
52	2	H. G. Wells, *The History of Mr. Polly* (New York, 1910), p. 6.
53	15	William James, *The Varieties of Religious Experience* (New York, 1914), p. 41.
54	6	Otto Rank, *Truth and Reality* (New York, 1936), p. 66.
57	24	Phyllis Bottome, *Alfred Adler; A Biography* (New York, 1939), p. 22.
58	4	*An Autobiography* (Garden City, 1916), p. 317.
59	8	John 21:22.
59	17	"Gunga Din," *Rudyard Kipling's Verse* (London, 1938), p. 401.
60	17	Edited by Allan Nevins (New York, 1929), p. 217.
60	26	"Self-Reliance," *Works of Ralph Waldo Emerson* (London, 1905), p. 10.
61	6	Gordon W. Allport, *Personality; A Psychological Interpretation* (New York, 1938), p. 174.
64	4	As quoted in George Ross Wells, *The Art of Being a Person* (New York, 1939), p. 228.
66	11	J. H. W. Stuckenberg, *The Life of Immanuel Kant* (London, 1882), p. 102.
67	22	Rupert Hughes, *George Washington; The Rebel & The Patriot* (New York, 1927), pp. 296-297.
68	17	"The Mikado," Act II, *Plays and Poems of W. S. Gilbert* (New York, 1935), p. 392.
69	20	As quoted in Emil Ludwig, *Genius and Character* (New York, 1928), p. 119.
70	1	John Stuart Mill, *Considerations on Representative Government* (London, 1876), p. 24.
70	7	Alexander Wheelock Thayer, *The Life of Ludwig van Beethoven* (New York, 1921), II, 55.
70	26	George Ross Wells, *op. cit.*, pp. 95-96.
71	15	*Op. cit.*, p. 19.

REFERENCES

PAGE	LINE	
71	27	Abram Lipsky, *Martin Luther; Germany's Angry Man* (New York, 1933), pp. 158-159.
71	28	William S. Sadler, *The Mind at Mischief* (New York, 1929), pp. 116-117.
72	5	March 19, 1921, p. 893.
73	12	*The Angel That Troubled the Waters* (New York, 1927), p. 149.
74	2	C. G. Jung, *Modern Man in Search of a Soul* (New York, 1933), p. 264.
74	30	Joseph Wood Krutch, *The Modern Temper* (New York, 1929), p. 235.
75	10	Georgiana Burne-Jones, *Memorials of Edward Burne-Jones* (New York, 1904), II, 256.
75	24	Bronislaw Malinowski, *Science and Religion; A Symposium* (New York, 1931), p. 78.
75	27	Joel 3:14.
76	22	*The Complete Poetical Works and Letters of John Keats,* Cambridge Edition (Boston, 1899), p. 369, letter to George and Georgiana Keats, April 28, 1819.
76	31	*Mechanism, Life and Personality* (New York, 1914), p. 139.
78	2	Marc Connelly (New York, 1929), Part I, Sc. VIII, p. 68.

CHAPTER IV
GETTING ONESELF OFF ONE'S HANDS

79	5	John C. Schroeder, *Modern Man and the Cross* (New York, 1940), p. 70.
79	18	Cf. George H. McKnight, *English Words and Their Background* (New York, 1923), p. 420.
80	5	*Middlemarch* (Boston, 1900), II, 267.
80	23	*The Wholesome Personality* (New York, 1932), p. 49.
81	15	Martha Ostenso, "Gardenias in Her Hair," *Pic-*

PAGE	LINE	
		torial Review Combined with *Delineator,* September, 1937.
82	9	A. A. Roback, *Self-Consciousness and Its Treatment* (Cambridge, 1933), p. 12.
82	19	*Confessions* (New York, 1931), I, 30.
82	27	Act I, Sc. V, *The Complete Works of William Shakespeare,* edited by William George Clark and William Aldis Wright (New York, 1911), p. 347.
83	21	Henrik Ibsen, Act IV, Sc. XIII, Everyman's Library Edition, p. 163.
84	23	Henry Seidel Canby, *Thoreau* (Boston, 1939), pp. 223-224.
86	2	Alfred North Whitehead, *Religion in the Making* (New York, 1930), p. 16.
86	20	*Expositions on the Book of Psalms,* Psalm LVIII, Section 1.
87	1	Shakespeare, "Hamlet," Act III, Sc. I, *op. cit.,* p. 1026.
87	3	*Speeches & Letters of Abraham Lincoln,* edited by Merwin Roe (New York, 1919), p. 13, letter to John T. Stuart, January 23, 1841.
89	28	A. A. Milne, "The Old Sailor," *Now We Are Six* (New York, 1927), p. 36.
90	25	"I die alive," *The Poetical Works of the Rev. Robert Southwell* (London, 1856), p. 68.
91	11	Matthew 25:40 (King James translation).
91	23	"To Marguerite—Continued," *Poetical Works of Matthew Arnold* (London, 1923), p. 197.
92	10	Elizabeth Barrett Browning, "Sonnets from the Portuguese," VI, *Poems* (New York, 1889), II, 288.
93	1	Thomas Craven, *Men of Art* (New York, 1931), p. 111.
93	23	J. A. Hadfield, *Psychology and Morals* (London, 1923), p. 100.

REFERENCES

PAGE	LINE	
94	8	*The Teacher; Essays and Addresses on Education* (Boston, 1908), p. 5.
94	11	"Stradivarius," *Complete Poems* (New York), pp. 400-401.
94	24	Gordon W. Allport, *Personality; A Psychological Interpretation* (New York, 1938), p. 213.
95	2	*The Times,* London, January 10, 1934, p. 12.
95	8	"The Answer," *The Poetical Works of John Greenleaf Whittier* (Boston, 1888), p. 338.
96	3	"Julian and Maddalo," *The Complete Poetical Works of Percy Bysshe Shelley* (Boston, 1901), p. 158.
96	22	"The Ballad of Reading Gaol," *The Writings of Oscar Wilde, Poems* (New York, 1907), p. 271.
98	10	"Table Talk," *The Works of Charles Lamb* (New York, 1903), IV, 266.
98	24	William Makepeace Thackeray, *The History of Pendennis* (Boston, 1883), II, 73.
98	31	*The New-York Times,* July 1, 1882, p. 1.
99	22	William Ernest Hocking, *Living Religions and a World Faith* (London, 1940), p. 220.
100	5	*Op. cit.,* p. 174.
100	10	*Lectures on Preaching* (New York, 1888), p. 41.
101	1	William McDougall, *The Energies of Men* (New York, 1933), p. 234.
101	19	"Lay Morals," *The Works of Robert Louis Stevenson* (New York, 1898), XXII, 575-576.
101	28	"Antioch Notes," January 15, 1931, Antioch College, Yellow Springs, Ohio.
102	17	*Human Nature and Its Remaking* (New Haven, 1918), p. 13.
104	20	"To A Louse, On Seeing One On A Lady's Bonnet At Church," *Poems by Robert Burns* (Edinburgh, 1811), I, 238.
105	5	John Gilbert Cooper, *The Life of Socrates* (London, 1749), pp. 54-56.
106	21	Vinton Adams Dearing, as quoted in John Lang-

PAGE   LINE

don Jones, "The Touch of the Intangible," p. 13.

106   32   Harold Begbie, *Life of William Booth the Founder of the Salvation Army* (London, 1920), II, 463.

CHAPTER V

DEALING WITH FEAR AND ANXIETY

108   1   "Gertrude the Governess," *Nonsense Novels* (London, 1925), p. 75.

108   5   As quoted in George S. Stewart, *The Lower Levels of Prayer* (Nashville, 1940), p. 10.

108   17   "Memories and Portraits," *The Works of Robert Louis Stevenson* (New York, 1897), XIII, 266.

109   9   "Bishop Blougram's Apology," *The Complete Poetic and Dramatic Works of Robert Browning* (New York, 1895), p. 355.

110   14   As quoted in William H. Burnham, *The Normal Mind* (New York, 1927), p. 417.

110   23   Herman Melville (New York, 1930), p. 101.

111   4   Psalm 111:10.

111   27   *The Psychology of Power* (New York, 1923), p. 36.

112   19   (Garden City, 1931).

113   19   William S. Sadler, *The Mind at Mischief* (New York, 1929), p. 127.

113   21   *Ibid.*, p. 123.

114   20   *Ibid.*, p. 142.

115   5   "Courage," *Works of Ralph Waldo Emerson* (London, 1905), p. 269.

115   20   *The Great Society* (New York, 1917), p. 89.

115   29   Douglas Southall Freeman, *R. E. Lee; A Biography* (New York, 1935), II, 462.

116   8   Harry Leon Wilson, *Oh, Doctor!* (New York, 1923), p. 327.

PAGE LINE
116   21   *Oeuvres Complètes de Voltaire* (Paris, 1830), XLVII, 173, letter to L'Abbe D'Olivet, April 25, 1764.

117   27   *The Letters of Robert Louis Stevenson to His Family and Friends* (New York, 1899), II, 360, to James Payn, August, 1893.

118   13   "A Midsummer-Night's Dream," Act V, Sc. I, *The Complete Works of William Shakespeare,* edited by William George Clark and William Aldis Wright (New York, 1911), pp. 214-215.

118   25   As quoted in Sadler, *The Physiology of Faith and Fear* (Chicago, 1912), p. 358.

120   11   Proverbs 23:7 (King James translation).

120   15   *The Rediscovery of Man* (New York, 1938), p. 99.

121   20   *Op. cit.,* p. 424.

121   28   W. Stekel, *Conditions of Nervous Anxiety and Their Treatment* (New York, 1923), p. 133.

123   12   "The Rime of the Ancient Mariner," Part VI, *The Complete Poetical Works of Samuel Taylor Coleridge* (Oxford, 1912), I, 203.

123   21   Shakespeare, "Hamlet," Act III, Sc. I, *op. cit.,* p. 1026.

123   31   Genesis 3:8, 10.

124   26   *The Light of the World and Other Sermons* (New York, 1891), pp. 96-97.

127   7   Albert Bigelow Paine, *Mark Twain: a Biography,* Centenary Edition (New York, 1912), II, 862.

127   23   Henry Thomas and Dana Lee Thomas, *Living Biographies of Great Composers* (New York, 1940), p. 78.

127   25   I John 4:18.

128   9   Richard C. Cabot, *The Meaning of Right and Wrong* (New York, 1933), p. 99.

129   3   Carl Sandburg, *Abraham Lincoln; The War Years* (New York, 1939), III, 515.

REFERENCES

PAGE LINE
130   16   C. G. Jung, *Modern Man in Search of a Soul* (New York, 1933), p. 70.
130   22   Theodore Dreiser, *Living Philosophies,* edited by Henry Goddard Leach (New York), p. 57.
131   2   "Vailima Letters," *The Works of Robert Louis Stevenson* (New York, 1897), XVII, 259, to Sidney Colvin, August 23, 1893.
131   24   Joseph Wood Krutch, *The Modern Temper* (New York, 1929), p. 226.
132   6   *The Mind at Mischief,* p. 43.

CHAPTER VI
HANDLING OUR MISCHIEVOUS CONSCIENCES

133   9   As quoted in William Allen White, *Masks in a Pageant* (New York, 1930), p. 29.
133   12   "The Life of King Henry V," Act III, Sc. III, *The Complete Works of William Shakespeare,* edited by William George Clark and William Aldis Wright (New York, 1911), p. 555.
134   12   William Lecky (New York, 1906), I, 251.
135   1   Salvador de Madariaga, *Christopher Columbus* (New York, 1940), p. 340.
135   24   Esmé Wingfield-Stratford, *New Minds for Old* (New York, 1935), p. 322, of William Ewart Gladstone.
135   27   As quoted in William P. King, *Right and Wrong* (New York, 1938), p. 81.
136   8   *Adventures of Huckleberry Finn* (New York, 1885), p. 292.
136   26   James M. Barrie, *The Admirable Crichton and Other Plays* (New York, 1926), p. 109.
137   5   John W. Dodds, *Thackeray: A Critical Portrait* (New York, 1941), p. vii.
137   29   David Seabury, *What Makes Us Seem So Queer?* (New York, 1934), p. 3.

REFERENCES

PAGE	LINE	
138	1	Luke 15:17, 18.
138	4	"Experience," *Works of Ralph Waldo Emerson* (London, 1905), p. 99.
138	30	Genesis 3:12, 13.
139	31	Samuel Butler, *Hudibras* (Cambridge, 1905), First Part, Canto I, p. 9.
140	4	Matthew 7:1-3.
141	25	Wallace Brockway & Herbert Weinstock, *Men of Music* (New York, 1939), p. 249.
142	20	Act I, Sc. II, *op. cit.*, p. 1058.
143	7	"Ode to Duty," *The Poetical Works of William Wordsworth*, edited by William Knight (New York, 1896), III, 38.
143	12	William S. Sadler, *The Mind at Mischief* (New York, 1929), pp. 181-183.
143	13	Matthew 12:36.
144	15	Matthew 23:23, 24.
144	20	Luke 18:11-12.
144	25	Luke 15:29.
146	3	"The Rime of the Ancient Mariner," Part IV, *The Complete Poetical Works of Samuel Taylor Coleridge* (Oxford, 1912), I, 197.
147	7	J. A. Hadfield, *Psychology and Morals* (London, 1923), p. 37.
148	11	Psalm 32:1.
148	22	*Les Miserables,* Everyman's Library Edition, I, 217.
149	5	*Boswell's Life of Johnson,* edited by George Birbeck Hill (New York, 1887), IV, 373.
150	1	Romans 13:10.
150	29	Alexander V. G. Allen, *Life and Letters of Phillips Brooks* (New York, 1900), II, 332.
153	15	*A Select Library of Nicene and Post-Nicene Fathers of The Christian Church,* edited by Philip Schaff and Henry Wace, Second Series, VI, 429.

REFERENCES

PAGE LINE

153   22   John 3:17 (King James translation).

153   27   John 8:11.

CHAPTER VII
USING ALL THERE IS IN US

158   8   Cf. Luke 11:24-26.

159   1   James 3:11.

159   16   "In Memoriam," LVI, *The Poetic and Dramatic Works of Alfred Lord Tennyson,* Cambridge Edition, p. 176.

160   19   Julius Köstlin, *The Life of Martin Luther* (Philadelphia, 1883), pp. 217, 218.

161   14   Carroll A. Wise, *Religion in Illness and Health* (New York, 1942), p. 14.

161   16   Matthew 5:44.

161   29   Helen Nicolay, *Personal Traits of Abraham Lincoln* (New York, 1913), p. 317.

162   29   *The Abbott, The Waverley Novels* (Edinburgh, 1856), XXI, 213.

163   3   David Seabury, *How Jesus Heals Our Minds Today* (Boston, 1940), p. 70.

163   20   W. H. P. Faunce, in address at the "Celebration of the Ninetieth Birthday of William Williams Keen, M.D., January 19, 1927."

163   29   Carl Sandburg, *Abraham Lincoln; The War Years* (New York, 1939), III, 495-496.

163   32   Seabury, *op. cit.,* p. 220.

164   17   "Singing Iceman," *The American Magazine,* April, 1936, p. 114.

165   11   II Timothy 2:3.

165   16   *Ibid.,* 4:7.

166   8   "Endymion," Book III, ll. 170-171, *The Complete Poetical Works and Letters of John Keats,* Cambridge Edition (Boston, 1899), p. 81.

REFERENCES

PAGE	LINE	
166	16	*Deucalion, The Works of John Ruskin,* Library Edition (New York, 1906), XXVI, 194.
167	19	Johann Goethe, *Sprüche in Prosa. Maximen und Reflexion,* V.
168	11	*The Varieties of Religious Experience* (New York, 1914), p. 283.
169	20	Henry Thomas and Dana Lee Thomas, *Living Biographies of Great Philosophers* (New York, 1941), p. 256.
170	28	J. A. Hadfield, *Psychology and Morals* (London, 1923), p. 127.
171	18	*The Correspondence of William Cowper* (New York, 1904), III, 36, to Lady Hesketh, May 15, 1786.
171	21	Robert E. Peary, *The North Pole* (London, 1910), p. 266.
171	24	Commander Booth Tucker, *Life of General William Booth* (New York, 1901), p. 78.
172	12	*Life of Henry Wadsworth Longfellow,* edited by Samuel Longfellow (Boston, 1891), I, 53.
173	6	Georgiana M. Taylor, *Gospel Hymns Consolidated,* edited by Philip Paul Bliss (Chicago, 1883), 74.
173	13	Matthew 23:11.
173	28	"The Life of King Henry V," Act II, Sc. IV, *The Complete Works of William Shakespeare,* edited by William George Clark and William Aldis Wright (New York, 1911), p. 551.
174	2	Luke 10:27.
174	6	Matthew 7:12.
174	15	Pietro Mascagni, as quoted in *The Reader's Digest Reader* (New York, 1940), p. 11.
175	8	"Worship," *Works of Ralph Waldo Emerson* (London, 1905), p. 403.
176	14	*Letters of Henrik Ibsen* (New York, 1905), p. 218, to George Brandes, September 24, 1871.

REFERENCES

PAGE	LINE	
176	27	William Mather Lewis, Baccalaureate Sermon, Lafayette College, May 22, 1938, p. 2.
177	5	*Facing Life* (New York, 1929), p. 44.
177	13	"Self-Dependence," *Poetical Works of Matthew Arnold* (London, 1923), p. 256.
177	28	"Le Général Vandamme," *Revue de Lille* (Paris), XXVII, 404.
179	7	Hadfield, *op. cit.,* p. 163.
180	12	David Ewen, *Men and Women Who Make Music* (New York, 1939), p. 34.
181	14	John Masefield, *In the Mill* (New York, 1941), pp. 96-97.
181	17	Luke 22:42.
182	3	George Matheson, *Hymns for the Living Age* (New York, 1923), 296.
184	28	As quoted in Ernest R. Groves, *Understanding Yourself* (New York, 1939), p. 231.
187	6	Frank Swinnerton, *Nocturne* (New York, 1917), p. 16.

CHAPTER VIII
MASTERING DEPRESSION

PAGE	LINE	
188	9	*Battles and Leaders of the Civil War,* edited by Robert Underwood Johnson and Clarence Clough Buel (New York, 1887), I, 603.
189	18	"Nobody Knows the Trouble I See," *Seventy Negro Spirituals,* edited by William Arms Fisher (Boston, 1926), p. 125.
190	20	*The Works of Thomas Gray,* edited by Edmund Gosse (London, 1884), II, 8.
190	24	*Ibid.,* I, 73.
192	5	"Ode Recited At The Harvard Commemoration," *The Complete Poetical Works of James Russell Lowell* (New York, 1896), p. 345.
192	16	"De Profundis," *The Poetic and Dramatic*

REFERENCES

PAGE	LINE	

Works of Alfred Lord Tennyson, **Cambridge** Edition, p. 484.

193   2   José Ortega y Gasset, *Toward a Philosophy of History* (New York, 1941), p. 116.

193   10   *The Pilgrim's Progress,* Part I, Seventh Stage, Special Tercentenary Edition, pp. 318-319.

195   1   *Epistles,* Book I, 2, to Lollius Maximus.

195   6   As quoted in John Langdon-Davies, *Man Comes of Age* (New York, 1932), p. 130.

196   10   *Kangaroo* (New York, 1923), p. 26.

196   24   *Unforgotten Years* (Boston, 1939), pp. 129, 130.

197   26   As quoted in Arthur John Gossip, *From the Edge of the Crowd* (Edinburgh, 1930), p. 33.

198   7   *About Ourselves* (New York, 1927), pp. 114-115.

200   4   John Masefield, "The Everlasting Mercy," *Poems* (New York, 1929), p. 84.

201   4   *Kabloona* (New York, 1941), pp. 116-117.

201   23   *Pygmalion, The Works of Bernard Shaw* (London, 1930), 14, 214.

202   26   "Compensation," *Works of Ralph Waldo Emerson* (London, 1905), p. 27.

203   9   Wallace Brockway & Herbert Weinstock, *Men of Music* (New York, 1939), p. 228.

204   3   "The Life of King Henry V," Act IV, Sc. I, *The Complete Works of William Shakespeare,* edited by William George Clark and William Aldis Wright (New York, 1911), p. 561.

205   4   Harold E. B. Speight, *The Life and Writings of John Bunyan* (New York, 1928), pp. 18-19.

206   31   Hebrews 12:2.

207   5   Henry Thomas and Dana Lee Thomas, *Living Biographies of Great Painters* (New York, 1940), p. 227.

207   23   *The Normal Mind* (New York, 1927), pp. 600, 617.

REFERENCES

CHAPTER IX
THE PRINCIPLE OF RELEASED POWER

PAGE	LINE	
214	4	William James, *The Varieties of Religious Experience* (New York, 1914), pp. 515, 516-517.
214	17	Joseph Wood Krutch, *The Modern Temper* (New York, 1929), p. 10.
214	20	James, *op. cit.*, p. 508.
217	1	1:3 (King James translation).
217	2	J. A. Hadfield, *The Psychology of Power* (New York, 1923), pp. 51-52.
217	25	Alexis Carrel, "Prayer is Power," *The Reader's Digest*, March, 1941, p. 34.
218	6	*Modern Painters*, "Of Modern Landscape," *The Works of John Ruskin*, Library Edition (New York, 1904), V, 331.
218	13	*George Eliot's Life as Related in her Letters and Journals* (New York, 1899), II, 262, letter to R. H. Hutton, August 8, 1863.
218	17	"The Over-Soul," *Works of Ralph Waldo Emerson* (London, 1905), p. 59.
219	13	*The Last Chronicle of Barset* (London, 1869), II, 218.
221	21	*Op. cit.*, p. 35.
222	6	*And Gladly Teach* (New York, 1935), p. 118.
222	17	*The Works of Robert Louis Stevenson* (New York, 1897), VII, 351.
223	3	Henry Seidel Canby, *Thoreau* (Boston, 1939), p. 73.
224	20	Cf. Carrel, *Man the Unknown* (New York, 1935), p. 154.
225	3	George Eliot, "Stradivarius," *Complete Poems* (New York), p. 400.
225	8	*Passages From the Life and Writings of William Penn*, edited by T. Pym Cope (Philadelphia, 1882), p. 36.

PAGE	LINE	
225	12	Galatians 2:20 (King James translation).
225	18	*Joseph in Egypt* (New York, 1938), I, 4.
226	2	H. E. Bates, "Joseph Conrad and Thomas Hardy," *The English Novelists; A Survey of the Novel,* by Twenty Contemporary Novelists (New York, 1936), p. 256.
226	19	*Psychology, Briefer Course* (New York, 1900), p. 186.
227	14	Matthew 7:18.
228	1	"Mandalay," *Rudyard Kipling's Verse* (London, 1938), p. 413.
228	28	Cf. Matthew 5:21-37.
229	1	Matthew 23:26.
230	5	Romans 12:2.
230	18	Julius Harrison, *Brahms and His Four Symphonies* (London, 1939), p. 253.
231	15	Gordon W. Allport, *Personality; A Psychological Interpretation* (New York, 1938), p. 206.
231	21	II Corinthians 5:17.
232	5	Allport, *op. cit.,* p. 209.
233	18	Romans 7:19.
233	24	Philippians 4:13 (Moffatt translation).
234	7	Hadfield, *op. cit.,* p. 21.
235	13	Ephesians 3:16 (King James translation).
238	4	Philip Doddridge, *Hymns for the Living Age* (New York, 1923), 313.
238	6	George Croly, *ibid.,* 184.

CHAPTER X

THE PRACTICAL USE OF FAITH

240	7	As quoted in W. A. Visser 't Hooft, *None Other Gods* (New York, 1937), p. 161.
241	5	I John 5:4 (King James translation).
241	12	Samuel Putnam, *François Rabelais, Man of the*

PAGE LINE

Renaissance; A Spiritual Biography (New York, 1929), p. 527.

242   14   "The Poet at the Breakfast Table," The Writings of Oliver Wendell Holmes, Riverside Edition, III, 82.

243   18   The Life and Letters of Charles Darwin, edited by his son Francis Darwin (New York, 1887), I, 30.

243   25   "The Gospel of Relaxation," Selected Papers on Philosophy, Everyman's Library Edition, p. 37.

245   4   The Will to Believe (New York, 1915), p. 213.

245   19   As quoted in John C. Schroeder, "A Deeper Social Gospel," The Christian Century, July 26, 1939, p. 925.

246   27   The Conflict of Religions in the Early Roman Empire (London, 1910), p. 198.

247   20   Lloyd Morris, The Rebellious Puritan: Portrait of Mr. Hawthorne (New York, 1927), p. 110.

248   1   William Makepeace Thackeray, The History of Pendennis (Boston, 1883), I, 148.

248   13   Ephesians 3:17 (King James translation).

249   10   Clifford Hazeldine Osborne, The Religion of John Burroughs (New York, 1930), p. 2.

249   20   Clara Barrus, The Life and Letters of John Burroughs (New York, 1925), I, 318.

249   26   "Waiting," ibid., p. 67.

250   4   As quoted in The Reader's Digest, October, 1941, p. 84.

250   11   C. G. Jung, Modern Man In Search of a Soul (New York, 1933), pp. 277, 278.

251   16   William Ernest Hocking, What Man Can Make of Man (New York, 1942), pp. 60-61.

253   7   Edward A. Strecker, "Mental Hygiene," Nelson New Loose-Leaf Medicine, VII, 413, 1927.

254   22   "Observations on the Life-History of Chronic

PAGE	LINE	
		Peptic Ulcer," *The Lancet*, London, December 11, 1937, p. 1360.
255	6	Josephine A. Jackson, M.D., *Outwitting Our Nerves* (New York, 1934), p. 11.
255	11	I am greatly indebted throughout this section to a book by Carroll A. Wise, *Religion in Illness and Health* (New York, 1942), especially the second chapter. Most of my direct quotations from medical specialists concerning the non-physical causes of disease are drawn from works to which this chapter calls attention.
256	9	Charles P. Emerson, "The Importance of the Emotions in the Etiology and Prognosis of Disease," *Bulletin of the New York Academy of Medicine,* November, 1929, p. 986.
256	16	Carl Binger, "The Psycho-Biology of Breathing," *Annals of Internal Medicine,* July, 1937, p. 207.
256	19	Harlow Brooks, "Concerning Certain Phases of Angina Pectoris," *International Clinics,* December, 1928, IV, 32.
258	12	*Mark Twain's Notebook,* edited by Albert Bigelow Paine (New York, 1935), p. 256.
258	19	*Op. cit.,* p. 266.
258	28	Gordon W. Allport, *Personality; A Psychological Interpretation* (New York, 1938), p. 172.
259	20	"Macbeth," Act V, Sc. V, *The Complete Works of William Shakespeare,* edited by William George Clark and William Aldis Wright (New York, 1911), p. 1004.
259	28	"A Reconsideration of Proust," *The Saturday Review of Literature,* October 27, 1934, p. 1.
260	16	Bertrand Russell, *Religion and Science* (New York, 1935), p. 233.
260	21	*The Modern Temper* (New York, 1929), p. 249.
261	29	Edwin Holt Hughes, *Christianity and Success* (Nashville, 1928), p. 51.

REFERENCES

PAGE LINE

262   7   As quoted in the *Yale Alumni Weekly*, March 4, 1932, p. 448.

262   26 James Branch Cabell, *Something About Eve* (New York, 1929), pp. 136-137.

263   10 Phyllis Bottome, *Alfred Adler; A Biography* (New York, 1939), p. 91.

263   13 Hesketh Pearson, *G. B. S.; A Full Length Portrait* (New York, 1942), p. 29.

263   21 *Psychology, Briefer Course* (New York, 1900), p. 186.

Index

INDEX

INDEX

7

In the popular mind, ᴵ Fosdick stands as a great American preacher and pastor of Riverside Church, New York. What is generally unknown—and what makes this volume so exciting—is that for twenty years he has been consulted by thousands of persons, concerned with problems that for the most part have no relation whatever to religion. Thousands more have written to him for help on all sorts of personal problems as a result of his fifteen years of week-by-week broadcasts.

Now out of this vast experience comes this book, unquestionably of greater appeal to the general reader than anything Dr. Fosdick has written. While it promises no short, easy road to personal well-being, this book will help any intelligent person to get a better hold on himself. It shows how best to deal with fear and anxiety, how to master depression and how to handle one's "mischievous conscience."

The book starts with a clear, fresh discussion of how a person can and readers would profit from a glimpse of what Dr. Fosdick is saying about Being a Real Person.

This book seems destined to reach a wider audience than any book Dr. Fosdick has written, even though a total of more than a million copies of his eighteen earlier books have been sold.